D1084290

SOCIETY FOR NEW TESTAMENT STUDIES

MONOGRAPH SERIES

General Editor: G. N. Stanton

56

PAUL, JUDAISM AND THE GENTILES

PAUL, JUDAISM AND THE GENTILES

A SOCIOLOGICAL APPROACH

FRANCIS WATSON

Lecturer in New Testament Studies
King's College London

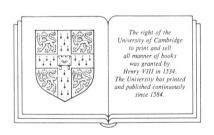

The right of the
University of Cambridge
to print and sell
all manner of books
was granted by
Henry VIII in 1534.
The University has printed
and published continuously
since 1584.

CAMBRIDGE UNIVERSITY PRESS

CAMBRIDGE
LONDON   NEW YORK   NEW ROCHELLE
MELBOURNE   SYDNEY

Published by the Press Syndicate of the University of Cambridge
The Pitt Building, Trumpington Street, Cambridge CB2 1RP
32 East 57th Street, New York, NY 10022, USA
10 Stamford Road, Oakleigh, Melbourne 3166, Australia

First published 1986

Printed in Great Britain at
the University Press, Cambridge

British Library cataloguing in publication data
Watson, Francis
Paul, Judaism and the Gentiles : a sociological
approach. − (Monograph series/Society for New
Testament studies; no. 56)
1. Paul, *the Apostle, Saint*   2. Judaism
3. Christianity and other religions − Judaism
I. Title   II. Series
261.2'6   BS2506

Library of Congress cataloguing in publication data
Watson, Francis, 1956−
Paul, Judaism, and the Gentiles.
(Monograph series / Society for New Testament
Studies ; 56)
Originally presented as the author's thesis (Ph.D. −
University of Oxford, 1984).
Bibliography: p.
1. Paul, the Apostle, Saint.   2. Bible. N.T.
Epistles of Paul − Criticism, interpretation, etc.
3. Sociology, Christian − History − Early church, *ca.* 30−
600.   4. Law and gospel − History of doctrines − Early
church, *ca.* 30−600.   5. Church history − Primitive and
early church, *ca.* 30−600.   I. Title.   II. Series:
Monograph series (Society for New Testament Studies) ; 56.
BS2506.W37   1986   225.9'24   86−6062

ISBN 0 521 32573 0

CONTENTS

v

PREFACE

The present work has grown out of a doctoral thesis which was accepted by the Faculty of Theology in the University of Oxford in January 1984. The thesis was prepared under the supervision of the late Professor G. B. Caird, who patiently watched and assisted its rather wayward progress over a period of five years. Mr Robert Morgan too was a source of much encouragement and many helpful suggestions. However, the thesis has been very thoroughly rewritten from the standpoint of a much more rigorous historical and sociological perspective. The aim is to demonstrate from this perspective that the view of Paul's controversy with Judaism and Jewish Christianity which derives from the Reformation is seriously misleading, and that the Pauline texts become much more readily comprehensible when one abandons this overtly theological approach.

It may be as well at the outset to explain the way in which I have tried to use sociological insights in the study of Paul. Much valuable recent work applying sociology to the New Testament has been interdisciplinary in nature. The methods and the terminology of professional sociologists are used, and accounts are given of their research into religious movements far removed from early Christianity. In this way, the New Testament is set against a very broad background. There is a great deal of merit in this approach; but the danger is that sociology will come to be regarded as an alien and exotic newcomer to traditional New Testament studies, rather than a natural and inevitable concomitant of the historical-critical method − which is what I take it to be. New Testament scholars have always been interested in the *Sitz im Leben* of a tradition or text − i.e. the social reality underlying a tradition or text. A sociological analysis of how sectarian groups work may enable one to reconstruct a *Sitz im Leben* with much greater clarity and precision, but as a natural extension of accepted historical method rather than as a radically new departure.

This sociological analysis takes as its starting-point the hypothesis that a text presupposes an existing social situation and is intended to function within that situation in ways not necessarily immediately apparent from the text itself. This is a working hypothesis, and not an *a priori* assumption that all theoretical statements *must* be socially determined. The application of this hypothesis will be much more fruitful with some texts than it is with others. In some cases, a writer may be writing in a genuinely theoretical manner without any significant relation to social realities; in other cases, lack of evidence may make it impossible to reconstruct the social realities underlying a text. Sociological analysis is not a satisfactory way of filling in the gaps in our historical knowledge. It is not a substitute for historical evidence, but a way of interpreting the evidence. It is the argument of the present work that such an approach to Paul's controversies with Judaism and Jewish Christianity sheds a great deal of unexpected light on familiar texts such as Galatians and Romans, and thus shows up serious shortcomings in the more traditional theologically-oriented approach.

I would like to thank Professor G. N. Stanton for the encouragement that he has given during the preparation of this work, and for accepting it for the SNTS monograph series.

FRANCIS WATSON

King's College London
May 1985

ABBREVIATIONS

AB	Anchor Bible
AnBib	Analecta Biblica
AThANT	Abhandlungen zur Theologie des Alten und Neuen Testaments
BBB	Bonner Biblische Beiträge
BDF	F. Blass, R. Debrunner and R. W. Funk, *Greek Grammar of the New Testament*
BevTh	Beiträge zur evangelischen Theologie
BJRL	*Bulletin of the John Rylands Library*
BNTC	Black's New Testament Commentaries
EKKNT	Evangelisch-katholisch Kommentar zum Neuen Testament
ET	English translation
EvTh	*Evangelische Theologie*
ExT	*Expository Times*
FRLANT	Forschungen zur Religion und Literatur des Alten und Neuen Testaments
FS	Festschrift
HNT	Handbuch zum Neuen Testament
HTKNT	Herders theologischer Kommentar zum Neuen Testament
HTR	*Harvard Theological Review*
ICC	International Critical Commentary
Int.	*Interpretation*
JAAR	*Journal of the American Academy of Religion*
JBL	*Journal of Biblical Literature*
JES	*Journal of Ecumenical Studies*
JR	*Journal of Religion*
JSNT	*Journal for the Study of the New Testament*
JTS	*Journal of Theological Studies*

KEKNT	Kritisch-exegetischer Kommentar über das Neue Testament
LCL	Loeb Classical Library
LW	Luther's Works (ET St Louis)
MNTC	Moffatt New Testament Commentary
MTZ	*Münchener theologische Zeitschrift*
NCBC	New Century Bible Commentary
NIGTC	New International Greek Testament Commentary
NLC	New London Commentaries
NovT	*Novum Testamentum*
NovTSup	*Supplement to Novum Testamentum*
NTS	*New Testament Studies*
RSV	Revised Standard Version
SB	H. L. Strack and P. Billerbeck, *Kommentar zum Neuen Testament aus Talmud und Midrasch*
SBL Diss.	Society for Biblical Literature, Dissertation Series
SBM	Stuttgarter Biblische Monographien
SBT	Studies in Biblical Theology
SJT	*Scottish Journal of Theology*
SNTSMS	Society for New Testament Studies Monograph Series
SNTW	Studies of the New Testament and its World
StBib	*Studia Biblica*
StEv	*Studia Evangelica*
StNT	Studien zum Neuen Testament
StTh	*Studia Theologica*
TB	*Theologische Blätter*
TDNT	Theological Dictionary of the New Testament
THKNT	Theologischer Handkommentar zum Alten und Neuen Testament
TNTC	Tyndale New Testament Commentary
TZ	*Theologische Zeitschrift*
WMANT	Wissenschaftliche Monographien zum Alten und Neuen Testament
WUNT	Wissenschaftliche Untersuchungen zum Neuen Testament
ZBK	Zürcher Bibelkommentare
ZNW	*Zeitschrift für die neutestamentliche Wissenschaft*
ZTK	*Zeitschrift für Theologie und Kirche*

1

PAUL, THE REFORMATION AND MODERN SCHOLARSHIP

What is the nature of Paul's attack on Judaism and Judaizing Christianity? It is increasingly being recognized by New Testament scholars that the answer to this question can no longer be taken for granted.

According to the traditional approach stemming from the Reformation, Paul is attacking the idea that salvation can be earned by acts of obedience to the law, as held by his Jewish or Jewish Christian opponents. He himself preaches the gospel of salvation solely by the grace of God, and the idea that salvation is to be earned by man's achievement is therefore anathema to him. Judaism is thus presented as a religion of 'works righteousness', a form of Pelagianism according to which God has given us the law so that we might earn salvation by fulfilling it. Paul's gospel opposes such arrogance with its insistence on grace and faith alone. On this view, what is at issue between Paul and his opponents is a matter of pure theology and pure theory: they debate the merits of two rival answers to the question, How can man be accepted by God? Many scholars still believe that this interpretation of the Pauline texts is essentially correct.

But other scholars are dissatisfied with this approach. The fundamental question is whether or not such an approach can do justice to the historical and sociological context in which Paul was writing. Paul understood himself as the apostle to the Gentiles, and the problem of the status of the Gentiles dominated his life and work. Can the highly theological interpretation given by the Reformation tradition be reconciled with this very specific historical situation? Or does it result in a distorted view both of Paul and of the Judaism he opposed? It will be the argument of the present work that the latter is the case: the Reformation tradition's approach to Paul is fundamentally wrong. But before embarking on this argument, a more detailed survey is needed first of the Lutheran approach, and secondly of the modern dissatisfaction with it.

1 The Lutheran approach

It is commonly asserted that 'modern Pauline studies began with the Tübingen scholar, F. C. Baur' (Howard, *Crisis*, 1). In one sense, this is obviously true: Baur was the first great exponent of the study of Paul by historical methods. But in another sense, the statement is misleading, for modern Pauline studies are still dominated to a remarkable extent by Luther's interpretation of the apostle.[1] Whereas endeavours such as synoptic source criticism and the quest for the historical Jesus can be traced back to quite definite beginnings in eighteenth- and early nineteenth-century rationalism, we must go back to Luther to find the origin and inspiration of much contemporary work on Paul. Of no area of Paul's thought is this more the case than with his attack on the adherents of the law, which is our present concern.[2]

Luther's interpretation of Paul is dominated by opposition to what he conceives as a terrible misuse of the law as a means by which sinful and deluded man seeks to earn salvation by his own efforts. In the 1535 lectures on Galatians, he comments on Gal. 3:10:

> To want to be justified by works of the Law is to deny the righteousness of faith. On this basis, when those who are self-righteous keep the Law, they deny the righteousness of faith and sin against the First, Second and Third Commandments, and against the entire Law, because God commands that He be worshipped by believing and fearing Him. But they, on the contrary, make their works into righteousness, without faith and against faith. Therefore in their very keeping of the Law they act in a manner that is most contrary to the Law, and they sin most seriously and grievously ... The righteousness of the Law which they think they are producing is in fact nothing but idolatry and blasphemy against God. (253–4)

Luther here and elsewhere shifts the emphasis away from the traditional view of sin as transgression of particular commandments, and asserts that it is precisely those who keep the commandments who in doing so manifest the essence of sin, since they rely on themselves and reject the grace of God.[3]

All this presupposes that when Paul condemns 'works', he means moral activity in general, and not just the Jewish 'ceremonies' which are abolished by the coming of Christ. Luther considers the latter view a disastrous error. In *De Servo Arbitrio* (1526), he writes:

> That is the ignorant error of Jerome, which, in spite of Augustine's strenuous resistance, – God having withdrawn and let Satan prevail – has spread out into the world and has persisted to the present day. It has consequently become impossible to understand Paul, and the knowledge of Christ has been inevitably obscured. Even if there had never been any other error in the Church, this one alone was pestilent and potent enough to make havoc of the gospel. (258)

If 'ceremonies' are all that Rom. 3:20 refers to, how would this help the argument that all are unrighteous? In fact, in the law of Moses ceremonies and the Decalogue are one, equally binding. Thus, freedom from the law means freedom from the whole law (285). Paul's condemnation of 'works' refers quite generally to 'all workers and all their works', but especially to 'their good and virtuous works' (271–2).

This, then, is Luther's view of the misuse of the law. We turn now to his view of its correct use: it was given in order to reveal sin, so as to terrify man's conscience and cause him to seek grace in Christ. In *The Freedom of a Christian* (1520), he sums this up as follows:

> We must point out that the entire Scripture of God is divided into two parts: commandments and promises. Although the commandments teach things that are good, the things taught are not done as soon as they are taught, for the commandments show us what we ought to do but do not give us the power to do it. They are intended to teach man to know himself, that through them he may recognize his inability to do good and may despair of his own ability ... Now when a man has learned through the commandments to recognize his own helplessness and is distressed about how he might satisfy the law – since the law must be fulfilled so that not a jot or tittle shall be lost, otherwise man will be condemned without hope – then, being truly humbled and reduced to nothing in his own eyes, he finds in himself nothing whereby he may be justified or saved. Here, the second part of Scripture comes to our aid, namely, the promises of God ... (348)

All this does not make good works unnecessary, although they contribute nothing to salvation. The reason for this is as follows:

> Although, as I have said, a man is abundantly and sufficiently justified by faith inwardly, in his spirit, and so has all that he needs, except insofar as this faith and these riches must grow from day to day even to the future life; yet he remains in this mortal life on earth. (358)

Out of spontaneous love for God, the body must be reduced to subjection, which also enables one to serve others (358ff); 'Man, however, needs none of these things for his righteousness and salvation' (365).

Here, then, we have the ideas which were to become the second and third uses of the law in the classical Lutheran formulation: the law was given to provoke despair at one's own sinfulness, so that one might flee to Christ for mercy; it was also given to guide the earthly lives of those who are justified by faith. As Ebeling has pointed out, it is only the former that really deserves to be called a *usus legis* in Luther ('Triplex Usus Legis', 71).

We have discussed briefly Luther's interpretation of Paul's statements about the law under the two headings of the misuse of the law and its correct use.[4] Both of these spring from the fact that the law is a demand for complete obedience: it is misused when man attempts to earn salvation by fulfilling it, for it is intended to expose man's sin so that he seeks mercy in Christ. In the theology of *R. Bultmann*, the latter element recedes into the background.[5] In his article, 'Christ the End of the Law' (1940), Bultmann writes:

> As for the question of being inwardly weighed down by the law, it is absolutely clear that Paul never speaks of it. In its Lutheran form, this question is, at any rate, entirely foreign to Judaism ... His utterances about his past do not indicate that he suffered from an oppressive consciousness of sin. (39)

He warns that 'Paul is easily confused with Luther', which leads us to 'overlook the historical situation in which Paul is writing' (37). His complete rejection of the so-called *secundus usus legis* is accounted for by his view of the nature of sin.[6] In Luther, 'sin' may have its straightforward sense of acts which transgress the moral law, and which it is the function of the law to expose; or it may refer to the attempt to earn salvation, so that one is paradoxically disobeying the law in the very act of fulfilling it, because one does so in order to establish a claim on God.[7] Bultmann, with dialectical theology in general, emphasizes the latter idea at the expense of the former. In his article, 'Liberal Theology and the Latest Theological Movement' (1924), he writes:

> Man as such, the whole man, is called in question by God. Man stands under that question mark, whether he knows it or not. His moral transgressions are not his fundamental sin ... *Man's fundamental sin is his will to justify himself as man*, for thereby he makes himself God. When man becomes aware of this, the whole world is taken off its hinges; for man then puts himself under the judgment of God.   (46-7)

This view of sin and the law (and, by implication, of Judaism) dominates Bultmann's interpretation of Paul. Paul

> says not only that man *cannot* achieve salvation by works of the Law, but that he was not even *intended* to do so ... But why is this the case? Because man's effort to achieve salvation by keeping the Law only leads him into sin, indeed this effort itself in the end is already sin.
> (*Theology*, I, 263-4)

Sin is 'man's self-powered striving to undergird his own existence in forgetfulness of his creaturely existence, to procure his salvation by his own strength' (264), and this is precisely the nature of the Jewish keeping of the law. Thus, 'It is not only evil deeds already committed that make a man reprehensible in God's sight, but man's intention of becoming righteous before God by keeping the Law and thereby having his "boast" is already sin' (267). The Pauline term for this fundamental sin is 'boasting' (cf. Rom. 3:27), in radical contrast to the acceptance of God's grace as a gift, which is faith's attitude (281).

Bultmann's desire to refer as many as possible of Paul's statements about the law to its misuse as a means of achieving salvation is exemplified by his interpretation of Rom. 7, a chapter which had previously served as the *locus classicus* for the Lutheran *secundus usus legis*.[8] In 'Romans 7 and the Anthropology of Paul' (1932), he argues that it is to be understood against the background of Phil. 3:6 and Rom. 10:2ff, in which Paul speaks not of repentance from specific transgressions but of abandonment of zeal for the law (148ff); the essence of faith is therefore the renunciation of one's own righteousness (150). Thus, the sin discussed in Rom. 7 is the effort to achieve righteousness for oneself. 'The good' in vv. 14ff is to be understood not as what is morally good but as 'life', i.e. the authentic life which is the Creator's purpose for man. Man knows of the possibility of authentic existence, but fails to attain it because he strives to achieve it through his own efforts (152). All that he is able to procure by this means is death (155), which is the meaning of τὸ κακόν. ποιεῖν and πράσσειν are thus equivalent to κατεργάζεσθαι: man wills what is good (life) but only achieves what is evil (death). Far from helping man to overcome sin, the law has awakened sin in him (156). Thus, Rom. 7 is no longer seen as an account of the moral struggle, in which the moral man is continually frustrated by his failure to overcome sin. This is not a subjective struggle at all, but a 'trans-subjective' struggle underlying all human life but only disclosed in the gospel (151). Rom. 7 is thus a retrospective analysis by the Christian of his own past, which he now understands for the first time. This view of Rom. 7 accords with the view of dialectical theology that 'sin' refers primarily not to individual actions but to the self-assertion and desire for autonomy which underlies the quest to establish one's own righteousness before God.

It would be impossible to exaggerate the importance of this whole theme in Bultmann's general theological work as well as his exegesis,[9] and this may be illustrated from 'Christ the End of the Law', where Bultmann interprets Paul's critique of Judaism as follows:

> He sees that the striving of the Jews is basically motivated by the *need for recognition*, and that in this connection this need to be recognized means fundamentally not seeking to be accepted in the sight of other men (though this will always be a concomitant of it), but rather to be accepted in the sight of God, the court of appeal which stands high above every human judgment ... A specifically human striving has merely taken on its culturally, and in point of time, individually distinct form in Judaism. For it is in fact a striving common to all men, to gain recognition of one's achievement; and this generates pride. (43)

Bultmann concludes:

> Thus it is an error to think that belief in the grace of God requires a sense of sin or a confession of sin, in the sense that man must admit to himself how much or how often and grievously he has sinned and continually is sinning. He does not need to consider frantically or artificially his

immoralities, and does not need to contort his good works into bad. He is to consider the reason for his being, and to ask himself whence his life comes: whether it is from the grace of God or from his own powers, and whether his life is sustained from the effort to gain glory, whether he is driven this way and that by the need for recognition, or whether in the knowledge of his vanity he has seen through the comedy of this effort and so has become conscious of his sin in the sight of God. (48–9)

These excerpts indicate the immense significance that Paul's statements about the law have for Bultmann. His exegesis is motivated by a passionate theological concern.

According to *E. Käsemann*, the works of the law 'are for Paul a higher form of godlessness than transgressions of the law, and are thus incompatible with faith' (*Romans*, 103). Like Bultmann, Käsemann regards the Jew as an example of a general human phenomenon, although he is more concerned with 'the religious man' than with 'the need for recognition'. In 'Paul and Israel', he writes:

> The apostle's real adversary is the devout Jew ... as the reality of the religious man. For man, whether he knows it and acts correspondingly or not, is the being who is set before God: and this fact the devout Jew acknowledges. Certainly such a profession is no protection from illusion. In fact, religion always provides man with his most thorough-going possibility of confusing an illusion with God. Paul sees this possibility realized in the devout Jew: inasmuch as the announcement of God's will in the law is misunderstood as a summons to human achievement and therefore as a means to a righteousness of one's own. But that is for him the root sin, because an image is set in the place of God; man, in despairing presumption, erects his own work into the criterion of the universal judgment, and God becomes an approving spectator of our doings. (184–5)

Paul 'strikes at the hidden Jew in all of us' (186). His doctrine of the law is the 'radical spearhead' of the doctrine of justification ('Salvation History', 72), which now needs to be directed against a complacent, bourgeois church. The doctrine of justification

> undoubtedly grew up in the course of the anti-Jewish struggle and stands or falls with this antithesis. But the historian must

not make things easy for himself by simply, as historian, noting this incontrovertible fact. If he does, he could equally well call Jesus a pious Jew who had a memorable fate and left behind him a series of impressive sayings. Our task is to ask: what does the Jewish nomism against which Paul fought really represent? And our answer must be: it represents the community of 'good' people which turns God's promises into their own privileges and God's commandments into the instruments of self-sanctification.

(71−2)

Käsemann's statements are symptomatic of the fact that Paul functions in the Reformation tradition not primarily as a historical but as a quasi-mythological figure, whose gospel of grace was rejected by the church but who returns at certain key moments (notably the Reformation) to challenge the church's legalistic way of thinking.[10] Käsemann's version of this widespread Protestant myth may be illustrated from his article, 'Paul and Early Catholicism'. He claims that Paul was

> an individualist, doubtless one of the most significant in church history and surely the most controversial even in earliest Christianity. The later period was able to assimilate him only by setting the image of a saint in the place of his actual life ... Alongside this image of Paul, to which the ecclesiastical future belonged, there is, however, the real Paul as well. This Paul remains confined in seven letters and for the most part unintelligible to posterity, not only to the ancient church and the Middle Ages. However, whenever he is rediscovered − which happens almost exclusively in times of crisis − there issues from him explosive power which destroys as much as it opens up something new. His historical existence and activity is then repeated ... It is never long, to be sure, until orthodoxy and enthusiasm again master this Paul and banish him once more to his letters. However, the Church continues to preserve his letters in her canon and thereby latently preserves her own permanent crisis. She cannot get away from the one who for the most part only disturbs her. For he remains even for her the apostle of the heathen; the pious still hardly know what to make of him. (249−50)[11]

For Käsemann as for Bultmann, the essence of the Pauline doctrine of justification is the condemnation of the attempt to earn salvation by one's own efforts. Bultmann applies this to what he sees as a tendency of human life as a whole, self-assertion or the need for recognition. Käsemann uses it in a sharply polemical fashion against every form of conservatism, especially theological or ecclesiastical.

The approach to Paul taken by the representatives of dialectical theology (one thinks of scholars such as Bornkamm, Fuchs, Conzelmann, Klein and Hübner, as well as Bultmann and Käsemann) should not be lightly dismissed by those who cannot accept it. It represents much the most impressive modern attempt to reach to the heart of Paul's theology, and its theological seriousness compels respect, the more so as it has been engendered in part by the bitter experiences of modern German history. Although it can sometimes lead its advocates into bad-tempered and short-sighted polemic, on other occasions it attains a lucidity and profundity which makes New Testament scholarship from other traditions seem facile and superficial by comparison. On the other hand, this does not mean that its exegesis of Paul is correct: 'Profound theologians can be profoundly wrong.'[12]

This interpretation of Paul's controversy with Judaism obviously stems directly from the Reformation, and is not peculiar to dialectical theology.[13] But there has been a great deal of discussion about the extent to which opposition to the sinful attempt to put God under an obligation by one's obedience to the law is to be found in the Pauline texts. Whereas Bultmann and his followers have tended to see virtually every Pauline statement about the law in this light, scholars such as Althaus have emphasized that the traditional view of sin as transgression of the law is also of great significance to Paul.[14] More recently, U. Wilckens has rejected altogether the idea that Paul can see in 'works of the law' the essence of sin, arguing that Paul does not contest the desire to fulfil the law in itself, but only the possibility of such a fulfilment.[15] H. Hübner's recent book, *Law in Paul's Thought* (ET 1985) contains an attempt to mediate between these two positions; he argues that Bultmann's view is to be found in Romans but not in Galatians. Thus, in Gal. 3:10 Paul denies the possibility of a *quantitative* fulfilment of the law (38–41), whereas Rom. 3:27 criticizes boasting in one's fulfilment of the law (116). Similarly, Abraham is described as 'ungodly' in Rom. 4:5 in part because he wished to be justified by works (121), whereas there is no sign of this sinful boasting in Galatians (111).

On the whole, this debate has been carried on within the confines of the Reformation tradition. But other interpreters of Paul have questioned the Reformation approach *as a whole*. Is it really the case that at the heart of Paul's controversy with Judaism is an attack on the idea that righteousness is to be achieved by one's own efforts? Is there not a danger of reading back Luther's controversy with the Roman Catholic church into the first century, and so of failing to understand the historical circumstances of Paul's controversy with Judaism? We must now outline the views of some of the scholars who have questioned the traditional approach.

2 Opposition to the Lutheran approach

The first to claim that Paul's polemic against Judaism was motivated by a rather different concern was *Ferdinand Christian Baur*. He argued that Paul

> was the first to lay down expressly and distinctly the principle of Christian universalism as a thing essentially opposed to Jewish particularism. From the first he set this Christian principle before him as the sole rule and standard of his apostolic activity. In his Christian consciousness his own call to the apostolic office and the destination of Christianity to be the general principle of salvation for all people were two facts which were bound up inseparably in each other.
>
> (*Church History*, I, 47)

In his conversion, Paul 'broke through the barriers of Judaism and rose out of the particularism of Judaism into the universal idea of Christianity' (47). This contrast between universalism and particularism dominated his work. This was the point at issue in Galatians; in the debates described in Gal. 2,

> The alternatives ... were either to do away with the distinction between Jewish and Gentile Christians altogether, or to continue to be Jews, and deny to the Gentile Christians any privilege which would place them on the same level with the Jewish Christians. (55)

The Jerusalem apostles represented the particularist view, Paul the universalist: 'According to the former, it is in vain to be a Christian without being a Jew also. According to the latter, it is in vain to be a Christian if, as a Christian, one chooses to be a Jew as well' (57).

The significance of circumcision in this debate was that, as the means of entry into the Jewish community, it is a sign of the superiority of that community. On the other hand, Paul argues that this barrier between Jew and Gentile must be removed. The main point of Gal. 3 is thus that

> all who are baptized into Christ enter ... into a new community, in which all the causes of division between man and man, which are to be found in the outward circumstances of iife, are at once removed. (59)

The purpose of Romans is similarly

> to do away with the last remaining portions of the Jewish exclusiveness, by taking up and representing it as the mere introduction to the Christian universalism which extended to all nations. (*Paul*, I, 322)

> In the main part of the letter, from beginning to end, the theme is that each and every privilege of Jewish particularism, internal and external, is of no avail.
> ('Zweck und Gedankengang', 207)

Baur protests against the interpretation of the Epistle as a dogmatic handbook: it has *become* the basis of Protestant dogmatics, but that does not mean that this was its original intention. Such a view is reminiscent of the Catholic view of the apostles as bearers of the church's teaching, for in both, past and present are confused ('Zweck und Veranlassung', 154). It also means that Rom. 9–11 is quite unjustifiably regarded as an appendix of secondary importance, whereas it is in fact the heart of the letter (157f). Here Paul argues from the universalistic standpoint against the view of Jewish Christians that Gentiles could not participate in salvation until Israel accepted it (160), and claims that in the light of the success of the Gentile mission and the failure of the Jewish mission, 'the contrast between Jews and Gentiles, still firmly held by Jewish Christians, must lose its significance' (164). Contrary to the traditional view, Rom. 1–8 serves as a prelude to Rom. 9–11:

> Everything which the apostle develops in the first eight chapters is the necessary presupposition for cutting off at its roots the Jewish particularism, which opposes the apostle's universalism not in Judaism as a whole, but in the Christian church itself. (174)

The purpose of Rom. 1–8 is 'to indicate the opinions and scruples which still prevented his readers, as Jewish Christians, from giving complete adherence to the Pauline universalism' (*Paul*, I, 354). Thus, the denial that salvation is by works of the law is motivated by Paul's universalism:

> If men could attain righteousness and salvation by works of the law …, then the Jews alone would possess this righteousness, and God would only be the God of the Jews, but God is equally the God of the Gentiles as of the Jews … Faith alone corresponds to the universal conception of God.   (351)

Thus, Rom. 1–11 forms a unity derived from opposition to particularism:

> The absolute nullity of all its claims is the great idea which pervades the whole discussion, and which forms the connection between the two great sections of the Epistle (i.–viii. and ix.–xi.) … Its great significance lies not so much in its doctrinal discussions about sin and grace, as in its practical bearing on the most important controversy of these times, the relation between Jew and Gentile.
>
> (*Church History*, I, 72)

Baur and his critics believed that there was a conflict between his view, according to which Paul opposes Jewish exclusivism, and the Lutheran view, according to which he opposes the Jewish attempt to earn salvation ('Zweck und Gedankengang', 87ff).

By interpreting the so-called 'dogmatic' or 'theological' parts of Galatians and Romans in this way, Baur is able to link them with his reconstruction of early church history. It is well-known that he saw early church history as dominated by the conflict between Jewish Christianity, represented by James, and Pauline Gentile Christianity. But what needs to be emphasized here is that he perceives Paul's historical context and his theological reflection as a unity; Paul's theology is not abstract and theoretical but concrete and practical.

Modern interpreters in the Reformation tradition have made little use of Baur's insights in this area, despite his influence in other respects,[16] and in so far as they have, they have assumed that Baur and the Reformation are compatible. Thus, although Bultmann realizes that Paul's Jewish Christian opponents argued that 'the condition for sharing in salvation is belonging to the Jewish people' (*Theology*, I, 55), this is allowed no real significance for Pauline theology, for 'the real problem of the Law' is 'the problem of legalism, the problem of good works as the condition for participation in salvation' (111). In his article, 'Zur Geschichte der Paulus-Forschung' (1929), Bultmann commends Baur for maintaining the unity of Paul's thought and religious experience, as opposed to more recent scholars who disparage Paul's theology and seek to recover the religious experience underlying it: 'For Baur, Paul's thought *is* his experience' (314). Baur thus preserves the existential character of Paul's thought (331). But here and elsewhere, Bultmann and other representatives of dialectical theology remain studiously silent about the fact that Baur persistently opposed the Lutheran view of Paul's controversy with Judaism – the view which dialectical theology sought to revive. The idea that Paul's 'doctrine' might be closely related to his historical activity was implicitly rejected.

One reason why interpreters in the Reformation tradition have found it so hard to make use of Baur's insights is that their position depends on the possibility of generalizing Paul's attack on Jewish 'works of the law'. It is held that Paul is attacking not simply Judaism but, by implication, the universal human error of trying to earn salvation by one's own efforts. His attack on Judaism is an attack on 'religion' in general.[17] There is therefore no room here for a contrast between universality and exclusiveness, since both positions are in their own way 'universal'.[18] Käsemann and others quite rightly emphasize that it is not outside the scope of historical study to look for the general principles underlying a particular set of circumstances. But if one misunderstands the particular circumstances, one will also misunderstand the general principles.

K. Stendahl has strongly emphasized the conflict between the traditional Lutheran approach to Paul and the historical approach pioneered by Baur. He begins his well-known article, 'The Apostle Paul and the Introspective Conscience of the West' (1963), by contrasting the introspective element in Protestantism, typified by Luther's struggles with his conscience, with the 'robust' conscience displayed by Paul (200). The question, How can I find a gracious God?, was posed by late medieval piety, but it finds no echo in Paul. Paul was concerned instead with the question of the implications of the Messiah's coming for the status of the law and for the relationship between Jews and Gentiles (203). The early church rightly concluded that these issues were no longer relevant in a situation in which the separation of church and synagogue was taken for granted, and so Paul's teaching about justification and the law had little influence until the time of Augustine, when 'the Pauline thought about the Law and Justification was applied in a consistent and grand style to a more general and timeless human problem' (205). There thus arose the view (revived by Luther) that according to Paul, 'Nobody can attain a true faith in Christ unless his self-righteousness has been crushed by the Law'. Here, Paul's concern with the problem of the inclusion of the Gentiles in the church is completely ignored (206). The Lutheran belief that every man has a 'legalistic Jew' in his heart is thus a distortion of Paul's true meaning.

Stendahl returns to the attack in his book, *Paul among Jews and Gentiles* (1977). In Galatians, 'Paul's argument is that one does not have to go through Judaism into Christianity, but that there is a straight and direct way for the Gentiles apart from the law' (18). As regards Romans, 'the real centre of gravity' is chs.9–11, where the question of Israel is discussed (28). Rom. 1–8 merely forms a preface to this, and argues that 'since justification is by faith it is equally possible for both Jews and Gentiles to come to Christ' (29). All this indicates that Paul did not regard the Jewish–Gentile problem as a universally-applicable paradigm illustrating the human plight and its resolution:

> The doctrine of justification by faith was hammered out by Paul for the very specific and limited purpose of defending the rights of Gentile converts to be full and genuine heirs to the promise of God to Israel.   (2)

> Paul's doctrine of justification by faith has its theological context in his reflection on the relationship between Jews and Gentiles, and not within the problem of how *man* is to be saved ...   (26)

> When Paul speaks about the Jews, he really speaks about Jews, and not simply the fantasy Jews who stand as a symbol or as the prime example of a timeless legalism.   (36–7)

It should be apparent that Stendahl's position is very close indeed to that of Baur. The significance of his work is therefore that, over against the unhistorical existentialist approach of dialectical theology, he has revived Baur's insistence on the need to relate Paul's theological reflection to his historical context and his practical concerns.

W.D. Davies adopts a position in many ways similar to that of Stendahl. The main difference is that whereas Stendahl seems to regard Paul's reflection on the Jew–Gentile problem as more or less irrelevant, Davies regards it as extremely important in the contemporary dialogue between the church and the Jewish community. At the heart of his position is the view that prior to Jamnia the church and the Jewish community were not separated from one another; our understanding of Paul is distorted unless we constantly bear this fact in mind.

Thus, Paul was not a convert to a new religion but 'a Pharisee who had accepted Jesus as the Messiah' (*Paul*, 71). Although he rejected the imposition of the law on Gentile converts, he continued to observe it himself (73), for 'the observance of the law ... was Paul's passport with Judaism' (74). His aim in setting aside certain aspects of the law for his Gentile converts was not to distance himself from Judaism but to put into practice the universalism of parts of the Jewish scriptures (59ff), thus breaking away from the particularism of much contemporary Judaism while remaining true to Jewish tradition. He continued to believe in the unique privileges of Israel: 'Despite his noble universalism, he finds it impossible not to assign a special place to his own people' (75). Paul has thus been misunderstood because it has been forgotten that his debate with Judaism was a 'family dispute' about 'the true interpretation of their common Jewish tradition' ('People of Israel', 22). This disagreement was possible within Judaism because of the fluid, tolerant nature of Judaism prior to AD 70 (19). The fact that 'between us and Paul stands the Protestant Reformation' ('Law', 6) makes it easy for us to misunderstand his view of the law. As a Jew, he held that the Torah was not simply a commandment but also a gift of God's grace (5). He felt able to proclaim the end of the law because of the Jewish belief that the Messiah would inaugurate a new law at his coming (7–8). His statements about the law are not entirely consistent, and one should not emphasize the negative ones at the expense of the positive (8ff). Christianity was for Paul 'the fulfilment and not the annulment of Judaism' (12).

For Davies, all this has contemporary relevance. The Holocaust and the rise of the State of Israel are realities which 'demand that we sit again at the feet of Paul, whose mind is a clue to the pre-Jamnian period, to learn afresh that the debate between Jews and Christians, separated as they now are, is a familial one' ('People of Israel', 37). Paul 'provided ground in his day for mutual tolerance and respect between Jew and Gentile Christian', and it is bitterly ironical that he has been so tragically misinterpreted (38).[19]

Much the most formidable challenge to the Reformation tradition's interpretation of Paul has come in the work of *E. P. Sanders*. In his book, *Paul and Palestinian Judaism* (1977), he claims that the modern Lutheran interpretation of Paul makes use of a quite erroneous view of Judaism derived from the misleading textbooks of Weber and Bousset.[20] These teach that according to Judaism, man must earn salvation solely by his own efforts. Every good work establishes merit, and every transgression establishes demerit. Merits and demerits will be weighed at the Last Judgment, and one's destiny depends on which preponderates (37ff). Sanders also criticizes Strack–Billerbeck, claiming that the selection of the material often distorts the meaning of the texts and is based on the false view of Judaism just described (42–3). Bultmann seems not to have had 'substantial independent access to the literature of "late Judaism"', and particularly not to Rabbinic sources' (43), yet his support for the Weber–Bousset view has ensured its perpetuation in the work of Braun, Rössler, Jaubert, Black, Fuller, Conzelmann and Thyen (43ff). This view is based on 'a massive perversion and misunderstanding of the material' (59), caused by 'the retrojection of the Protestant–Catholic debate into ancient history, with Judaism taking the role of Catholicism and Christianity the role of Lutheranism' (57).

Sanders summarizes the true pattern of Rabbinic religion as follows:

> God has chosen Israel and Israel has accepted the election. In his role as King, God gave Israel commandments which they are to obey as best they can. Obedience is rewarded and disobedience punished. In case of failure to obey, however, man has recourse to divinely ordained means of atonement, in all of which repentance is required. As long as he maintains his desire to stay in the covenant, he has a share in God's covenantal promises, including life in the world to come. The intention and effort to be obedient constitute the *condition for remaining in the covenant*, but they do not *earn* it.
>
> (180)

If the Judaism Paul attacked is misunderstood by the Reformation tradition, this raises the possibility that Paul himself has been misunderstood.[21] In *Paul, the Law and the Jewish People* (1983), Sanders argues that this has indeed been the case. The Judaism attacked by Paul is not the Judaism of the Lutheran caricature but Judaism as it really was; Paul attacks 'the traditional understanding of the covenant and election' (46).[22] Sanders begins his work by listing four possible interpretations of Paul's exclusion of 'works of the law' (17). The first and second he describes as the 'quantitative' and 'qualitative' views, which are the positions represented by Wilckens and Bultmann respectively. The third interpretation is that of Paul's 'exclusivist soteriology', and the fourth view emphasizes the setting of the controversy in the Gentile mission (cf. Stendahl).

Some of Sanders' exegesis is similar to Stendahl's. Thus he writes: 'The subject of Galatians is not whether or not humans, abstractly conceived, can by doing good deeds earn enough merit to be declared righteous at the judgment; it is the condition on which Gentiles enter the people of God' (18). However, Sanders argues that Paul opposes this Jewish exclusiveness not with a universalistic gospel but with a different form of exclusiveness, based on Christology. Salvation is in Christ alone, and therefore it cannot be by the law (i.e. by membership of the Jewish people); this is the sole content of Paul's critique of Judaism. He does not argue that '*since* the law cannot be entirely fulfilled, *therefore* righteousness is by faith' (23), nor does he accuse the Jews of 'self-righteousness' or 'legalism' – that view is 'mere eisegesis which rests on long and venerated (perhaps too venerated) tradition' (155). Paul claims simply that as God's way of salvation is through faith in Christ, Judaism is automatically disqualified. He can tell us nothing about Judaism unless we share his *a priori* Christology.

The contrast in Phil. 3:9 between 'my own righteousness' and 'the righteousness from God which depends on faith' may serve as an example:

> Paul does not say that boasting in status and achievement was wrong because boasting is the wrong attitude, but that he boasted in things that *were gain*. They *became loss* because in his black and white world, there is no second best. His criticism of his own former life is not that he was guilty of the attitudinal sin of self-righteousness, but that he put confidence in something other than faith in Jesus Christ.   (44)

Again and again, by means of painstaking exegesis, Sanders seeks to show that both the 'quantitative' view (i.e. the view that works are wrong because it is impossible to fulfil the law in its entirety) and the 'qualitative' view (i.e. the view that to attempt to fulfil the law leads to the sin of boasting in one's own achievements) are false. Paul rejects the law not because it has any inherent defects but simply because it is something other than Christ.

The Finnish scholar *H. Räisänen* argues that Paul's statements about the law are so full of contradictions as to be completely incoherent. He draws attention to the 'uncritical praise of Paul's thought' (*Paul*, 7) which characterizes so much Protestant scholarship: 'modern Paulinism' may be described as 'the theological cult of the apostle' (15). Yet, as the profound disagreement between Käsemann and Cranfield shows, 'The followers of the apostle have hardly ever been able to agree on what he really wanted to say' (3). The dilemma may be stated as follows: 'On the one hand, the clarity, profundity and cogency of Paul's theological thinking is universally praised. On the other hand, it does not seem possible to reach any unanimity whatever as to what his message really was' (4). The inconsistencies are almost endless. For example, the meaning of νόμος is often unclear; Paul may be referring to the law, or to something else, and the meaning may shift even within a single passage. He holds that the law is abrogated but that its 'decree' (Rom. 8:4) is still in force. He teaches that nobody can fulfil the law but that some non-Christian Gentiles do. The law was given to bring 'life' (Rom. 7:10), but it never had even the theoretical power to do so (Rom. 8:3, Gal. 3:21). The law was a temporary addition to the divine testament (Gal. 3: 15ff), and yet a dramatic act of liberation from its power was needed (Gal. 3:13). Paul's Old Testament exegesis is often arbitrary, and his view that the law calls forth sin is incredible ('Paul's Theological Difficulties', 304–5). Contrary to the common view that there is a fundamental change of stance between the polemic against the law in Galatians and the calmer and more positive tone of Romans, the real problem is the deep contradictions *within* each letter (302). In Rom. 1–3, the commonplace observation that 'many live in grave sins' leads to the sweeping generalization, 'All are under sin' (310), which is 'a blatant ''non sequitur''' (309). Indeed, Rom. 2 is 'simply a piece of propagandist denigration' (*Paul*, 101); attempts to interpret it as a profound piece of theology are unconvincing. If this approach seems unduly negative, Räisänen's answer is that a corrective is needed, since Paul is still so widely regarded as theologically authoritative (14–15).

The work of Stendahl, Davies, Sanders and Räisänen is symptomatic of a very widespread feeling of dissatisfaction with the Lutheran approach to Paul. This is also apparent in the work of such scholars as M. Barth, G. Howard, J. D. G. Dunn, N. T. Wright and (perhaps most significantly) in the important new three-volume commentary on Romans by U. Wilckens.[23] The process of 'delutheranizing Paul' is already well under way.

3 A sociological approach

The scholars discussed in the previous section have criticized the Lutheran approach to Paul from a number of different points of view.[24] One problem that arises again and again in different forms is the relation between Paul's historical situation and his theology. The Lutheran approach has assumed that in Paul's teaching about justification and the law we have the permanent essence of the Christian gospel, which no doubt arose in a concrete historical situation, but which is to be interpreted existentially, in comparative isolation from its historical origins. Even historically conscious scholars such as Bultmann and Käsemann argue for the legitimacy of this approach.

In opposition to this isolation of theology from history, the present discussion will adopt a sociological perspective in order to examine how Paul's theorizing is related to the concrete problems which he faced — in particular, the legitimacy of the law-free gospel for the Gentiles and the status of the Jewish people. *The social reality which underlies Paul's discussions of Judaism and the law is his creation of Gentile Christian communities in sharp separation from the Jewish community*. His theological reflection legitimates the separation of church from synagogue.

Two sociological models will be used to shed light on this process; they will be discussed in detail in the second half of the following chapter. The first is *the transformation of a reform-movement into a sect*.[25] New religious movements (including early Christianity) often begin as reform-movements within an existing religious community (in this case, the Jewish community). When opposition is encountered, one possibility is that the reform-movement will be transformed into a sect — i.e. a closely-knit group which sets up rigid and clearly-defined barriers between itself and the parent community. It will be argued that this is an appropriate model for studying Paul's creation of churches which were separated from the Jewish community. For example, this means that the Galatian controversy may be interpreted as a controversy about the nature of the church: should it continue to be a reform-movement within the Jewish community (the Judaizers' view), or should it be a sect, clearly differentiated from the Jewish community (Paul's view)?

The second sociological model follows from the first. If a sectarian group is to establish and maintain separation from the religious body from which it originated, it will require *an ideology legitimating its state of separation* – i.e. a theoretical justification for its separate existence, which is shared by all the group's members and which helps to give it its cohesion.[26] This may involve first a denunciation of the group's opponents; secondly, the use of antitheses, of which the positive member (e.g. light, truth) defines the group's members, and of which the negative member (e.g. darkness, error) defines the community from which the group is trying to distance itself; and thirdly, a reinterpretation of the religious traditions of the community as a whole in the light of the belief that the sectarian group is the sole legitimate heir to those traditions. It will be argued that this is an appropriate model for interpreting Paul's theoretical reflections on Judaism and the law.

The purpose of this sociological approach is to emphasize the close link between the social and historical setting and the theological reflection; the first model (the transformation of a reform-movement into a sect) stresses the former, whereas the second model (the theoretical rationale for separation required by a sectarian group) stresses the relationship between the two.[27] In opposition to the Lutheran approach, it will be argued that Paul's theological reflection is completely misunderstood if it is isolated from its social context, the creation and maintaining of sectarian groups among the Gentiles, separated from the Jewish community.[28] It is important to state that this approach does not claim to exclude the possibility of *any* theological interpretation of Paul; it is obvious that Paul's letters can legitimately be interpreted from a number of different standpoints.[29] This approach simply claims that one particular theological interpretation of Paul, derived from Luther, misunderstands what the historical Paul was doing and saying.

How does the present interpretation relate to the work of the other scholars, discussed above, who have expressed dissatisfaction with the Lutheran approach? It endorses Baur's stress on the relationship between Paul's theological reflection and his historical activity, and it has affinities with his contrast between Pauline universalism and Jewish exclusiveness. But the latter view is not entirely satisfactory. In broad historical terms, it is true that, by emancipating Christianity from its origins within the Jewish community, Paul did enable it to transform itself into a 'world religion'; to that extent the contrast between universality and exclusiveness is justified. But it is also true that this was not what Paul himself intended. His eschatological expectations make it impossible that he should have foreseen or intended the way in which Christianity gradually extended its influence throughout the Roman empire until it became the official state religion, thus attaining a universality denied to Judaism. The term 'exclusiveness' is in some ways more applicable to the sectarian groups created by Paul himself than it is to the Jewish community. If in one sense it is true that Paul sought to break down the barrier between Jew and Gentile, he nevertheless did so only to re-establish exclusiveness in a new form.[30]

Stendahl's renewal of Baur's insight into the relationship between Paul's theological reflection and his historical situation is to be welcomed, as is his clear perception that this is incompatible with the Lutheran approach. But he does not make the crucial point that Paul's view of the rights of Gentiles involved the separation of the church from the Jewish community. The debate is not simply concerned with the rights of Gentiles to enter the church, but with the nature of the church: should it continue as a reform-movement within Judaism, or should it become a sect outside it?

This view, with its stress on separation from Judaism, is incompatible with the view of W. D. Davies and others, that Paul was a loyal though much misunderstood Jew. On the present view, it was Paul's Judaizing opponents who wished to remain loyal members of the Jewish community, and Paul who insisted that the gospel required separation. However liberal and fluid Judaism before Jamnia may have been, it could hardly have tolerated a man who proclaimed that Gentiles who ignored many of the law's requirements were accepted by God, whereas Jews who remained faithful to the law were rejected.

The present discussion will seek to develop further two of the ideas stressed by Sanders. The first is the claim that the fundamental category of the Judaism which Paul attacked is not 'earning salvation' but the covenant. The second is the claim that Paul does not oppose Judaism because of any theoretical shortcomings it may or may not have, but simply because it is not Christianity. These two points will be particularly important in the discussion of the fundamental antithesis between faith and works. The present emphasis on the social and historical realities underlying Paul's theological reflection will attempt to account for his insistence that Christ and the law are incompatible.

Räisänen emphasizes the inconsistencies in Paul's discussions of the law, and it is quite true that there are a large number of these inconsistencies, not only between Galatians and Romans (which would suggest developments in Paul's thought − the view of Hübner and others), but also within Romans and Galatians themselves. The present treatment sees the cohesiveness of Paul's statements about the law not primarily at the theoretical level but at the level of practical strategy.[31] It will be argued that Paul's sole aim in discussing Judaism and the law is to maintain and defend the separation of his Gentile Christian churches from the Jewish community. In fulfilling this aim, he makes use of various types of theoretical legitimation, which are not always compatible with one another as pure theory, but which all contribute to the same practical goal. In other words, in studying the Pauline texts, one should ask not simply about what Paul is *saying*, but also about what he is *doing*.[32]

The first question to which we must address ourselves is therefore: What was the historical and sociological situation which gave rise to the Pauline problem of the law?

2

THE ORIGINS OF PAUL'S VIEW OF THE LAW

1 Historical reconstruction

If we are to understand Paul's view of the law and of Judaism correctly, our starting-point should not be the complex theoretical discussions of the law found in his letters, but the situation in the history of the early church underlying these discussions. It is obvious that there is a close link between Paul's statements about the law and the mission to the Gentiles, and this suggests that the origins of the former are to be found in the origins of the latter.[1] In the first part of the present chapter, we shall investigate the way in which the mission to the Gentiles developed out of the mission to the Jews, and the reassessment of the law which this involved.

A The evidence of Acts

1. One version of the origins of the Gentile mission is given to us by the lengthy account of the conversion of Cornelius in Acts 10:1 – 11:18. Unlike the otherwise somewhat similar conversion-story in Acts 8:26ff, this one is intended to have a paradigmatic significance: what is being described is not an isolated event but the origin of the Gentile mission, to whose progress much of the rest of Acts is devoted. This is clear from 11:18, where those who had initially opposed Peter's conduct confess, 'Then to the Gentiles also God has granted repentance unto life.'[2] Likewise, in 15:7ff Peter's reference to this event serves to justify the preaching activity of Paul and Barnabas among the Gentiles. Luke therefore asserts that the origins of the Gentile mission are to be found in the conversion of Cornelius, and a discussion of this subject must take this narrative into account.

The narrative can hardly be historical as it stands.[3] In addition to its many Lucan and legendary features, it contradicts Gal. 2:7–9, where Peter is seen not as the pioneer of the Gentile mission, but as the one to whom the mission to the Jews was entrusted.[4] But it might be argued that although Luke has exaggerated the significance of the conversion of Cornelius, this narrative nevertheless preserves genuine historical reminiscences which provide valuable information about the origins of the Gentile mission. That is the position of Dibelius, who claims that two parts of the narrative are historically authentic: Peter's vision and the conversion of a God-fearing Gentile.[5] Dibelius thinks that these two parts of the narrative were originally separate, on the grounds that the vision (10:9–16) is describing the abolition of the food-laws, whereas 10:28 (cf. 11:12) applies it not to food but to men: 'God has shown me that I should not call *any man* common or unclean' ('Cornelius', 111–12). Dibelius further claims that this vision may have been used by Peter or his supporters to justify his abandonment of the food-laws at Antioch (Gal. 2:12). As regards the conversion of the God-fearing Gentile centurion, Dibelius thinks that it reproduces historical events, though in the style of a 'legend' (121). He writes: 'We must assume that there was a period of time ... during which such isolated cases [i.e. of the conversion of Gentiles] could have occurred, by chance and not in order to defend a principle' (122); Luke has exaggerated the significance of this story, but this and other similar incidents were an important preliminary to the fully-fledged Gentile mission.

But it is very doubtful whether the Cornelius narrative is of any historical value. The following features suggest that Acts 10 is a Lucan composition from beginning to end.

(i) Luke elsewhere shows an interest in devout centurions.[6] In his version of the Q story of the healing of the centurion's servant, he has added the Jewish elders' testimony to the centurion's piety (Lk. 7:4f). Julius the Centurion is favourably disposed towards Paul (Acts 27:1, 3, 31f, 42ff). This is simply one aspect of Luke's generally favourable attitude towards Roman authority.[7]

(ii) Divine guidance given through angels (10:1–8) is typically Lucan (Acts 8:26; 27:23f; cf. 5:19f; 12:7ff). The closest parallel to the present story is in Lk. 1:8ff (Zechariah's vision in the temple). The two stories have in common a stress on the previous piety of the recipients of the angelophany, the occurrence of the angelophany during worship, and the recipient's initial response of fear.

(iii) Peter's vision (10:9–16) involves a direct message from the Lord, and such visions are characteristic of Luke: Stephen (Acts 7:55f), Ananias (9:10ff), and above all Paul (in chronological order, 9:3ff; 22:6ff; 26:13ff; 22:17ff; 16:9; 18:9f; 23:11; 27:33ff) are all recipients of such visions. This suggests that 10:9ff is not independent but Lucan.[8] The use of animals to symbolize men (cf. 10:28) is not a serious difficulty.[9]

(iv) The supernatural proof of apostolic authority is the outpouring of the Spirit, in 10:44f just as in 2:1ff; 4:31; 8:14ff and 19:1ff.[10]

It therefore seems unlikely that any primitive traditions preserving historical reminiscences of the origins of the Gentile mission underlie 10:1–11:18. Luke's purpose is to vindicate the Gentile mission and the churches which it brought into being by tracing it back ultimately not to the questionable authority of Paul[11] but to the unquestioned authority of Peter and to unmistakable supernatural signs of divine guidance[12] (cf. Acts 15:6ff).

2. But Luke also gives us an alternative account of the origins of the Gentile mission which at first sight seems rather more credible. In Acts 11:20f, he tells us of men of Cyprus and Cyrene, who were among those driven out of Jerusalem by Saul's ferocious persecution of the church, and who took the momentous step of preaching the gospel to the Greeks, with considerable success. He also gives us information about the antecedents to this decision. In Acts 6:1, he tells us about a dispute between the 'Hellenists' and the 'Hebrews' in the Jerusalem church over the distribution of food. Many scholars have conjectured that, as in Acts 15:36–40, Luke is covering up a far more serious disagreement.[13] They note that the seven men named in 6:5 all have Greek names, and so probably belonged to the Hellenist party. The only two whose activities are described – Stephen and Philip – are not seen as welfare officers, as 6:2f would lead one to expect, but as preachers (6:8–8:40), precisely the function which according to 6:2–4 was reserved for the apostles alone. Thus (it is argued), the seven were leaders of the Greek-speaking wing of the Jerusalem church which was to a large extent independent of the Aramaic-speaking wing, led by the apostles. Even if it was language rather than theology which initially caused the Hellenists to separate from the Hebrews, they soon developed a radical theological stance, according to Martin Hengel: 'They called for the eschatological abolition of Temple worship and the revision of the law of Moses in the light of the true will of God' (*Acts* 72–3).[14] Although Luke portrays Paul's persecution as affecting the whole church (Acts 8:1), it is more likely that it affected only the Hellenists, according to Hengel (74). It was this which eventually led them to preach to the Gentiles: 'The "Hellenists", driven out of Jewish Palestine, were gradually forced to go beyond the circle of full Jews and also to turn to Gentiles who were interested in Judaism' (75).

Although the abandonment of circumcision and the whole ritual law was probably a gradual process (79), this decision was already implicit in the criticism of the law developed in Jerusalem (Hengel, 'Ursprünge', 27).[15] Thus, according to Hengel, it was the Hellenists' radical theology which eventually led to the law-free Gentile mission, and which prepared the way for the work of Paul. This theology was derived from Jesus' own critique of the law (*Acts*, 72), and the Hellenists thus bridge the gap between Jesus and Paul.

But this reconstruction of the origins of the Gentile mission is full of problems. Together with the majority of scholars, Hengel does not believe that Acts 7 (Stephen's speech) gives any reliable information about the Hellenists' theology,[16] and so the hypothesis of the Hellenists' radical view of the law relies entirely on Acts 6:13f, where 'false witnesses' accuse Stephen: 'This man never ceases to speak words against this holy place and the law; for we have heard him say that Jesus of Nazareth will destroy this place, and will change the customs which Moses delivered to us.'[17] To begin with, Hengel arbitrarily assumes that Luke's version of the accusation against Stephen is authentic, but that his view that it was produced by lying 'false witnesses' is not.[18] In addition, the accusation speaks of the abolition of Temple worship and the revision of the law *only at the Parousia*; until that occurs, the law presumably remains unchanged. The accusation therefore gives no basis for supposing that the Hellenists adopted a radical attitude towards the present practice of the law. In any case, there are good grounds for doubting the authenticity of this accusation, for it seems to be modelled on the charge against Jesus recorded in Mk 14:58: 'false witnesses' report, 'We heard him say, "I will destroy this temple that is made with hands, and in three days I will build another, not made with hands".' Luke omits this accusation from his account of Jesus' trial (Lk. 22:66–71), and makes it the basis of Stephen's trial instead.[19] Thus the main evidence for the hypothesis of the Hellenists' radical view of the law seems extremely precarious.[20]

Indeed, it seems very doubtful if there ever were two groups in the Jerusalem church, the Hellenists and the Hebrews. In Acts 11:19f, Luke's attribution of the beginning of the Gentile mission to Hellenists who had been driven out of Jerusalem by persecution agrees so well with his tendency to emphasize the centrality of Jerusalem at every point[21] that one must doubt its historicity.[22] Luke insists that the Gentile mission and its main protagonists originated in Jerusalem (perhaps under the influence of Is. 2:3, 'Out of Zion shall go forth the law, and the word of the Lord from Jerusalem'). This view leads to modifications of the earlier tradition on at least two occasions. First, Luke places the resurrection appearances in or near Jerusalem, in flat contradiction to the promise of Mk 14:28 and 16:7 that the risen Christ will appear in Galilee; his rewriting of Mk 16:7 (Lk 24:6f) is especially revealing. Secondly, he states that Paul's persecution of the church took place in Jerusalem. This contradicts Gal. 1:22f,[23] where Paul writes: 'And I was still not known by sight to the churches of Christ in Judaea; they only heard it said, "He who once persecuted us is now preaching the faith he once tried to destroy".' V.23 recounts what the Judaean churches have heard about Paul from his former victims, not their own experience of him; on the contrary, they have never seen him (v.22).[24] It therefore seems beyond doubt that Paul cannot have persecuted Christians in Jerusalem.[25] In the light of these two examples, one should treat with considerable scepticism Acts' claim that all the other protagonists in the Gentile mission came from Jerusalem: the Hellenists (6:1; 11:20), Barnabas (4:36f; 11:22ff), John Mark (12:12, 25) and Silas (15:22, 27, 40). This fits the programme outlined in 1:8, but one suspects that the historical reality was rather more complicated. In the case of the Hellenists, it may be that later tension between Jerusalem and Antioch (cf. Gal. 2) has been retrojected back into the earliest days of the Jerusalem church.[26]

The historicity of a Hellenist party in the Jerusalem church becomes still more doubtful when one observes how Luke understands the term 'Hellenist'. According to 9:29, when Paul came to Jerusalem soon after his conversion, he disputed with 'Hellenists', who sought to kill him. These people are probably to be identified with the Jews from Cyrene, Alexandria, Cilicia and Asia who disputed with Stephen (6:9), in his case successfully bringing about his death.[27] In other words, 'Hellenists' are for Luke neither Gentiles,[28] nor Jews with a lax attitude towards the law,[29] nor even Greek-speaking Jews *per se*,[30] but Jews from the Diaspora now resident in Jerusalem.[31] If this is the case, then Luke has earlier explained the origin of the Hellenist group in the Jerusalem church:[32] in the Pentecost story, Peter's hearers consist not of native Jews but of 'Jews, devout men from every nation under heaven' (Acts 2:5) − a long list of their various places of origin is given in 2:9−11. It is because these many Jews from the Diaspora are converted by Peter's sermon (cf. Acts 2:41) that Luke can introduce the 'Hellenists' in Acts 6:1.[33] But Acts 2:5ff is manifestly unhistorical; the view that the only people to show any interest in the earliest Christian preaching were Jews from the remotest parts of the Diaspora, who became Christians in vast numbers, lacks all credibility. Luke's portrayal is determined by his view of the church's world-wide mission as intended primarily for the Jews of the Dispersion, and only secondarily for the Gentiles (cf. Acts 13:14–49; 18:4ff; 19:8ff; 28:23ff).[34] If this is correct, then the historicity not only of Acts 2 but also of the Hellenist group in Acts 6 becomes extremely doubtful.

Acts therefore gives us virtually no reliable information about the origins of the mission to the Gentiles. Even the claim of 11:19f, that men from Cyprus and Cyrene preached to Greeks in Antioch, before the arrival of Barnabas and Paul, seems very doubtful in view of Paul's decisive influence on the decision to turn to the Gentiles (on which see below). We thus learn nothing from Acts about the process in which important elements of the law were first set aside to facilitate the entry of Gentiles into the church.[35]

B The evidence of Paul's letters

If we are to reconstruct this process at all, we must turn not to Acts but to Paul's letters. Although the evidence is extremely scanty, a convincing picture does emerge from this source. The process seems to have had five main aspects. First, Paul began his Christian career as a missionary to Jews and not to Gentiles. Secondly, he and others first preached to Gentiles in response to the failure of their preaching among the Jews. Thirdly, they did not require full submission to the law from their Gentile converts; in particular, circumcision, the food-laws, the Sabbath and the feast days were set aside. Fourthly, the purpose of this was to make it easier for Gentiles to enter the church, and so to ensure the success of the preaching of the gospel. Fifthly, this involved the separation of Pauline Gentile Christians from the Jewish community. Thus, the origins of Paul's theology of the law are to be found in a specific social situation, and not in his conversion experience, his psychological problems or his insight into the existential plight of humanity.[36] Each of these five points must now be substantiated in detail.

1. *At an early stage of his Christian activity, Paul had preached the gospel only to Jews.* In 2 Cor. 11:24, Paul writes: 'Five times I have received at the hands of the Jews the forty lashes less one.' This reference to the discipline of the synagogue is strange, since nowhere

else in Paul's letters is it implied that he retained any links with the synagogue (even in 1 Cor. 9:20, on which see below). In Rom. 11:13f, Paul states that his work as apostle to the Gentiles affects Jews only indirectly, through their becoming 'jealous', and this seems to exclude the possibility that he still preached to Jews.[37] The problem is solved if 2 Cor. 11:24 refers to an earlier phase in Paul's career when he *was* preaching to the Jews.[38]

In 1 Cor. 9:20f, Paul writes:

> To the Jews I became as a Jew, in order to win Jews; to those under the law I became as one under the law — though not being myself under the law — that I might win those under the law. To those outside the law I became as one outside the law — not being without law toward God but under the law of Christ — that I might win those outside the law.

This passage cannot mean that Paul carried on a mission to the Jews at the same time as his mission to the Gentiles, changing chameleon-like from one way of life to another according to the company he was in.[39] Occasional conformity to the law is entirely alien to the Jewish way of life, and could never have helped him to 'win those under the law'. It is much more likely that Paul is referring in v. 20 to the earliest days of his Christian commitment, in which he continued to live as a Jew and preached to Jews only, and that v. 21 describes his irrevocable break with the Jewish way of life when he began to think of himself as 'apostle to the Gentiles'.[40] That would explain the use of the aorist tense rather than the present. Paul's insistence that when he was preaching to Jews he observed the law for purely pragmatic reasons, while regarding himself as free from the law, should not be taken literally. He wishes his readers to think that throughout his life as a Christian he has always understood himself as free from the law, even during the earliest period.[41] But there is in fact no reason to suppose that during the period of mission to the Jews he already held his later doctrine of freedom from the law. As we shall see, this arose in the context of mission to the Gentiles after the abandonment of the mission to the Jews.

Two passages in Galatians also point to an early period of mission-ary activity among the Jews. Gal. 1:18–24 suggests that three years after his conversion there was no hint of any tension between Paul and the churches of Jerusalem and Judaea.[42] Whatever Paul may have discussed with Cephas and James, it cannot have been Gentile entry into the church without submission to the law, for that did not become a problem until fourteen years later (2:1–10);[43] but it surely would have been a problem if Paul had already been permitting it. At this stage, the Judaean churches still regarded Paul's conversion as grounds for praise and thanksgiving (1:23f).[44] In Gal. 5:11, Paul writes: 'But if I, brethren, still preach circumcision, why am I still persecuted?' This verse must surely be a reply to an accusation by Paul's opponents: Paul still preaches circumcision. They cannot have meant that he consistently preached circumcision, for it was obvious that he had not done so in Galatia. They must therefore have meant that when with Gentiles he opposed circumcision, but that when with Jews he affirmed it – i.e. that he 'pleased men' (1:10).[45] Since κηρύσσειν is a technical term for Christian proclamation, 'preaching circumcision' is probably equivalent to preaching τὸ εὐαγγέλιον τῆς περιτομῆς (Gal. 2:7) – proclaiming Jesus as the Jewish Messiah who came to save the Jewish community, the community of the circumcised. That Paul might have been understood in this way is clear from Rom. 3:1f and 15:8, where he uses remarkably positive language about the significance of (physical) circumcision. But for our present purposes, it is Paul's response to the charge of inconsistency which is important: 'If I, brethren, still preach circumcision, why am I still persecuted?' Paul acknowledges that he had once preached τὸ εὐαγγέλιον τῆς περιτομῆς,[46] but uses his experiences of persecution by the Jewish community to prove that he does so no more. As in 1 Cor. 9:20f, we therefore have here a clear indication that Paul began his career as a missionary by preaching to Jews, but at a later stage abandoned this practice and embarked on his Gentile mission. Gal. 5:11 thus alludes to the period before the Gentile mission referred to in Gal. 1:18ff.

It might be argued that the call to preach to the Gentiles was part of Paul's conversion, according to Gal. 1:16; this would leave no room for a preliminary period of preaching among the Jews. But in Gal. 1:16, Paul is reflecting on his conversion as he now understands it, about seventeen years after the event. This passage cannot be safely used as evidence for Paul's self-understanding at the time of his conversion.[47] One should not assume that his understanding of himself as called to preach to the Gentiles was an integral part of his conversion experience,[48] any more than one should assume that his entire theology was somehow already contained in that experience[49] – common though both views are. All we know of Paul's conversion is how he chose to understand it in polemical contexts many years later.

The view that Paul was engaged in preaching only to the Jews in his early years as a Christian accounts for the curious fact that we know so much about the last decade or so of his career, but so little about the previous seventeen years. Paul would not have been likely to have had much to say about his years of preaching to the Jews once he had embarked on his mission to the Gentiles. It also accounts for the fact that the admission of Gentiles to the church became a problem at such a late date (Gal. 2:1ff). If Paul had preached to the Gentiles and practised and taught freedom from the law from the beginning, it is hard to see why this did not become an issue for so many years.

2. *Paul (and others) first preached to the Gentiles as a response to the failure of their preaching among the Jews.* In Rom. 11:11, Paul writes of Israel: 'Through their failure salvation has come to the Gentiles'; Israel's 'trespass' is the failure to believe in Jesus as the Christ (cf. Rom. 9:32f). This idea is repeated constantly during the course of Rom. 11: 'If their trespass means riches for the world, and if their failure means riches for the Gentiles...' (11:12); 'If their rejection means the reconciliation of the world ...' (11:15); 'If some of the branches were broken off, and you, a wild olive shoot, were grafted in their place to share the richness of the olive tree ...' (11:17); 'You will say, "Branches were broken off so that I might be grafted in"' (11:19); 'A hardening has come upon part of Israel until the full number of the Gentiles comes in' (11:25); 'As regards the gospel, they are enemies of God, for your sake' (11:28); 'You ... have received mercy because of their disobedience' (11:30). In its present context, this idea is to be understood theologically: God has hardened the hearts of the Jews (11:8–10) because it was his will to remove them from their privileged position and to install Gentiles in their place. But this is to be understood as a secondary theological reflection on a primary historical and social reality. When Paul states in v. 11 that salvation has come to the Gentiles, he is referring to the successful results of his own Gentile mission; thus, in v. 13 he mentions that he is 'apostle to the Gentiles'. We may therefore paraphrase the statements of vv. 11, 12, etc., quoted above, as follows: Jewish failure to believe the gospel has led to Paul's mission to the Gentiles, and so to the salvation of many Gentiles. Faced with the problem of Jewish failure to believe their gospel, Paul and his colleagues turned to the Gentiles, who did believe it. In order to legitimate their action, they claimed that God had hardened the Jews so as to save Gentiles in their place.

It is this historical and social situation alone which can account for the remarkable series of statements in Rom. 11 to the effect that Israel's unbelief has led to the salvation of the Gentiles, for it is hard to imagine how Paul could have come to such a view except through reflection on what had actually happened.[50] Here at last we are on solid ground in our investigation of the origins of the Gentile mission: it began in response to Jewish failure to believe the gospel.[51]

Who was responsible for this momentous decision to turn to the Gentiles? Gal. 2 provides the answer: it was Paul, Barnabas and the other Jewish Christians at Antioch. In 2:1, 9, Paul links Barnabas with himself as sharing a commission to preach to the Gentiles, and he was therefore incensed that '*even* Barnabas' later succumbed to pressure from Jerusalem to force Gentiles to accept the Jewish law (Gal. 2:13f). It was probably Paul and Barnabas who initiated the revolutionary new attitude towards the Gentiles, for they are to be seen not merely as delegates from Antioch but as leaders;[52] 2:9 confirms their leading position. But they were also supported at first by 'the rest of the Jews', i.e. the other Jewish Christians at Antioch, until they defected alongside Peter and Barnabas (Gal. 2:13). One may therefore say that the Gentile mission was initiated as a communal venture by the Jewish Christian congregation of Antioch, in response to the failure of its preaching among the Jews.[53]

According to Acts 13:46–8; 18:4–7; 19:8f, etc., Paul's practice was to preach first in the synagogue and to turn to the Gentiles only after being rejected by the Jews. But Paul's description of himself as apostle to the Gentiles (Rom. 1:5; 11:13; 15:16; Gal. 1:16; 2:7–9) suggests that at the time when the letters were written he was devoting his energies entirely to preaching to the Gentiles. This is in agreement with Rom. 11:11ff,[54] which does not suggest that Paul's preaching to the Gentiles always followed unsuccessful preaching in the local synagogue,[55] and indeed apparently excludes any further direct preaching to Jews (NB 11:13f). Rom. 11:11ff implies a period of transition, in which Paul and others gradually came to the conclusion that the Jews had been hardened and that they were called to preach to the Gentiles instead. This transition now lies in the past, so that Paul can describe himself as apostle exclusively to the Gentiles. The portrayal of his activity in Acts is in keeping with the author's utterly unhistorical insistence that Paul continued to live as a Pharisee and that his belief in Jesus as the Messiah made no difference at all to his attitude towards the law (Acts 18:18; 21:20ff; 23:6; 25:8; 26:4f; 28:17).[56]

3. *Paul and the other Antiochene Jewish Christians did not require full submission to the law from their Gentile converts.* According to Gal. 2:3, Paul took the uncircumcised Titus with him to Jerusalem, and this shows that the Antiochene church had dispensed with circumcision for Gentiles. In Gal. 2:12, Paul says that when Peter came to Antioch, he at first ate with Gentiles; this must mean that he shared in the custom of communal meals which was already established in the Antiochene church, for there is no reason why Peter himself should have introduced this practice.

It is not quite clear what 'eating with Gentiles' meant for the Antiochene Jewish Christians: did it mean the abandonment of the Mosaic dietary laws?[57] Paul claims in Gal. 2:14 that in eating with Gentiles, Peter has been living 'like a Gentile' (ἐθνικῶς), and if taken literally this would mean that Peter and the Jewish Christians of Antioch had abandoned the observance of the law and their Jewish identity.[58] But it is hard to imagine the apostle to the circumcised (2:7–9) doing this, and it is perhaps more likely that Paul has exaggerated the extent of Peter's departure from the law, since his aim in 2:11ff is to present Peter as agreeing with his own doctrines of justification by faith and freedom from the law, even though his actual conduct was inconsistent with this. The example given – eating with Gentiles – perhaps suggests a relaxed attitude towards the law on the part of the Antiochene Jewish Christians, rather than a complete renunciation of the law.

The situation may have been rather different for the Antiochene Gentile Christians. In 2:14, Paul accuses Peter of 'compelling the Gentiles to Judaize' i.e. to adopt the Jewish way of life, and this suggests that prior to the arrival of the 'men from James' (2:12), Gentile Christians were exempted from certain of the requirements of the law. With the exception of exemption from circumcision (2:3), it is impossible to know exactly what this 'freedom' (2:4) consisted of, but since Paul had been a leader in the church of Antioch, his own later attitude towards Gentile exemption from the law may be cautiously used as evidence for the practice of Gentile Christians at Antioch. Paul tells his converts to 'eat whatever is sold in the meat market without raising any question on the ground of conscience' (1 Cor. 10:25),[59] and aligns himself with those who believe that no food is unclean (Rom. 14:14f, 20f). It is therefore probable that at Antioch too, Gentile Christians were exempted from the Jewish food-laws.

As regards observance of the Sabbath and of the Jewish feasts, Paul's later attitude may again serve as evidence for Gentile Christian practice at Antioch. Paul criticizes the Galatians for observing 'days and months and seasons and years' (Gal. 4:10). He commends the man who 'esteems all days alike', who is just as able to give honour to God as the man who 'esteems one day as better than another' (Rom. 14:5f). There is no reference anywhere in Paul to abstention from work or meeting together to worship on the Sabbath; 1 Cor. 16:1 suggests that even at this early stage, Christian worship took place on the first day of the week. Although Paul's Gentile converts are still aware of the annual Jewish feasts (1 Cor. 16:8), they interpret them in an allegorical and Christological sense which destroys their character as specific holy days (1 Cor. 5:6–8). All this suggests that at Antioch too, Gentile Christians did not observe the Jewish Sabbaths and annual feasts.[60]

Thus, the Antiochene Gentile Christians were apparently exempted from circumcision, the food-laws, the Sabbath and the feast-days. L. Goppelt has described the reason for the Antiochene church's liberal attitude towards the law as 'obscure' (*Apostolic Times*, 66).[61] On the contrary, the reason is very clear, and this takes us on to our next point.

4. *The abandonment of parts of the law of Moses was intended to make it easier for Gentiles to become Christians;*[62] *it helped to increase the success of Christian preaching.* The main features of the Jewish ritual law were objects of ridicule in the Graeco-Roman world. According to Josephus, Apion 'denounces us … for not eating pork, and he derides the practice of circumcision' (*Ap.* 2.137). Philo admits that circumcision is 'an object of ridicule among many people' (*Spec. Leg.* I.2).[63] When the delegation of Alexandrian Jews appealed to the Emperor Gaius, he mockingly asked them, 'Why do you refuse to eat pork?' (Philo, *Leg.* 361).[64] Seneca and Juvenal regarded the Jewish observance of the Sabbath as a sign of indolence (Augustine, *Civ. D.* 6.11; *Sat.* 14.95–106);[65] Agatharcides saw it as sheer folly (Josephus, *Ap.* 1.205–12). It was because of their awareness of such reproaches that certain Jews 'removed the marks of circumcision' (1 Macc. 1:15) and 'gladly adopted' the king's religion, which involved the prohibition of Sabbaths, feasts and food-laws (1 Macc. 1:43–9). The same is true of those Jews condemned by Philo who used a spiritualized interpretation of the Sabbath, the festivals and circumcision as an excuse for ignoring the literal commandments (*Mig.* 86–93).[66] Christian writers did not hesitate to exploit these general anti-Jewish sentiments. The author of the Epistle to Diognetus writes:

I do not suppose that you need to learn from me that, after all, their scruples about food and superstition about the Sabbath, and their pride in circumcision and the sham of their fasting and feast of the new moon, are ridiculous and unworthy of any argument. (4.1)

Paul himself compares circumcision to mutilation (Phil. 3:2) and castration (Gal. 5:12).

These features of the Jewish law must have severely inhibited the success of the Jewish mission to the Gentile world.[67] Josephus' story of the conversion of Izates illustrates both the problem which circumcision posed for Gentiles attracted to Judaism, and differences of opinion among Jews about whether it should be imposed on them (*Ant.* 20.38−48).[68] The abandonment of this commandment and of other objectionable parts of the law of Moses must have greatly assisted the success of the early Christian mission to the Gentiles.[69]

Indeed, Paul quite frankly admits that he abandoned the Jewish law precisely in order to ensure the success of his preaching among the Gentiles. In 1 Cor. 9:21, he writes: 'To those outside the law I became as one outside the law ... that I might win those outside the law.' This is contrasted with living as a Jew, described in 9:20. Similarly, in 10:32f, he writes: 'Give no offence to Jews or to Greeks or to the church of God, just as I try to please all men in everything I do, not seeking my own advantage, but that of many, that they may be saved.' In these passages, Paul states that his reason for abandoning the law of Moses in the context of the Gentile mission is 'that I might win the more' (1 Cor. 9:19). To insist on strict observance of the law of Moses would make it very hard to make Gentile converts; conversely, the law is set aside to make it easier for Gentiles to become Christians. Paul insists that his object is 'the advantage of many', but another way of putting the same point would be to say that his practice was intended to ensure the success of his own preaching.

Paul's opponents recognized that this was his reason for setting aside parts of the law.[70] In 1 Thes. 2, he defends his own sincerity and honesty, and the reference to Jewish hostility in 2:15f may suggest (if it is authentic) that throughout the chapter he is defending himself against specifically Jewish charges. In 2:4 he states that he and his companions speak 'not to please men, but to please God who tests our hearts'. It may well be that the charge that Paul sought to 'please men' was directed against his refusal to insist on a strict observance of the law of Moses. The charge would then be that Paul was so eager to gain converts for his cause that he was not ashamed to tamper with the commandments of God in order to make conversion easier. Gal. 1:10 is a clearer example of the same thing. In answer to the charge that he 'pleases men', Paul angrily retorts: 'Am I now seeking the favour of men, or of God? Or am I trying to please men? If I were still pleasing men, I should not be a servant of Christ.' It seems to have been the Judaizers' case that Paul had been commissioned by the apostles (cf. 1:1; 1:11–2:10), but that at Antioch he opposed the imposition of the Jewish way of life on Gentile converts (cf. 2:11ff), *because he wished to please men.*[71] He recognized that observance of the law would make it harder to gain Gentile converts, but instead of respecting the commandments he preached a gospel of 'cheap grace', arbitrarily setting aside requirements such as circumcision in order to gain converts and increase his reputation and power; so they appear to have argued.

Paul protests that his reasons for dispensing with the law are strictly theological (2:15–5:11), but his own words in 1 Cor. 9:21 and 10:32f prove that the setting aside of parts of the law was originally not a matter of theological principle but of practical expediency. Paul, Barnabas and other missionaries at Antioch had failed to persuade their Jewish hearers that Jesus was the Christ. They gradually came to the conclusion that God had hardened the hearts of the Jews; he was calling them to abandon their mission to the Jews and to go to the Gentiles instead. To prevent their bitter experience of almost total rejection being repeated, they set aside some of the requirements of the law which would be most offensive to Gentiles, and so ensured the success of their preaching. Paul's theological discussions about the law are therefore attempts to justify this essentially non-theological decision.

5. *The Gentile mission thus involved the separation of the church from the synagogue.* Christian missionaries had already been alienated from the synagogue by Jewish rejection of their message, and the Gentile mission set the seal on that alienation, for the abandonment of essential parts of the law of Moses would have been quite incompatible with continuing membership of the synagogue.[72] Acts 11:26b hints at this when it tells us that 'in Antioch the disciples were for the first time called Christians'.[73] The inhabitants of Antioch realized that they needed a new name to differentiate the followers of Jesus from the Jews because they realized that an irrevocable separation between the two groups had taken place.

The Antiochene church's attitude towards the law was incompatible with membership of the synagogue not only because it rejected individual commandments, but because it dispensed with the whole notion of the uniquely privileged relationship between God and Israel – the fundamental tenet of Judaism. For the Jewish community, customs such as circumcision and abstention from pork were of value as outward signs of Israel's privileged position, elected by God and separated from the nations. Thus, Philo paraphrases one of Balaam's oracles as follows:

> How shall I curse them whom God hath not cursed? ... I shall not be able to harm the people which shall dwell alone, not reckoned among other nations; and that, not because their dwelling-place is set apart and their land severed from others, but because in virtue of the distinction of their peculiar customs they do not mix with others to depart from the ways of their fathers ... Their bodies have been moulded from human seeds, but their souls are sprung from divine seeds, and therefore their stock is akin to God. (*Mos.* 1.278–9)

The Jews' 'peculiar customs' are thus an outward sign of their unique relationship to God. Above all, this was true of circumcision, which was already seen in Gen. 17 as the sign of the covenant between God and Israel. From the time of the Maccabees, there was an increasing emphasis on this rite as the sign of the unique Jewish identity. According to Jub. 15:26,

> Every one that is born, the flesh of whose foreskin is not circumcised on the eighth day, belongs not to the children of the covenant which the Lord made with Abraham, but to the children of destruction; nor is there, moreover, any sign on him that he is the Lord's, but (he is destined) to be destroyed.

In a well-known passage, Philo criticizes those Jews who regard the laws concerning the Sabbath, the festivals and circumcision as mere symbols of spiritual realities, and who do not regard the literal sense as binding (*Mig.* 86–93), and his chief objection is that by doing so they cut themselves off from the Jewish community (90); if they wish to avoid 'the censure of the many' (93), they should 'interfere with no established custom' (88). This again illustrates how the customs differentiating the Jewish community from the Gentiles were regarded not as peripheral but as essential for membership of that community. To disregard them was to separate oneself from the synagogue.

The link between the abandonment of these laws and separation from the Jewish community suggests that the statement (or 'slogan'),[74] 'There is neither Jew nor Greek ...' (Gal. 3:28; 1 Cor. 12:13; Col. 3:11) was originally part of the tradition of the church of Antioch.[75] Its abolition of the distinction between Jew and Gentile was symbolized by means of the common meals (Gal. 2:12).[76] Early Antiochene Christianity should therefore not be seen merely as a form of liberal Judaism, for its attitude towards the Jewish ritual law involved a more or less complete separation from the Jewish community.[77]

This, then, is the social and historical context of Paul's discussions of the law.[78] To sum up: 1. Paul began his missionary career by preaching to Jews only. 2. He and others first preached to Gentiles as a response to their failure among Jews. 3. They did not require full submission to the law from their Gentile converts. 4. Their abandonment of parts of the law of Moses was intended to make it easier for Gentiles to become Christians. 5. The Gentile mission thus involved the complete separation of the church from the synagogue. The law was a problem for Paul not primarily for theological reasons, but because he needed to justify the fundamental decision to abandon parts of it and break with the Jewish community, in the face of criticisms from Jews and Jewish Christians.[79]

2 Sociological analysis

A Two sociological models

1. If we consider this transition from mission to the Jews to mission to the Gentiles from a sociological standpoint, we may describe it as *the transformation of a reform-movement into a sect*.[80] A new religious movement does not arise in a vacuum, but is always related to the old religion which preceded it; positively, it draws much of its content from what has gone before, and negatively, it rebels against certain elements of the old. In many cases, it is the intention of the leader or leaders not to found a new religion, but to reform the existing one. The aim may be to purge the existing religion of its present corruption and to restore its original purity (real or imagined), or to foster new beliefs or patterns of conduct within the structure of the old religion. The reform-movement intends nothing less than the transformation of the old religion; it claims the old religion for itself.

Its advocates do not see themselves merely as a righteous remnant in a corrupt society. They are more ambitious than that, for they believe that the tremendous new impetus which has grasped them will sweep away every obstacle from its path until corruption is destroyed and reformation is complete. Thus, the religious movement initiated by Jesus was at first a movement to reform Judaism in preparation for the imminent coming of the kingdom of God;[81] it was not a sect.[82] Even after Jesus' death, the impetus continued unabated, as his disciples preached throughout Judaea and Galilee in the hope of the conversion of the Jewish people to their understanding of the imminent redemption of Israel.[83]

But a reform-movement is bound to encounter opposition from a very early stage.[84] Its reliance on charismatic leadership inevitably brings it into conflict with the traditional authority-structures of the old religion.[85] For a while, this conflict may help the movement to define and clarify its goals. But it may gradually become clear that the original goals of the movement are unattainable. Political power usually remains firmly in the hands of the traditional authorities, and society as a whole may prove resistant to change, taking the view that 'the old is good' (Lk. 5:39). Slowly, the seemingly irresistible power of the original religious impulse begins to wane, as again and again it encounters resistance and rejection.

If the reform-movement is able to survive the initial conflict with the traditional authority-structures, it is likely that it will be gradually transformed into a sect. The distinctions between the two are fluid; they represent opposite ends of the spectrum, and there are a large number of possible gradations between them. The essential difference between the two is that the reform-movement adopts a hopeful attitude towards society, believing that with divine help it will be able to transform it, whereas the sect adopts a hostile and undifferentiated view of society.[86] On the latter view, there are only two categories of people, the righteous and the unrighteous (i.e. members of the sect and non-members); all the distinctions of rank and status which seem so important to society at large fade into insignificance by comparison with this fundamental distinction. Although missionary work may continue (for recruits still have to be found), the sect no longer believes in an irresistible divine power operating in the present, causing its message to transform society as a whole. It places its trust in a future eschatological vindication, which will prove to its opponents that, despite its weak and marginal position in society, God is on the side of its members. Society outside the sect is written off. It stands condemned; it is liable to God's judgment. Salvation is to be found exclusively through membership of the sect. The sect is thus differentiated from the reform-movement by its alienation from society.

2. One of the sect's main needs is for *an ideology legitimating its separation from society*;[87] an ideological barrier must be erected between the two.[88] The sect's members need to know exactly where they stand, for if they are unclear about this they may fall victim to the specious arguments of the sect's opponents (especially the traditional religious authorities). There is nothing more disastrous for the coherence or morale of a sectarian group than the apostasy of some of its members; this is the reason why such opprobrium is heaped upon apostates. Separation may be legitimated in any or all of the following ways.

(i) *Denunciation.* The sect's opponents may be attacked either for their general moral depravity or for their crimes against the sect. Such charges may bear little resemblance to an 'objective' view of reality, for the sect is not interested in 'objective truth' but in its own inner coherence. To secure this, a hostile portrayal of its opponents must be perpetuated.

(ii) *Antithesis.* The gulf which is perceived between the sect and society may be crystallized in antitheses.[89] These antitheses take the form of a contrast between the two groups: the righteous and the unrighteous; the holy and the unholy; the godly and the ungodly; and so on. The antithesis may express a predestinarian outlook: the elect and those whose hearts are hardened. The advantage of predestinarian language is that on the one hand it reinforces the sense of an elite status experienced by members of the sect,[90] and on the other hand it provides an explanation for the potentially damaging fact of the unbelief of the majority.[91]

(iii) *Reinterpretation.* A reform-movement seeks the renewal and revitalization of the religious traditions of the whole community. In contrast to this, the sect regards itself as the sole legitimate possessor of those traditions, and denies the legitimacy of the claim to them made by society as a whole. The traditions must therefore be reinterpreted to apply exclusively to the sect.

The sequence, reform-movement − rejection − sect, is not intended to be a fixed sociological law to be rigidly applied in all cases; nor will a sectarian group's legitimation of separation from a parent religious community inevitably involve denunciation, antithesis and reinterpretation. Historical phenomena rarely follow such simple models exactly: there are too many variables involved, and each case is unique. Even when these patterns do seem broadly to fit the evidence, ambiguities and complicating factors will remain. Nevertheless, one should not regard the uniqueness of each individual historical phenomenon as a reason for ignoring the possibility of common underlying sociological patterns.[92] If carefully handled, such patterns can illuminate the subject rather than distorting it. We shall attempt to apply the patterns outlined above first to the Qumran community, secondly to the Johannine community, and thirdly to Paul himself.[93] Only the broad outlines will be described, since our purpose is not the general study of sectarianism in early Judaism and Christianity, but the study of Paul's separation from Judaism.

B Qumran

1. We know very little about the early history of the Essene movement, but the evidence suggests that in the early stages it would be more correct to regard it as a reform-movement than as a sect. According to CD 1:7–10, in the twenty years before the advent of the Teacher of righteousness there emerged a group who 'understood their iniquities, and became conscious that they were guilty men; but they were like the blind and like them that grope for their way for twenty years'. The language suggests a comparatively unstructured movement. If it is correct to identify this group with the 'Asideans' of 1 Macc. 2:42; 7:13–17,[94] this would again suggest a reform-movement: at one time they aligned themselves with the Maccabees (1 Macc. 2:42), and at another they submitted to the high priest, with disastrous results (1 Macc. 7:13–17). But their programme of reform was defeated in their unsuccessful struggle against the non-Aaronite Hasmoneans – a defeat which the Essenes blamed on the 'house of Absalom' (1QpHab 5:9–12; cf. 1 Macc. 11:69f; 13:11). The only possibility open for the Teacher of righteousness and his followers was exile:

> They did not reckon that I was the instrument of thy power,
> And so they chased me from my homeland like a bird from
>   his nest;
> And all my friends were driven away from me.
>
> (1QH 4:8–9)[95]

Thus, through rejection the reform-movement became a sect, characterized by intense opposition to all non-members: 'Everlasting hatred in a spirit of secrecy for the men of perdition!' (1QS 9:21–2).

2. The Essenes therefore required an ideology legitimating their separation from the Jewish community as a whole, and this may be summarized in the categories outlined above.

(i) *Denunciation.* In CD 4:12–5:11, a bitter polemic is directed against the sect's chief opponents. They are guilty of fornication, in that they take a second wife while the first is still alive; they profane the Temple through intercourse during menstruation; they marry their nieces, contrary to the sect's interpretation of Lev. 18:13. The sect describes as the constant practice of its enemies what are in fact purely theoretical differences over matters of *halakhah*.[96] It needs these differences, and it needs to exaggerate them, in order to justify and perpetuate its own separate existence.

(ii) *Antithesis.* Humanity is divided into two classes: 'the sons of light' and 'the sons of darkness' (1QS 1:9–10), 'the sons of righteousness' and 'the sons of wickedness' (1QS 3:20–1), 'the men of the lot of God' and 'the men of the lot of Belial' (1QS 2:1, 4–5). Whether one walks in righteousness or wickedness depends on divine predestination: 'From the God of knowledge comes all that is and shall be', and he has appointed for man 'two spirits', i.e. 'the spirits of truth and falsehood' (1QS 3:15, 18–19). Thus the separation between the sect and the world is legitimated by being ascribed to the work of God himself. The frequent repetition of such antithetical descriptions of insiders and outsiders helps to create and perpetuate the sect's alienation from the wider society.[97]

(iii) *Reinterpretation.* The sect claims that it is the sole legitimate possessor of the religious traditions which in fact it shares with the whole community, and it must therefore reinterpret these traditions in the light of this claim. The Qumran community's reinterpretation of religious traditions takes a wide variety of different forms, only a few of which can be briefly mentioned: (a) Membership of the covenant through circumcision is denied to the Jewish community as a whole and claimed for the sect alone; circumcision is thus spiritualized (1QS 5:1–5). (b) True observance of the Jewish community's holy days (Sabbaths, feasts, the day of atonement) is to be found only within the sect (CD 6:18–19). (c) The sect alone offers true sacrifices, through obedience and prayer (1QS 9:4–5). (d) Scripture belongs only to the sect, and not to the community as a whole: Scripture frequently speaks of the sect and the key events in its history (1QS 8:7, 13−16, CD 3:21−4:5, the *pesharim*); the sect's formation was the climax of biblical history (CD 3:1−20); Scripture confirms its fervent messianism (4QPatr; 4QTest; 4QFlor 1:10−13).

In all these ways, the boundary between the sect and society is established, defined and strengthened. The sect's continued existence is entirely dependent on whether its legitimation of separation remains plausible for its members. For this reason, apostates are bitterly denounced (CD 8), for in their case the ideology has proved ineffective, so that the sect's very existence is threatened.

C The Johannine community

These same two sociological phenomena − the transformation of a reform-movement into a sect and the creation of an ideology legitimating separation − are also in evidence in the Fourth Gospel.[98]

1. The gospel of John contains several references to expulsion from the synagogue. Jesus warns the disciples in 16:2, 'They will put you out of the synagogue', and adds in v. 4, 'I have said these things to you, that when their hour comes you may remember that I told you of them.' This passage is obviously a *vaticinium ex eventu*: the Johannine community has experienced expulsion from the synagogue, and one way of coming to terms with this crisis was to ascribe foreknowledge of it to Jesus.[99] In the light of 15:18ff, expulsion from the synagogue may be seen as the concrete manifestation of the world's hatred towards Jesus and his community. Here, another way of coping with the crisis of expulsion is seen: the suffering of the community at the hands of the Jews is not to disturb its members, since it is the logical consequence of the Jews' hostility towards Jesus himself (15:18−21). This tendency to explain suffering by tracing it back to Jewish hostility towards Jesus accounts for the fact that the expulsion from the synagogue experienced by the Johannine community (16:2) is retrojected into the earthly life of Jesus in 9:22, 34 and 12:42.[100] The blind man's parents 'feared the Jews, for the Jews had already agreed that if any one should confess him to be the Christ, he was to be put out of the synagogue' (9:22). Here, 'already' (ἤδη) is significant: expulsion from the synagogue is grounded in the Jewish attitude towards the earthly Jesus. In 9:34, the blind man, now cured, is duly 'cast out' (i.e. expelled from the synagogue) because of his confession that Jesus is 'from God' (v. 33). He contrasts with the

believers among the authorities who did not confess their faith 'lest they should be put out of the synagogue' (12:42).[101]

Thus, at an earlier stage of its history, the Johannine community had existed as a reform-movement within the Jewish community, dedicated to persuading fellow-Jews that Jesus was the Christ. This led in the end to a clash with the traditional authorities, i.e. the Pharisees (cf. 12:42), which resulted in expulsion from the synagogue for those who openly acknowledged Jesus as the Christ.[102] Those who were expelled had to reorganize themselves in sectarian separation from the Jewish community, and judging from the language of 15:18−16:4, the expulsion with its aftermath was a traumatic experience.[103]

2. In order to survive this crisis, separation had to be legitimated; an attempt had to be made to explain and justify the new position outside the Jewish community to the group's members. This may be summed up in the same three headings used above.

(i) *Denunciation*. The Jewish leaders 'receive glory from one another and do not seek the glory that comes from the only God' (5:44). Their concern for the scriptures (5:39) is thus hypocritical and self-seeking. In 7:19, the people are condemned: 'None of you keeps the law.' In 8:44 it is said that their father is the devil, and that they carry out his desires. Their failure to believe in Jesus is quite simply 'sin' (15:22, 24), hatred of the Father (15:23). Jn 7−8 shows how the people came to share their leaders' hostility towards Jesus, initially taking his claims seriously (7:12, 15, 25−7, 31, 40−3), but eventually repudiating him (8:48, 52f, 57) and seeking to kill him (8:59). Thus, the verdict on the people as a whole at the end of Jesus' public ministry is that 'though he had done so many signs before them, yet they did not believe in him' (12:37), in accordance with Is. 53:1 and 6:10 (Jn 12:38−40). The sectarian character of the Johannine community is thus seen in its undifferentiated hostility towards the Jewish community as a whole, and not just towards its leaders.[104] Leaders and people alike are denounced.

(ii) *Antithesis*. The sect's separation from the Jewish community is expressed and justified by means of antitheses. The structure of the gospel as a whole is antithetical: the unbelief of the Jewish community (a central theme of Jn 1−12) is contrasted with the true followers of Jesus, to whom private instruction is given (Jn 13−17).[105] Antithetical pairs of words are a vital element in John's theology, and it is important to realize that the metaphysical dualism which they apparently imply is grounded in the sociological dualism which is the sectarian group's response to hostility from the wider community.[106] In its context, the antithesis between flesh and Spirit in 3:6 is an antithesis between the 'rulers of the Jews' (3:1) and the Johannine community, those who have been 'born of the Spirit' (3:5, 8). The Jews are 'from below', 'of this world' (8:23), 'slaves' (8:32ff), in 'darkness' (8:12). But Jesus is 'from above', 'not of this world' (8:23), and likewise his followers are 'not of this world' (17:16); they are 'free' (8:32ff), they have 'the light of life' (8:12, cf. 12:46). The function of such antitheses is to express and justify the sect's separation from the Jewish community.[107]

(iii) *Reinterpretation.* Reinterpretation of religious traditions denies the legitimacy of the wider community's use of these traditions, and claims them exclusively for the sect. The Jewish theology of the covenant is reinterpreted in 8:54f: the Jews claim that God is 'their God', but it is Jesus and his followers who truly know him. The Jews claim to be the seed of Abraham (8:33, 37, 39), yet they deny their kinship with Abraham by their desire to kill the one whose coming Abraham longed for (8:39f, 56ff). The Jewish community also lays claim to Moses: 'We are disciples of Moses' (9:28); 'We know that God has spoken to Moses' (9:29). But in fact, Moses will convict them at the Judgment, for he bears witness to Jesus (5:45ff; cf. 1:45; 3:14). The same is true of the prophets (2:17, 22b; 6:45; 10:34ff; 12:14ff, 38ff; 15:25, etc.). The Johannine community thus claims to be the sole legitimate possessor of Jewish religious traditions.

D Paul

1. Paul and his congregations seem to have been the only early Christians to have adopted an attitude of sectarian separation from the Jewish community prior to AD 70; we have already traced the process by which this took place in the first half of this chapter. Paul abandoned preaching to the Jews because he became convinced that God had hardened their hearts against the gospel. He turned instead to the Gentiles, and in order to ensure the success of his preaching, he did not insist on full observance of the law of Moses.[108] This involved the complete separation of his churches from the synagogue.

2. It follows that, like the Qumran and Johannine communities, he had to develop a theoretical rationale for separation from the Jewish community.[109] Since most of the rest of the present work will be devoted to an exploration of the implications of this statement, only

a brief summary is necessary here. Once again, the categories of denunciation, antithesis and reinterpretation are appropriate.

(i) *Denunciation.* The clearest example of this is Rom. 2. In Rom. 2:1–3, Paul turns on the Jew who, like Paul himself in 1:18ff, condemns the idolatry and immorality of the pagans; the judge is being utterly hypocritical, for he is doing exactly the same things himself. The Jew who sets himself up as an expert in the law and who delights to instruct others is in fact guilty of stealing, adultery, temple-robbery and transgression in general (2:17–24). He is not in the least concerned about this inconsistency because he is convinced that because he is circumcised (2:25) and a Jew his salvation is secure (2:4). He has a 'hard and impenitent heart' (2:5). Such people will experience 'wrath and fury' (2:8), 'tribulation and distress' (2:9) on the Day of Judgment.

Not the least of the problems which commentators have found with Rom. 2 is the exaggerated nature of these charges. But this is only surprising if one takes an idealistic view of Paul as a man concerned only with the disinterested pursuit of the truth. If one abandons the attempt to read Rom. 2 as pure theology and asks instead what Paul is trying to *do*, the reason for this polemic becomes clear: he wishes to reinforce the barrier separating the church from the synagogue. What matters is not whether the charges are 'true', but whether his readers find them plausible.[110]

(ii) *Antithesis.* Paul uses a wide variety of antithetical terms in the course of controversy with Judaism. The following are some of the most important: works of the law, faith in Christ Jesus (Gal. 2:16, abbreviated to works, faith in Rom. 3:27; 4:16; 9:32); law, Christ (Gal. 2:21); flesh, Spirit (Gal. 3:3; 4:29); curse, blessing (Gal. 3:10, 13f); law, promise (Gal. 3:15–18, 21); slavery, sonship (Gal. 4:1–7); slavery, freedom (Gal. 4:22–5:1); circumcision, Christ (Gal. 5:2): circumcision, cross (Gal. 5:11; 6:12); law, grace (Gal. 5:4; Rom. 6:14f); death, life (2 Cor. 3:6); letter, Spirit (2 Cor. 3:6; Rom. 7:6); condemnation, righteousness (2 Cor. 3:9); confidence in the flesh, glorying in Christ Jesus (Phil. 3:4): a righteousness of my own, based on law, righteousness from God that depends on faith (Phil. 3:9; cf. Rom. 10:3); sin, grace (Rom. 5:20f); works, God's call (Rom. 9:11); works, grace (Rom. 11:6). As in the examples of antithesis from Qumran and the Johannine community, the function of these antithetical contrasts is to express the ineradicable distinction between the sect (in which salvation is to be found) and the parent religious community (where there is only condemnation). The sect's members must be quite clear about the boundary separating the two groups, for to be unclear about it is to risk losing one's salvation (cf. Gal. 5:2−4). These antitheses therefore legitimate the separation of church from synagogue, a separation which took place for practical reasons and not because of any theoretical incompatibility between the practice of Judaism and faith in Jesus Christ. To put it another way: *faith in Christ is incompatible with works of the law because the church is separate from the synagogue.*

(iii) *Reinterpretation.* In Gal. 3:6ff and 4:21ff, and in Rom. 4:1ff and 9:6ff, Paul discusses the figure of Abraham. He does so not simply because Abraham was an outstanding figure in Jewish tradition, but because its relationship to Abraham was an essential part of the Jewish community's self-definition. Jews regarded themselves as 'the seed of Abraham', members of God's covenant with Abraham and his descendants through the rite of circumcision, and so heirs to the promises made to him. Paul claims that these things are the exclusive property of his (largely Gentile) communities of those who have faith in Jesus Christ. In doing so, he seeks to reinforce the barrier separating the church from the Jewish community.

One might expect Paul to repeat this procedure with the law − wresting it from the hands of his Jewish opponents and claiming that it was truly observed only in the church. He is aware of the possibility of a spiritualized interpretation of circumcision (Rom. 2:29; Phil. 3:2f), but in general he concedes the law to his opponents, arguing that it is in fact the bringer of sin, death and condemnation to its adherents (Gal. 3:10; 2 Cor. 3:6−9; Rom. 5:20f; 6:14; 7:5f). In other words, he claims that a true *understanding* of the law is to be found only in the Christian community (cf. 2 Cor. 3:14f). If the reinterpretation of Abraham serves to emphasize the privileged position of the church by comparison with the Jewish community, the reinterpretation of the law serves to emphasize the terrible plight of the Jewish community by comparison with the church. Both are concerned to reinforce the barrier between the two. Paul wishes to inculcate in his converts a horror of life under the law, i.e. life in the Jewish community: there, the reign of sin and death, under which the whole of humanity stands with the exception of the sect's members, is seen at its most powerful.

The reinterpretation of what are for Paul the two great themes of Scripture − promise and law − is backed up at every point by the use of individual texts. For Paul, Scripture was not written for the benefit of the Jewish community, but 'for our instruction, upon whom the end of the ages has come' (1 Cor. 10:11; cf. Rom. 15:4). Scripture is thus invoked to justify sectarian separation from the synagogue.

In the first part of this chapter, we examined the origins of Paul's mission to the Gentiles, in the context of which the law first became a problem. Using the evidence of the epistles rather than Acts, we concluded that Paul and his colleagues at Antioch abandoned their mission to the Jews because they became convinced that their failure to make converts was due to their hearers' divinely ordained hardness of heart. This led them to preach to Gentiles instead, and in order to ensure the success of their preaching, certain offensive commandments of the law were set aside. This involved a complete break between the church and the synagogue. In the second half of the chapter, this process was examined from a sociological point of view. It represents an attempt to transform a reform-movement into a sect, in response to rejection. The sect is characterized by hostility towards the society from which it has separated itself, and in order to legitimate this separation an ideology is necessary. We found that Paul's attitude towards Judaism exactly fitted the structure of an ideology legitimating separation, derived initially from other sources. This combination of historical and sociological perspectives seems to offer a more appropriate approach to the interpretation of Paul's view of Judaism than the exclusively theological models so often propounded.

3

THE GALATIAN CRISIS

1 The origins of the crisis

We have now traced the process in which Paul and other Jewish Christians at Antioch transformed what was originally a reform-movement within Judaism into a sect outside it. What has not yet been emphasized is the extent to which this decision was controversial within the church itself. Not all early Christians were as ready as Paul was to conclude that the Jewish people as a whole were irretrievably hard of heart, and that the attempt to gain converts should therefore be pursued outside the Jewish community and its way of life. Most Jewish Christians were not yet ready to abandon the original dream that the Jewish people as a whole would soon be united in their expectation of the coming of Jesus as the Messiah. They would have regarded Paul's preaching of freedom from the law to Gentiles as based on a disastrously false presupposition (that God had abandoned the Jewish people), and as gravely hindering their own mission. This disagreement came to a head in the controversy between Paul and the Judaizing missionaries who were achieving considerable success among his own converts in Galatia, and in the events which led up to it, described in Gal. 2. The essential issue in Galatians is thus whether the church should be a reform-movement within Judaism or a sect outside it.[1]

This view is in contrast to one highly influential interpretation of Galatians. Ever since the Reformation, Paul's opponents in Galatia have been seen as the archetypal protagonists of legalistic religion.[2] Their claim that righteousness must be earned, so it is said, forms the dark background against which the Pauline gospel of an unearned righteousness through faith shines forth all the more brightly. Their doctrine of merit acts as the foil for Paul's doctrine of grace. Their insistence that good works must be added to faith if one is to be saved gives Paul the opportunity for asserting in the most uncompromising way that one is saved by faith alone. For example, Munck comments on the Galatians' eagerness to accept Judaizing ideas as follows:

Wherever salvation by faith without the works of the law is preached, we find people who cannot satisfy their longing for holiness — it was then called righteousness; they want to be doing something, they want to build up a world of holiness; they do not want to be content with the grace which they feel is debased and sullied by everyday human life, but to prepare a human vessel that is worthy to receive God's heavenly grace.   (*Paul*, 132−3)

This homiletical passage reveals the presuppositions with which scholars in the Reformation tradition still tend to approach Galatians.[3] The analysis in the previous chapter should already have shown that this isolation of theology from history is at best grossly over-simplified and at worst a complete misunderstanding. In the present chapter, we shall attempt to apply the historical and sociological results achieved so far to Galatians.

A Controversy at Antioch (Gal. 2:4f)

In the last chapter, we saw how the fateful decision to preach a law-free gospel to the Gentiles was reached. Gal. 2 takes up the story from this point on. V.4 refers to 'false brethren secretly brought in, who slipped in to spy out our freedom which we have in Christ Jesus', and it is likely that this refers to Jewish Christians who came to Antioch because they were concerned that Christians there had abandoned the mission to the Jews and were preaching a gospel of freedom from the law to the Gentiles.[4] It is true that v.4 occurs in the middle of a passage about Paul's second visit to Jerusalem, and for that reason it has commonly been assumed that he encountered these 'false brethren' in Jerusalem.[5] But this is unlikely, for vv.3−5 should be regarded as a parenthesis. In v.2, Paul tells how he explained his activity to 'those who were of repute' in Jerusalem, and v.6 describes their response: they had nothing to add.[6] The intervening material is therefore a digression. In v.3, Paul says that Titus, his companion, was not compelled to be circumcised, and v.4 begins with the words, 'But because of false brethren ...' Unfortunately, Paul never tells us what it was that happened 'because of false brethren', for he does not complete the sentence, but merely asserts in v.5 that he did not compromise with these people.[7] What was it that happened 'because of false brethren'? The references to Titus and to circumcision in v.3 may provide a clue; Paul probably intended to say, 'Because of false brethren, I had to go with Titus to Jerusalem to discuss the question of his circumcision and the circumcision of other Gentile converts.' If so, then v. 4 refers to Jewish Christians who came to Antioch and expressed their grave concern over the new policies which had been adopted there.[8]

Several other points support this interpretation.

(i) V. 4 says that the false brethren were 'secretly brought in' and that they 'slipped in to spy out our freedom', and these expressions suggest an encounter at Antioch rather than Jerusalem. If this took place at Jerusalem, the meaning is presumably that the false brethren somehow managed to infiltrate the supposedly secret meeting between Paul and those of repute (cf. 2:2);[9] but this seems somewhat implausible. Antiochene freedom from the law could best be spied on at Antioch itself.

(ii) Paul must have had some urgent reason for going up to Jerusalem, at least eleven years (and probably fourteen) after his previous visit.[10] He tells us in v. 2 that he went up 'by revelation', but it is likely that this 'revelation' was occasioned by a crisis in the church at Antioch over the question of the Gentiles and the law[11] – a crisis so grave that it led Paul to fear that his work so far had been 'in vain' (v. 2). It must have been the false brethren of v. 4 who caused this crisis.[12] They expressed their concern about the new policies at Antioch, and demanded that Gentile converts should be circumcised, and although Paul did not yield to them (v. 5), they must have weakened his position considerably, for the decision to submit the matter to the pillars in Jerusalem would have been something of a gamble.

(iii) Acts 15:1f tells us that men came down from Judaea to Antioch teaching that Gentile converts should be circumcised; after Paul and Barnabas had failed to resolve the matter in debate, they were appointed to go to Jerusalem to ask for the guidance of the apostle and elders.[13] This again confirms that Gal. 2:4–5 refers to controversies in the church at Antioch prior to the Jerusalem conference.

In the letter supposedly sent from the church at Jerusalem to the churches of Antioch, Syria and Cilicia, we read: 'Since we have heard that some persons from us have troubled you with words, unsettling your minds, although we gave them no instructions ...' (Acts 15:24). Here it is admitted that the false brethren came 'from us', i.e. from Jerusalem. But it is also asserted that they were acting entirely on their own initiative, and not on the instructions of the apostles. In inserting the phrase, 'although we gave them no instructions', Luke appears to be countering the idea that the teachers of 15:1f *were* sent by the apostles.[14] Elsewhere in Acts 15, he clearly covers up major conflicts in the early church in the interests of his idealized view of the apostolic age as a time of church unity and harmony: Paul himself becomes one of the 'men from James' whose task is to impose the Jewish food-laws on Gentile converts (15:22, 25, 30f; 16:4), despite the fact that in reality he had vehemently opposed such an imposition (Gal. 2:11ff),[15] and his conflict with Barnabas on this issue (Gal. 2:13) becomes in Acts 15:36ff a conflict over the trivial matter of whether or not John Mark should accompany them.[16] In the light of these distortions, it is perhaps legitimate to use Acts 15:24 as evidence that the false brethren *were* sent to Antioch by the authorities in Jerusalem.[17] This is also suggested by Paul's reference to them as 'spies' (cf. Gal. 2:4); a spy acts on someone else's behalf.[18] Paul says that their aim was to 'bring us into bondage' (Gal. 2:4), and it is unlikely that these newcomers to the Antiochene church should have attempted to assert their authority in this way without the backing of Jerusalem.[19] We know from Gal. 2:12 that James later sent emissaries from Jerusalem to Antioch to try to impose the Jewish law on Gentile converts (cf. 2:14),[20] and so there is no reason why he should not have done so earlier.[21] This would also explain why Paul had to go to Jerusalem to resolve the problem: he would have been appealing to James and the Jerusalem church to abandon their hostility towards the new policy with regard to the Gentiles and the law.

All this gives a coherent and consistent account of the origins of the Gentile mission and initial Christian opposition to it. Paul, Barnabas and other Jewish Christians at Antioch preached the gospel to their fellow-Jews, with little success. Perhaps over a period of a number of years, they gradually became convinced that God had hardened the hearts of the Jewish people as a whole (with the exception of the Jewish Christian remnant), and that he was calling them to preach to Gentiles instead. In order to ensure the success of their preaching among the Gentiles, they did not require observance of some of the distinctively Jewish features of the law (circumcision, the food-laws, the Sabbath and the feast-days), and so in effect separated themselves from the Jewish community. What had started as a reform-movement within Judaism thus became a sect outside it. However, the Jerusalem church did not accept that the time had come for the abandonment of the mission to the Jews (cf. Gal. 2:7–9), and they would have been seriously concerned about the new developments in Antioch because of their potentially disastrous effects on their own mission, and because they remained loyal adherents of the Jewish law.[22] So they sent emissaries to Antioch to see whether the rumours about what was happening there were true, and if so to bring the Antiochene church back to allegiance to the law. These people were firmly opposed by Paul and Barnabas, but they must have caused a crisis of confidence in the Antiochene congregation; after all, the Antiochenes too revered James the brother of the Lord and the chief apostles as 'those who are of repute' and as 'pillars'. So Paul and Barnabas took the desperate step of going to Jerusalem to appeal to the leaders there and to seek recognition for their policies.[23]

B The council in Jerusalem and the Antioch incident

Paul claims in Gal. 2:7–9 that he and Barnabas obtained this recognition in Jerusalem. The pillars 'saw that I had been entrusted with the gospel of the uncircumcision' (2:7); they 'perceived the grace that was given to me', and so 'gave to me and to Barnabas the right hand of fellowship, that we should go to the Gentiles' (2.9). Thus Paul claims that 'those who were of repute' accepted the legitimacy of his activities because they recognized that he had been called by God. But it is hard to see how they could have done so. As we have seen, the presupposition of Paul's mission to the Gentiles was that the Jewish people as a whole had been hardened by God, so that preaching to them was useless. It is unlikely that James, Cephas and John should have accepted this, since they were still carrying on a mission to the Jews (2:7–9).[24] In addition, to have accepted the legitimacy of the principle of freedom from the law (cf. 2:4) would have fatally undermined their own mission: non-Christian Jews would be unlikely to accept the proclamation of people who associated themselves with those who had thrown off the yoke of the Torah.[25] This problem is alluded to by Paul when he attributes Peter's withdrawal from table-fellowship with the Gentiles to his 'fearing those of the circumcision' (2:12). This phrase should not be understood as a reference to a 'circumcision party' within the early church,[26] for in 2:7–9 'the circumcision' is three times used to refer to the whole Jewish people, the objects of the Jerusalem church's mission, and this suggests that 'the circumcision' in 2:12 has the same sense.[27] Peter 'feared those of the circumcision' in the sense that he realized that association with those who held a lax view of the law would expose him to persecution and rejection by the Jews to whom he preached. Thus, if the Jerusalem leaders gave Paul the whole-hearted recognition that he claims, they would have seriously undermined their own mission. It seems highly unlikely that they did so.

One must face the fact that the narrative of Gal. 2 is thoroughly tendentious.[28] The denials of Gal. 1:1,10–12, together with the oath of 1:20, indicate that Paul is responding to a quite different understanding of the relevant events, and there is no *a priori* reason why one should take his account at face value and reject any other possible interpretation. The problem with Paul's account of his agreement with the Jerusalem leaders is not only that it is incompatible with what we can deduce about the origins of the Gentile mission from other Pauline sources (the argument of this section so far), but also that it makes the behaviour of James, Peter and Barnabas, as described in Gal. 2:11–14, incomprehensible.

In Gal. 2:14, Paul accuses Peter of 'compelling the Gentiles to Judaize' (i.e. to adopt the Jewish way of life). In an attempt to reconcile this statement with the recognition for his Gentile mission that Paul claims in 2:7–9, commentators have assumed that the necessity for the withdrawal of Jewish Christians from Gentiles is a legitimate inference from the terms of the agreement of 2:7–9,[29] and that Peter can only be said to have 'compelled the Gentiles to Judaize' in a very indirect sense.[30] But Gal. 2:11ff cannot be so easily harmonized with the agreement as recounted by Paul. First, the withdrawal from the Gentiles not only of Peter, the apostle to the circumcision (2:8), but also of Barnabas, the apostle to the Gentiles (2:9), becomes hard to understand. Secondly, the text gives not the slightest reason for weakening the sense of 'compelling the Gentiles to Judaize' to 'unintentionally putting pressure on Gentiles who misunderstood his action to adopt the Jewish way of life'. On the contrary, this phrase is to be understood in the light of the reference in 6:12 to those who 'compel you to be circumcised'. If Paul does not mean what he says in 2:14, he has expressed himself most unfortunately, for his opponents in Galatia would be able to claim that in compelling the Galatians to be circumcised (6:12), they are following the precedent set by Peter at Antioch, who *on Paul's own admission* 'compelled the Gentiles to Judaize'. Why should Paul gratuitously offer his opponents Peter as their chief ally? 2:13f should therefore be taken absolutely literally: in response to instructions from James,[31] Peter, Barnabas and the Antiochene Jewish Christians other than Paul withdrew from fellowship with the Gentile Christians, demanding that they adopt the Jewish way of life.

On this view, the behaviour of James, Peter and Barnabas in Gal. 2:11 – 14 is inconsistent with 2:7 – 9. In the one case, the legitimacy of the Gentile mission is accepted, in the other it is denied. Paul's claim is that he was in the right and that the others had suddenly and unilaterally abandoned the Jerusalem agreement.[32] But it is more likely that in 2:7 – 9 Paul exaggerates the extent to which his own understanding of the Gentile mission was accepted.[33] He asserts in 2:5 that (at Antioch and, by implication, in Jerusalem) he was utterly uncompromising in his defence of his Gentile mission. But, as we have seen, there was another view of the Jerusalem conference in existence, which Paul here attacks: according to this view, Paul was commissioned (at the Jerusalem conference?) to be the emissary of the Jerusalem apostles (cf. 1:1, 11), but disobeyed them at Antioch (cf. 2:11ff) because he desired to 'please men' (cf. 1:10) by refusing to impose objectionable requirements of the law on Gentile converts. In other words, Paul's opponents blamed him for having behaved at Antioch in a manner inconsistent with what was decided at Jerusalem. They apparently asserted that he 'still preaches circumcision' (cf. 5:11), and since this cannot be a reference to his preaching in Galatia, it may refer to what he said in Jerusalem. If so, his assertion that Titus was not compelled to be circumcised and his stress on his uncompromising attitude (2:3, 5) may be intended to refute the claim that he *had* accepted the imposition of the law on Gentiles while at Jerusalem (cf. the tradition underlying Acts 16:3).[34]

If one accepts at face value Paul's self-dramatizing view of himself in Gal. 2 as the heroic defender of the true gospel against its legalistic opponents (a view which those influenced by the Reformation find almost irresistible), one will find it incredible that he should ever have been understood to 'preach circumcision' at the Jerusalem conference. The charge to which Paul responds in Gal. 1 – 2 and 5:11 – that his conduct at Antioch contradicted his acceptance in Jerusalem of Jewish privilege, as maintained by the 'pillars' – would then be the result of pure malice. But Paul's own statements indicate that he could give the appearance of regarding circumcision and Jewish privilege very highly, even while carrying on his work of establishing sectarian Gentile congregations which were incompatible with them. 'What advantage has the Jew? Or what is the value of circumcision? Much in every way ...' (Rom. 3:1f); for 'Christ became a servant to the circumcision to show God's truthfulness, in order to confirm the promises given to the patriarchs' (Rom. 15:8), and this means that 'all Israel will be saved' (Rom. 11:26; cf. vv. 28f). If Paul made statements like this at the Jerusalem conference, one can understand the existence of an alternative account of that conference (rejected by Paul in Gal. 1–2 and 5:11), which accused him of hypocrisy – saying one thing and doing another. One should therefore be very cautious about accepting his claim that the pillars at first gladly accepted his and Barnabas' apostleship to the Gentiles, but that a little while later James, Peter and Barnabas (!) unaccountably changed their minds and began to impose the law on Gentile converts. It is impossible to be sure exactly what happened in Jerusalem, but Paul's own account does not seem very plausible.

It seems that James' attempt to impose the law on the Antiochene Gentile Christians was successful.[35] If Paul had won the argument, he would surely have said so. But instead, he merely tells us in 2:13f that the Jews at Antioch were hypocritical and that the Gentiles had no choice – they were 'compelled to Judaize'. This event therefore represented a disaster for Paul: his work in Antioch, based on the premise of the law-free gospel for the Gentiles, had been destroyed at a stroke. It is not surprising that as he recalls what had happened, he gives vent to his anger in sarcastic references to the leaders of the Jerusalem church.[36] They are 'those who are supposed to be something', but 'what they were makes no difference to me',[37] for 'God shows no partiality' (2:6); they are 'those who are supposed to be pillars' (2:9).[38] Apart from Paul, the Antiochenes had submitted to the authority of the leaders in Jerusalem, and this in effect constituted a vote of no confidence in Paul's leadership. He left Antioch because he had to.[39]

C The founding of the Galatian churches

Recent work on Pauline chronology tends to acknowledge the general chronological accuracy of Acts 16ff, but also to deny that the Jerusalem conference preceded Paul's missionary activity in Macedonia and Achaia, as Acts 15 suggests. It is held that the conference in Jerusalem took place on the visit to Jerusalem alluded to in Acts 18:22, *after* the visit to Greece.[40] This view is in some ways attractive, but there is one point which seems to tell decisively against it, and it concerns Paul's relationship with Barnabas. We may infer from Gal. 2:1, 9 that Barnabas was Paul's partner in his early missionary activity among the Gentiles. This partnership must have come to an end with their disagreement about whether Gentile converts should submit to the Jewish law (Gal. 2:13). According to 1 Thes. 1:1 and 2 Cor. 1:19, Paul was accompanied during the initial evangelization of Greece not by Barnabas but by Silvanus and Timothy, and this suggests that the mission to Greece belongs to the period after the break with Barnabas, and so after the Jerusalem conference. The present reconstruction of the situation in Galatia therefore assumes that the chronology of Acts 15ff is substantially correct; it can be confirmed at numerous points from Paul's letters.

Soon after the break with Jerusalem and Antioch, Paul 'went through the region of Phrygia and Galatia', according to Acts 16:6. Although nothing is said about founding churches there, we are told in Acts 18:23 that at a later date Paul 'went from place to place through the region of Galatia and Phrygia strengthening all the disciples' – i.e. consolidating the work that had been done on his first visit. These two references to 'Galatia' strongly imply that the so-called 'north Galatian' theory about the destination of Galatians is correct. Acts itself is clearly referring to north Galatia, since 16:1–6 distinguishes between 'the region of Galatia' and the (south Galatian) cities which Paul has just visited.[41] Paul too must have north Galatia in mind. After his second visit (Acts 18:23), Paul arrived at Ephesus (Acts 19:1), from where he wrote 1 Corinthians (cf. 1 Cor. 16:8). In 1 Cor. 16:1, Paul mentions his recent instructions to the churches of Galatia about the collection for the Jerusalem Christians, and it is surely probable that these instructions had been given during the visit to 'the region of Galatia' mentioned in Acts 18:23. In its chronological context, 1 Cor. 16:1 fits perfectly with Acts 18:23, and this is a very strong argument in favour of the north Galatian view.[42] If this is correct, then Paul's defiant response to the disastrous setback in Antioch was to found new Gentile churches in Galatia.[43]

In Gal. 4:12b–15, Paul recalls the circumstances in which he founded the Galatian churches:

> You did me no wrong; you know that it was because of a bodily ailment that I preached the gospel to you at first;[44] and though my condition was a trial to you, you did not scorn or despise me, but received me as an angel, as Christ Jesus. What has become of the satisfaction you felt? For I bear you witness that, if possible, you would have plucked out your eyes and given them to me.

Paul is here referring to an illness, presumably of the eyes. His plan must have been to pass through Galatia on his way to somewhere else (cf. Acts 16:6f). But because of his illness, he was delayed in Galatia, and used the opportunity to establish churches there. Having lost one sphere of influence, he began to create another.

From Galatia, Paul and his companions went on to Troas (Acts 16:8), to Philippi (16:12), Thessalonica (17:1) and Beroea (17:10) in Macedonia, and to Athens (17:15) and Corinth (18:1) in Achaea. This itinerary is confirmed in Paul's letters: Philippi and then Thessalonica (1 Thes. 2:1; Phil. 4:16), Athens (1 Thes. 3:1) and Corinth (1 Cor. 2:3; 2 Cor. 1:19; cf. Phil. 4:15). Corinth became Paul's home for eighteen months (Acts 18:11), and it may well have been there that he received news of the crisis in the Galatian churches.[45]

The dating of Galatians is disputed, even among those who hold the north Galatian view,[46] and is not a matter of crucial importance for the present argument. But it is the aim of the following section to argue that Paul's opponents in Galatia were the 'men from James' (Gal. 2:12) who had previously opposed him in Antioch, and this is more plausible if it can be shown that the Antioch incident, the founding of the Galatian churches and their infiltration by Paul's opponents followed fairly closely after each other. The key to the problem is 1 Cor. 16:1, where Paul refers to his instructions to the Galatian churches to begin collecting money for Jerusalem: does this refer to a period after the Galatian crisis or before it? It has been argued that no money was ever received from the Galatian churches, since Rom. 15:26 states that the collection was the gift of the Macedonian and Achaean churches alone; this suggests that the collection was a failure in Galatia, and that 1 Cor. 16:1 therefore *precedes* the Galatian crisis.[47] But this argument is incorrect, for despite Rom. 15:26 it was not only the Macedonians and the Achaeans who contributed to the collection. In 2 Cor. 9:1–5, Paul tells his readers that he has boasted to the Macedonians about the Achaeans' enthusiasm for the collection, and he is therefore sending certain 'brethren' to Corinth to complete the collection before he himself arrives with the Macedonian delegates, so as to avoid embarrassment. These 'brethren' are clearly differentiated from the Macedonians of 9:3f.[48] They are described in 8:23 as 'apostles of the churches', and the nature of their apostleship is indicated in 8:19: 'He has been appointed by the churches to travel with us in this gracious work.' In other words, the 'brethren' are the representatives of the churches which have contributed to the collection.[49] The churches who appointed them cannot be the churches of

Macedonia (cf. 9:3f), nor (for obvious reasons) the churches of Achaea. Thus, despite Rom. 15:26, churches other than those of Macedonia and Achaea were involved in the collection, and in the light of 1 Cor. 16:1, the Galatians may well have been among them. 1 Cor. 16:1 does not prove that Galatians was written after 1 Corinthians.

Indeed, 1 Cor. 16:1 proves the opposite: Galatians must have been written *before* 1 Corinthians. Paul refers in Gal. 2:10 to his eagerness to fulfil the request of the 'pillars' for a collection from the Gentile churches, but nowhere in Galatians does he indicate that such a collection is or has been in progress in Galatia.[50] Since so much of the letter is concerned to prove his independence of the church of Jerusalem, he would have had to refer to the collection if he had already initiated it in Galatia, in order to explain why the collection did not imply any subordination to Jerusalem or any compromise with its desire to 'compel the Gentiles to Judaize' (2:14). The fact that the intention of 2:10 had not been carried out at this stage is accounted for by the break with Jerusalem described in 2:11ff.[51] (For further discussion of the collection, see the Excursus at the end of Chapter 9.) Thus, Galatians must have preceded the writing of 1 Corinthians.[52] As stated above, Corinth is the most likely place of origin.

Paul himself states in Gal. 1:6 that the crisis in Galatia occurred soon after he founded the churches there: 'I am astonished that you are *so quickly* deserting him who called you ...' He could hardly have used this expression if a period of several years had elapsed since he had preached to them.[53] The possible objection that Galatians is unlikely to belong to the same period as 1 Thessalonians, since the two letters are so different, is unconvincing, since Paul is not dealing with the problem of Judaizers in 1 Thessalonians. But the Thessalonian congregation was apparently independent of the synagogue, and this suggests that Paul had already worked out the theoretical rationale for separation which he develops in Galatians. This early dating of Galatians means that the crisis in the Galatian churches occurred fairly shortly after the crisis in Antioch (Gal. 2:11ff), and this has important implications for understanding the nature of the Galatian crisis.

D The 'men from James' in Galatia

What had happened in Galatia? By far the most likely answer (especially in the light of this early dating of Galatians) is that the 'men from James' (Gal. 2:12) had extended their activity beyond

Antioch;[54] hearing that Paul had founded new churches in Galatia, they too went there in order to put into practice the policies which had already been successful at Antioch. That is precisely what one would have expected them to do. Indeed, Paul too seems to have expected it. In Gal. 1:9, he writes: '*As we have said before*, so now I say again, If anyone is preaching to you a gospel contrary to that which you received, let him be accursed.' The phrase, 'As we have said before, so now I say again', should not be understood as a reference to 1:8.[55] On several other occasions, Paul makes it clear that he is repeating by letter what he had said when he was actually present: 'I warn you, as I warned you before ...' (Gal. 5:21); 'I warned those who sinned before and all the others, and I warn them now while absent, as I did on my second visit ...' (2 Cor. 13:2); 'For many, of whom I have often told you and now tell you even with tears ...' (Phil. 3:18). Thus, Gal. 1:9 shows that Paul had warned the Galatians during his first visit to beware of those who preached a different gospel to his. He had expected trouble, and in the light of his experiences in the period preceding the founding of the Galatian churches, he could only have expected trouble from one quarter: the men from James.[56]

W. Schmithals has argued that Paul's opponents cannot have been Jewish Christians from Jerusalem, because they criticize Paul for his own dependence on the Jerusalem church; this is why in Gal. 1–2 Paul goes to such lengths to argue that his apostleship is not 'from men nor through men, but through Jesus Christ ...' (1:1).[57] On this view, the purpose of Gal. 2:11ff (the quarrel at Antioch) is the same as that of 1:10–2:10: to stress Paul's independence from Jerusalem, proved above all by his public opposition to Peter. His opponents would then be Gnostics who believed in direct, unmediated and authoritative experience of God, and who were critical of the notion of hierarchical authority, passed on from one person to another. But the problem for Schmithals is that the discussion of Abraham and the law in Gal. 3–4 would then be irrelevant;[58] this discussion must surely be directed against Jewish Christians.

Another solution to the problem raised by Schmithals is more probable. It is not necessarily true to say that Paul's opponents *criticized* him for his dependence on Jerusalem. It seems that their case against him was in two parts: they *asserted* that his authority was dependent on the Jerusalem leaders, and they *criticized* him for defying those leaders at Antioch.[59] Gal. 1:10–2:10 answers the first point. Paul claims that his apostleship came directly from God, that for years he had virtually no contact with Jerusalem, and that when he went there with Barnabas and Titus the leaders there acknowledged the commission which had already been given to him by God. Gal. 2:11–21 answers the second point. Paul admits that he opposed Cephas, but argues that he was merely exposing the inconsistency of Cephas's behaviour, even on his own presuppositions; Cephas believed in justification by faith apart from the law, but his cowardice caused him to abandon the practical expression of this belief. The nature of the argument of Gal. 1–2 therefore cannot be used against the view that Paul's opponents were Jewish Christians from Jerusalem. On the contrary, this long explanation of the pre-history of the Galatian crisis only makes sense if the Galatian crisis was a continuation of the controversy described in Gal. 2.[60]

But the strongest reason for identifying Paul's opponents in Galatia with the 'men from James' is that exactly the same problem had arisen in Galatia as at Antioch: Should Gentiles submit to the law of Moses?[61] That is: Should the church remain a reform-movement within the Jewish community, to a large extent sharing its traditions and patterns of conduct? Or should it become a sect, separated from the Jewish community by its different beliefs and practices, and drawing its membership primarily from Gentiles?[62]

2 Paul's response to the crisis

In Galatians, Paul argues vehemently against the view that Gentile Christians should be incorporated into the Jewish community through submission to the law; in other words, he opposes the view of the church which still sees it as a reform-movement within Judaism. He argues for a sectarian view of the church: separation from the Jewish community is essential. His attempt to legitimate this separation may be summarized under the three headings of denunciation, antithesis and reinterpretation.

A Denunciation

In Galatians, denunciation is directed primarily against the Judaizers, and not the Jewish community as a whole. However, the Judaizers are seen as the representatives of the Jewish community (cf. 4:25), so the distinction is not significant. Paul begins the main body of his letter by cursing them twice (1:8f).[63] The curse is the strongest possible form of denunciation. It tacitly assumes that God shares the speaker's utter abhorrence for the person cursed, and seeks to evoke in its hearers the sense that they are confronted with a horrifying, super-human evil, which divine power will soon annihilate. Elsewhere, Paul seeks to win over the Galatians to his point of view by ridiculing his opponents and by undermining belief in their sincerity. Ridicule occurs chiefly in 5:12, where Paul identifies circumcision with castration.[64] He thus encourages his readers to see circumcision as a barbarous and degrading rite to which no civilized person could submit. There are few passages in Paul which express his alienation from the Jewish community more clearly.[65] In other passages, Paul tries to persuade his readers to suspect the motives of his opponents. Their apparent concern for the Galatians' welfare is in fact mere flattery which conceals their self-seeking (4:17). They are motivated by cowardice (6:12).[66] Their supposed zeal for the law is hypocrisy, for they are secretly transgressors of the law (6:13).[67] Paul is not interested in the slightest in an 'objective' assessment of his opponents' character; thus it is mistaken to read 6:13 as evidence that they were antinomians.[68] He is concerned only that his converts should reject their call for integration into the Jewish community, and one way of doing this is to give a hostile assessment of their character.

For our present purposes, much the most interesting aspect of Paul's denunciation of his opponents is his claim that in trying to impose the Jewish law on Gentile Christians, they are showing a cowardly unwillingness to endure persecution (2:12; 6:12). Persecution is a social phenomenon requiring sociological analysis. If it is to function successfully, any society must tolerate a certain amount of variety and dissent among its members. Conversely, if it is to retain its cohesion, it must set limits to possible dissent. Persecution is society's reaction to a minority group in its midst which it feels has transgressed those limits,[69] and may take a wide variety of forms: verbal abuse, exclusion from particular areas of life, physical violence, and so on. Persecution expresses the view that the norms of the minority group are incompatible with membership of the wider community. Any minority group faces the threat of persecution in some form, and two main responses are possible. The group may stress its continued acceptance of the norms and traditions of society as a whole, thus asserting its right to continued membership of that society. Or it may defiantly reject the old norms and traditions, and accept the persecution and separation which this will entail.[70] From this standpoint, the former response is sheer cowardice. Thus Paul accuses Peter of cowardice at Antioch: Peter 'feared those of the circumcision' (Gal. 2:12), i.e. he realized that his behaviour was exposing him to the danger of persecution because from the standpoint of Jewish society he had transgressed the limits of tolerable dissent.

Paul levels the same accusation against the Judaizers in Galatia: 'It is those who want to make a good showing in the flesh that would compel you to be circumcised, and only in order that they may not be persecuted for the cross of Christ' (6:12). To put this point more positively, the Judaizers wished to circumcise the Galatians, and so to integrate them into the Jewish community, because they held that the whole church should remain a part of that community.[71] Paul, on the other hand, in denying the necessity for circumcision denies the basis of the Jewish community, and accepts the persecution and separation which inevitably follows (cf. 5:11). The link between persecution and membership of a society is clearly expressed in 4:25–31. One can see oneself either as a member of the community centred on 'the Jerusalem above' (4:26) or of the community centred on 'the present Jerusalem' (4:25). To understand oneself in terms of the former will mean that one exposes oneself to persecution from those 'born according to the flesh' (4:29), i.e. the 'children' of 'the present Jerusalem' (4:25).

B Antithesis

The theological argument of Galatians is characterized by its frequent use of antithesis, and especially the fundamental antithesis between faith and works which has played such an important part in Western theology since the Reformation. According to the Reformation tradition, this antithesis portrays two possible human responses to God. One is the way of 'works', the way of morality, in which one tries to please God and earn salvation by one's scrupulous obedience to his commandments. The other is the way of 'faith', the way of submission to his grace, which comes to us only as a free gift quite apart from all moral achievement. It could be argued that even if the present interpretation of Paul is correct, this does not affect the validity of the exegesis of Paul inspired by the Reformation: whatever the underlying historical and social realities, the important thing is that for Paul the separation from Judaism was ultimately grounded in the profound theological insight expressed in the antithesis between faith and works. In this way, historical and theological approaches to Paul might be reconciled.

But such a reconciliation would be illusory. It is the purpose of the present argument not to show that the theology which the Reformation tradition finds in Paul springs from a particular sociological context, but to show that this theology is not present in Paul at all. For Paul, the term 'works of the law' refers not to morality in general but to the practice of the law within the Jewish community; and the term 'faith in Jesus Christ' refers not to a willingness to receive God's grace as a free gift and to renounce reliance on one's own achievements, but to the Christian confession of Jesus as the Messiah and the social reorientation which this entails.[72] There is no theoretical reason why the practice of the Jewish law and confession of Jesus as the Messiah should be incompatible, as Jewish Christians demonstrated.[73] The antithesis between faith and works does not express a general theoretical opposition between two incompatible views of the divine–human relationship. It merely expresses Paul's conviction that the church should be separate from the Jewish community. In itself, the antithesis does not provide a reason for this separation; it simply asserts the necessity for such a separation.

The antithesis therefore has an extremely limited function. It plays absolutely no part in Paul's portrayal of the inner life of his congregations; he does not play off faith against Christian behaviour, as though one were saved only by means of the former. On the contrary, for Paul faith includes within itself submission to Christian standards of behaviour. The decision of faith means the decision to abandon many of the norms and beliefs of one's previous social environment, and to adopt new norms and beliefs within a new social environment. The transition from the old to the new takes place in baptism. For Paul, faith is inconceivable without, for example, the abandonment of participation in idolatry (1 Thes. 1:9) or the practice of 'love', i.e. commitment to the new community of the church (Gal. 5:6). It is not simply that these things inevitably *follow* from faith, so that one could theoretically distinguish them from faith; on the contrary, faith *is* the abandonment of old norms and beliefs and the adoption of new ones.[74]

Faith for Paul is thus essentially active; there is no question of an antithesis between a passive reception of the gift of salvation followed by secondary active consequences. He is therefore able quite consistently to say that certain prohibited forms of conduct prevent people from entering the kingdom of God (Gal. 5:20f), and he is able to make salvation dependent on satisfactory conduct:

> Do not be deceived; God is not mocked, for whatever a man
> sows, that he will also reap. For he who sows to the flesh will
> from the flesh reap corruption; but he who sows to the Spirit
> will from the Spirit reap eternal life.   (Gal. 6:7f)

Paul is not contradicting himself when he makes salvation dependent
here on one's behaviour and elsewhere on one's faith,[75] for Christian
conduct is a vital constituent element of faith. The faith—works
antithesis is not an antithesis between faith and morality-in-general,
but an antithesis between life as a Christian, with its distinctive beliefs
and practices, and life as a Jew.

Thus, Paul does not separate Christian faith from Christian ethics
in his account of the inner life of his congregations. Nor, on the other
hand, does he isolate Jewish 'works of the law' from their true
context, the Jew's response to the divine gift of the covenant. He is
fully aware that his opponents in Galatia ground their appeal for
submission to the law on their own understanding of God's grace:
God's choice of Abraham and his seed from among the nations, to
be the recipients of salvation. Abraham and the promises of salvation
would hardly be so prominent a feature of his own argument in Gal.
3–4 if his opponents had not first introduced the subject.[76] In Phil.
3:4–6 and Rom. 9:4f, he again shows that on his view Jewish
obedience to the law is a response to the divine privileges of which
the Jews believe themselves the beneficiaries. He does not present
Judaism as a religion of pure 'achievement', any more than he
presents his gospel as a religion of pure passivity, i.e. the renunciation
of achievement. The antithesis between faith and works merely asserts
the separation of the church from the Jewish community; it does not
provide a theoretical rationale for that separation.[77]

It is obvious that Paul's attack on 'works' occurs in the context
of his attack on Judaism. But, according to Käsemann, 'the exegete
must not make things easier for himself by simply, as historian, noting
this incontrovertible fact ... Our task is to ask: what does the Jewish
nomism against which Paul fought really represent?' ('Salvation
History', 72). His answer is that of Luther: Paul is attacking the
upright and religious man.[78] But the assumption that for Paul the
Jew merely represents the *homo religiosus* is completely false, and
an analogy may make this clearer. One might take as one's starting-
point in interpreting Galatians Paul's opposition to the demand for
circumcision, and then ask: what does circumcision really represent?
One's answer might then be that circumcision is an external religious

rite, and that in opposing it Paul is expressing his undying hostility towards all forms of sacramentalism. But one would then be faced with the difficulty that Paul sanctions the use of sacraments (baptism and the Lord's Supper) within his own congregations. The reason for this difficulty is simply that the assumption that circumcision represents sacramentalism is incorrect; circumcision is rather the rite of entry into a particular religious community. Similarly, the assumption that submission to the law of Moses within the Jewish community represents the religious man's striving after moral achievement is incorrect. For Paul, one must accept not only Christian beliefs but also Christian norms of conduct in order to be saved. His opposition to 'works of the law' merely expresses his conviction that the acceptance of those beliefs and norms is incompatible with continued membership of the Jewish community.[79]

It is quite true that in one sense Paul's view of grace is more 'radical' than that of the Judaism he opposes. But this is merely the result of the fact that membership of the Jewish community is dependent on birth, whereas membership of a Pauline community is dependent on conversion.[80] Any religious group which proclaims the necessity of conversion is likely to emphasize the distinction between the old life and the new. The old life is characterized by sin, ignorance and death, and against this dark background the nature of the new life as a miraculous divine gift will shine out all the more brightly.[81] Rom. 5:12–6:23 is perhaps the clearest Pauline exposition of this viewpoint, which might also be illustrated from the Qumran *Hodayoth* and the literature of other conversionist groups, both ancient and modern. Such groups take a *dynamic* view of God's grace, and this contrasts with the more *static* view of grace taken by groups in which membership is determined by birth. But this is by no means the same as the allegedly Pauline contrast between salvation as a pure gift and salvation as a human achievement. Even if, in some passages, Paul does stress the idea of the miraculous divine gift, in others he stresses the human activity through which the gift is appropriated. The first group of passages has the function of reinforcing the community's sense of possessing incomparable privileges which mark it off from the social environment which its members have now left; the second group has the function of reinforcing the norms of conduct which give the community its identity. It is a mistake to find the essence of Paul's gospel only in the first group of passages, implicitly commending him for the profound insight into the existential plight of humanity supposedly expressed in them.

It is therefore correct to say, as E. P. Sanders does, that Paul opposes Judaism not because of any inherent errors such as 'self-righteousness' or 'legalism', but simply *because it is not Christianity*.[82] The present discussion attempts to give a historical and sociological grounding for this viewpoint. The next step is to examine some of the passages in Galatians in which antitheses are used, and to argue that the point at issue in all of them is not 'theology' as such but the separation of the church from the Jewish community.

1. Gal. 2:14–16 clearly indicates the very specific context of Paul's faith–works contrast. In his previous course of action Peter had (according to Paul) renounced his Jewish identity by living 'like a Gentile and not like a Jew' (2:14), and had thus proclaimed that 'in Christ there is neither Jew nor Greek'. Now, however, he has returned to the Jewish way of life, 'building up' the barrier between Jew and Gentile which he had previously 'torn down', and so admitting that in his previous course of action he had been a 'transgressor' (2:18).[83] In Paul's view, the controversy at Antioch was concerned with the question: Should Jews live ἐθνικῶς, or should Gentiles live ἰουδαϊκῶς (2:14b)? Paul argues for the former. V. 14b is parallel to vv. 15f: 'You, though a Jew ...' (v. 14) corresponds to, 'We ourselves, who are Jews by birth and not Gentile sinners' (v. 15);[84] 'You live like a Gentile and not like a Jew' (v. 14) corresponds to, 'Even we have believed in Christ Jesus, in order to be justified by faith in Christ, and not by works of the law, because by works of the law shall no-one be justified' (v. 16).[85] To seek to be justified by faith in Christ thus means to live like a Gentile, i.e. to live as a member of a Pauline congregation, separated from the Jewish community. To seek to be justified by works of the law is to remain within the community into which one was born (ἡμεῖς φύσει Ἰουδαῖοι, v. 15) by continuing to accept the appropriate way of life (ἰουδαϊκῶς, v. 14; ἔργα νόμου, v. 16).[86]

2. This must be borne in mind when interpreting other parts of Galatians. Thus, when in 3:12 Paul quotes Lev. 18:5 ('He who does them shall live by them'), he does not mean that faith is opposed to 'doing' in general, i.e. to human moral endeavour as a whole.[87] The text reads, 'He who does *them*' – he who lives by the law of Moses and so remains a loyal member of the Jewish community.[88] Nor does faith in this passage mean an attitude of receptivity towards God; it means the active acceptance of Christian beliefs and norms, together

with the social reorientation which this involves.[89] Paul's argument is not that faith and law as abstract theological principles are incompatible with one another.[90] He has simply read back his own conviction that Christianity is incompatible with the practice of Judaism into the Old Testament.[91]

3. In Gal. 2:17, Paul writes: 'But if, in our endeavour to be justified in Christ, we ourselves were found to be sinners, is Christ then an agent of sin?'[92] The latter part of this verse appears to allude to a Jewish Christian charge (perhaps a part of James' message): 'Your view of Christ has led you into sin' − i.e. by disregarding requirements such as circumcision and the food-laws.[93] Paul admits in v.18 that this would have been the case if he recognized the law as still in force.[94] But, according to vv.19f, the old norms are no longer in force. The traditional belief in Christ's death and resurrection is here pressed into the service of a revolutionary rejection of the old norms: 'I through the law died to the law that I might live to God.'[95] This sense of newness is classically expressed in 2 Cor. 5:17: 'The old has passed away, behold, the new has come.' Such revolutionary sentiments are typically sectarian; they are part of the means by which the sect expresses the gulf that it perceives between itself and society. Attempts are made to put such statements into practice; for example, social distinctions may be abolished, as in the Antiochene rejection of the Jew−Gentile divide. But revolutionary statements may disguise a great deal of conformity. The creation of a new identity may not be left to the spontaneity of the sect's members; it needs to be carefully structured, and so the old may reappear in a new guise. The tension between revolutionary theory and surprisingly conservative practice is perfectly exemplified by 1 Cor. 6:12 and 10:23. 'All things are lawful': this statement (perhaps a part of Paul's original preaching to the Corinthians)[96] expresses the liberating and exhilarating rejection of the old norms, whether Jewish or Gentile. But the practical application of this principle is another matter: it may not be used to justify free sexual love or participation in idolatrous worship. Old Jewish norms have reappeared in a new guise. The same is true of Galatians. Paul claims that the old norms belong to a life which is now dead and gone (Gal. 2:19f) and enthusiastically proclaims 'freedom' from them (2:4; 4:1−10, 21−31; 5:1, 13), yet in 5:19−21, the old Jewish attitudes towards fornication, idolatry, sorcery and so on reappear. The Christ−law antithesis is thus revolutionary only in the sense that it reflects the separation of Pauline churches from

the Jewish community, and the abandonment of a limited number of the norms of that community, such as circumcision and the food-laws.

4. In Gal. 5:2ff, Christ and circumcision are contrasted with each other. Bultmann rightly notes that the demand for circumcision means that 'the condition for sharing in salvation is belonging to the Jewish people' (*Theology*, I, 55),[97] but he can still claim that Paul's discussion of circumcision brings us to the heart of 'the Pauline problem of legalism' (112), i.e. 'the problem of good works as the condition for participation in salvation' (111).[98] This mental leap from circumcision to a wrong understanding of good works is quite illegitimate. Paul opposes circumcision because it is the rite of entry into the Jewish people, *and for that reason alone*.[99] Thus, denial of circumcision means exclusion from the Jewish community, i.e. persecution (Gal. 5:11). Christ is incompatible with circumcision not because 'Christ' involves a theological principle (receiving salvation as a sheer gift) which is incompatible with an alleged principle underlying circumcision (earning salvation), but because Paul has already decided that the church is only the church when it is separate from the Jewish community.[100] In 5:2 Paul writes, 'Now I, Paul, say to you that if you receive circumcision Christ will be of no advantage to you', and not the least significant part of this is the phrase, 'Now I, Paul, say to you ...' Paul here grounds his insistence on the incompatibility of allegiance to Christ with membership of the Jewish community not on rational theological argument but on his apostolic authority: the two things are incompatible because he says they are. Once again, it is clear that Paul's use of antithesis *asserts* the separation of church from synagogue, but does not *explain* theologically why such a separation is necessary.

C Reinterpretation

In the previous chapter it was argued that one of the main differences between a reform-movement and a sect is that the former is conscious of sharing the religious traditions of the wider group to whose reform it dedicates itself, whereas the latter regards itself as the sole legitimate possessor of those traditions and denies that they belong in any significant sense to the wider society. These two attitudes to tradition are at the heart of the theological discussions of Gal. 3–4. It seems that the Judaizers claimed that the promises of salvation were originally given to Abraham and to his seed, and that the seed of Abraham are those who are circumcised and who have submitted to the requirements of the law;[101] that is the theological basis for their demand that the Galatians be circumcised. Thus, their understanding of Christ is set in the framework of the religious traditions of the Jewish community as a whole; for them, although no longer for Paul, Jesus is still the Jewish Messiah.[102]

Gal. 3 only makes sense on the supposition that this was the Judaizers' message, for Paul argues there that his Gentile converts are *already* sons of Abraham, and this must be intended polemically. The question at issue is: Who is the seed of Abraham? The Judaizers claim that this refers to the Jewish community. But according to Paul, the Galatians must 'know therefore that those who are of faith, *these* are the sons of Abraham' (vv. 6f; οὗτοι is emphatic, and obviously contests the Judaizers' claim). It may be that the Judaizers also made use of Gen. 12:3,[103] for Paul goes to great lengths to explain his own interpretation of it (vv. 8f). His opponents would have argued: 'God indeed promised that he would grant salvation to the Gentiles, but only if they join themselves to the seed of Abraham − as it is written, "*In you* shall all the Gentiles be blessed".' According to Paul, this refers to a sharing by the Gentiles in the blessing with which Abraham himself was blessed, i.e. righteousness by faith (vv. 8f, 14).[104] The Judaizers claim that if the Galatians join the Jewish community, they will become heirs to the promise of salvation, for 'the promises were made to Abraham and to his seed' (v. 16a). But Paul argues that 'seed' here refers not to the Jewish people but to Christ (v. 16b) and to those who are in Christ, Jews and Gentiles indiscriminately (vv. 26−9).[105] In each case, the Judaizers are conscious of sharing religious traditions with the Jewish community as a whole, whereas Paul disinherits the Jewish community and claims that his congregations of mainly Gentile Christians are the sole legitimate possessors of these traditions.

For the Judaizers, being a son of Abraham meant submission to the law. In opposition to this, Paul in Gal. 3 is concerned to drive a wedge between sonship of Abraham and obedience to the law. Gentile believers share in 'the blessing of Abraham', but on the other hand 'those who are of works of the law' are under a curse (vv. 9f). The law can have nothing to do with God's promises to Abraham, for that would mean that God's will or covenant had been altered or made void (vv. 15−18). The law marked a purely temporary phase between the promise to Abraham and the coming of Christ to fulfil it (3:19−29; 4:1−7). Such arguments are only relevant if the Judaizers had claimed that obedience to the law was the essential consequence of sonship of Abraham. Once again, they share the traditions of non-Christian Jews.

In Gal. 3:10, Paul writes: 'For all who are of works of the law are under a curse, for it is written, "Cursed be everyone who does not abide by all things written in the book of the law, and do them".' The argument is such a startling *non sequitur* that it is likely that Paul is taking up a text used by his opponents[106] (as perhaps in v. 8), for on the face of it Dt. 27:26 says precisely the opposite of what Paul claims. A curse is pronounced not on those who are under the law, as Paul says, but on those who reject the law, and it is not immediately obvious why the Judaizers and those of the Galatians who 'desire to be under law' (4:21) should be thought to be doing this. Whether or not his opponents used this text, it perfectly sums up what must have been their position. Because Scripture pronounces a curse on those who do not submit to the law, the Galatians must do so, joining the Jewish community and living accordingly.[107] But this does not mean that, according to the Judaizers, perfect obedience is necessary if one is to gain salvation. It is Paul, not his opponents, who insists that this is necessary if one follows the way of the law:[108] 'I testify to every man who receives circumcision that he is bound to keep the whole law' (5:3). The reason for this is that according to Paul the law is an absolute demand which must be perfectly fulfilled; but that was not the position of his opponents. Nor does Gal. 5:3 mean that they required submission only to some of the commandments, as some scholars have claimed.[109] It simply means that they took seriously the possibility of forgiveness for transgressions within the covenant through the Messiah who 'died for our sins'.

Thus for the Judaizers the law is one of the gifts of God to the Jewish community as a whole; they do not claim to possess it exclusively. In 5:14, Paul does claim that the kernel of the law ('You shall love your neighbour as yourself') is a Christian possession, but his characteristic view in Galatians is to concede possession of the law to the Jewish community, but to claim that far from bringing a blessing it brings a curse (3:10). It does so because its demand for obedience is absolute, and no-one can attain it; such seems to be the meaning of 3:10 (cf. 5:3).[110] Thus we need to be redeemed from the law by the death of Christ (3:13f). If this absolute law remained in force, the promise of salvation could never be fulfilled (3:15–18). In fact, the law was only temporary, and remained in force only until Christ (3:19–4:11). Here, Paul grounds the separation of the church from the synagogue in the horrifying consequence of life under the law, that one inevitably falls prey to the curse it pronounces on the disobedient. The Jews, he claims, are utterly deluded in imagining that the law is an instrument of blessing. It is the bringer of a curse, and the Galatians would be well advised to reject the demands of its advocates.

In one sense, Paul has conceded possession of the law to the Jewish community. In another sense, he is arguing that Christians alone possess insight into the true meaning of the law, which is exactly the opposite of what its adherents think. Thus, here too the sectarian group is in possession of the true interpretation of an element of the tradition. The radical reinterpretation of the traditional understanding of the seed of Abraham and the law serves to justify the Pauline congregations' separation from the life of the Jewish community.[111] In the case of the Judaizers, no such reinterpretation has taken place, for they remain loyal members of the Jewish community as a whole, and not just of the Christian church. For them, Jerusalem was both the city of James and the church there, who had sent them (cf. 2:12), and the city of the whole Jewish community (cf. 4:25).

Returning to Käsemann's question, we may ask: What does the Jewish Christianity against which Paul fought really represent? The answer has nothing to do with 'the upright and religious man', or 'legalism', or 'good works as the condition for participation in salvation'. It represents continued loyalty to the religious community it was trying to reform, and to the traditions of that community.[112] All this meant nothing to Paul, who was convinced that God had hardened the Jews and that Jewish tradition, truly interpreted, was the exclusive possession of his sectarian Gentile communities.

4

PHILIPPI, CORINTH AND THE JUDAIZERS

1 A warning to the Philippians

A Place and time of writing

Like 1 Corinthians (cf. 1 Cor. 16:8f), Philippians was probably written from Ephesus during the three-year stay there which began soon after the second visit to Galatia (Acts 19:1ff; 20:31).[1] It is true that there is no certain evidence for Paul having been imprisoned in Ephesus, whereas in Philippians it is clear that Paul is writing from prison (1:7, 13f, 17).[2] But in 1 Cor. 16:9, he mentions his many adversaries there, and in 15:32 he seems to be contemplating the possibility of 'fighting with wild beasts' in the theatre there. (Paul cannot be there referring to an incident which has already taken place,[3] for v. 32 requires his death to function as an argument for the resurrection of the dead: i.e. 'If the dead are not raised, what would I gain if I ended my life in the arena at Ephesus, as may well happen?')[4] In 2 Cor. 6:5 and 11:23, he mentions 'imprisonments' among his sufferings. He tells in 2 Cor. 1:8−10 of his recent experiences at Ephesus:

> For we do not want you to be ignorant, brethren, of the affliction we experienced in Asia; for we were so utterly, unbearably crushed that we despaired of life itself. Why, we felt that we had received the sentence of death; but that was to make us rely not on ourselves but on God who raises the dead; he delivered us from so deadly a peril, and he will deliver us ...

Paul here says that he had expected to be condemned to death; but in fact, God had ensured that he was not. It seems clear that the possibility of death was genuine, and that Paul is not simply speaking hyperbolically about his despair. If the death sentence was really a possibility, Paul was probably in prison at the time, and an Ephesian imprisonment therefore seems highly likely.[5]

In Philippians too, Paul, in prison (1:7, 13, 14), faces the possibility of the death sentence. He believes that he will be released, because he thinks that Christ still has work for him to do (1:24–6; 2:24). But he is by no means certain: death is still a possibility (1:20–3), and despite the apparent confidence of release in 1:24–6, he delays sending Timothy until he sees 'how it will go with me' (2:23), i.e. whether or not 'I am to be poured out as a libation upon the sacrificial offering of your faith' (2:17).[6] It is true that the joy so emphasized in Philippians contrasts with the despair mentioned in 2 Cor. 1:8ff. But the latter passage may refer to the period of his imprisonment before the arrival of Epaphroditus from Philippi (4:18). Although Paul claims in 4:11–13 to have been 'content' even before the Philippians' gift arrived, the reference to 'sorrow' in 2:28 suggests a different story. When he writes in 4:10, 'I rejoice in the Lord greatly that now at length you have revived your concern for me', and in 4:14, 'Yet it was kind of you to share my trouble', he seems to imply that it is only since the arrival of Epaphroditus (or since his recovery from illness, 2:25ff) that he has been able to view his situation with such serenity. Paul's situation in Philippians is thus fully compatible with 2 Cor. 1:8ff.[7]

But the strongest argument for the view that Philippians was written in Ephesus is the fact that Paul's chief reason for hoping to be released is that he wishes to visit the Philippians (1:24–6; 2:24).[8] According to 2 Corinthians, after Paul's release (1:10), he did in fact go straight to Macedonia, via Troas (2:12f; 7:5; 8:1ff; 9:2), i.e. to Philippi. Philippians thus fits perfectly with Paul's plans towards the end of his time at Ephesus, and the same cannot be said for the rival theories that Philippians was written in Caesarea or in Rome,[9] for in neither case did Paul intend to visit Philippi when released (cf. Rom. 1:10–15; 15:22–9).[10] Furthermore, the reference in Phil. 2:19–24 to Paul's intention to send Timothy to the Philippians before him agrees with Acts 19:21f.[11]

B Paul's opponents in Phil. 3:2ff

Paul is serene at the prospect of death, but he is by no means serene at the prospect of Judaizers entering the Philippian church and trying to seduce his converts away from his own understanding of the gospel (3:2ff). These people are Christians,[12] for ἐργάτης (3:2) is an early Christian technical term for a missionary.[13] They proclaimed the necessity of circumcision, for Paul refers to them in 3:2 as the κατατομή, a parody of the true περιτομή, the Pauline congregation (3:3). Once again, circumcision is not regarded as an isolated ritual ordinance[14] but as the rite of entry into the people of God. Paul's opponents understand the people of God to be 'the circumcision' (cf. Gal. 2:7–9), i.e. the Jewish community, which they invite Gentile Christians to join.[15] Paul too understands the people of God as 'the circumcision', but interprets this in a spiritualized way (3:3). Here he is again insisting on the absolute separation between the church and the Jewish community, in contrast to his opponents, who still wish to belong to that community. He also refers to his opponents as 'dogs', a pejorative Jewish term for Gentiles, who are outside the covenant (cf. Mt. 15:26f; Rev. 22:15).[16] He seems here to be taking up his opponents' distinction between themselves, members of the true people of God, and the Gentiles, and reversing its application:[17] Gentile Christians (together with Paul) are 'the circumcision' and the Jewish Christian missionaries are 'the dogs'.[18]

It is often suggested on the basis of 3:12–16 that these Judaizers were also Gnostics who believed that the resurrection of the dead was a present reality.[19] But this is unlikely, for in this passage Paul is addressing not Judaizers but his own congregation;[20] the references in vv. 15f to 'us' and 'you' show that this is a purely internal matter. 3:9–11 marks a transition between an attack on Judaism ('a righteousness of my own, based on law', 3:9) and a much gentler corrective to 'enthusiasm' in 3:12–16 ('that if possible I may attain the resurrection from the dead', 3:11).[21] Here as elsewhere Paul is 'fighting on two fronts'. Thus 3:12–16 cannot be used against the view (which follows naturally from the discussion of Galatians in the previous chapter) that Paul's opponents are the emissaries of the Jerusalem church, who are trying to preserve the church's original character as a reform-movement within the Jewish community, and so opposing Paul's sectarian separation from that community.

After the gentle admonitions of 3:12–16, Paul reverts in vv. 18f to the violent denunciations of v. 2:[22]

> For many, of whom I have often told you and now tell you even with tears, live as enemies of the cross of Christ. Their end is destruction, their god is the belly, and their glory is in their shame, with minds set on earthly things.

Some scholars think that we have here a second group of opponents, who are antinomians,[23] or that the original Judaizing opponents are themselves revealed here to be antinomians.[24] But both views read this passage in much too literal a manner; it is not a literal description but a piece of violent polemic.[25] There is nothing here which cannot apply to straightforward Judaizers. In Gal. 2:21; 3:1; 5:11 and 6:12–14, Paul asserts that circumcision and the law are utterly opposed to the cross, and it is therefore likely that 'enemies of the cross of Christ' (Phil. 3:18) also refers to the advocates of circumcision (cf. vv. 2f). The claim that their minds are 'set on earthly things' (3:19) is exactly the same as the claim that they put their confidence in the flesh (vv. 3f), which unambiguously refers to Judaizers. This leaves us with the statement, 'Their god is the belly, and their glory is in their shame.'[26] 'Shame' (αἰσχύνη) is probably to be understood as a euphemism for the genitals. ἀσχημοσύνη has this euphemistic sense in Ex. 20:26 and Rev. 16:15, and so does τὰ ἀσχήμονα ἡμῶν in 1 Cor. 12:23; cf. also the phrase used by Artapanos, the second-century BC Hellenistic Jewish writer (quoted by Eusebius in *Praep. Evan.* 9.27.10), ἡ περιτομὴ τῶν αἰδοίων. 'Their glory is in their shame' is thus an abusive reference to circumcision. But in Phil. 3:19, Paul also says, 'their god is the belly', and this is probably not to be understood as a reference to the Jewish food-laws,[27] for κοιλία may have the same euphemistic sense as αἰσχύνη.[28] But why then should Paul say that '*their god* is the belly'? It seems that he is here alluding to Graeco-Roman phallic worship, such as the cult of Priapus, which spread to Greece and the great Hellenistic cities after the time of Alexander, and the Dionysia, which originated in Athens but spread almost everywhere.[29] If this is correct, Paul is saying: 'They worship their genitals.' This would again be a reference to his opponents' emphasis on circumcision.

Since in Gal. 5:11 Paul links circumcision with castration, and since in Phil. 3:2 he identifies it with the 'mutilation' practised in some forms of paganism and banned in the Old Testament,[30] it is not at all unlikely that he should also identify it with phallic worship.[31] This will only seem implausible if one is determined to maintain that Paul the Christian remained a loyal Jew, or if one cannot believe that the great apostle should stoop so low.[32] One way in which Paul really did resemble Luther was in the offensiveness of his abuse. Paul is probably here drawing on a tradition of hostile Gentile taunts against Jews. Philo (*Spec. Leg.* 1.2) and Josephus (*Ap.* 2.137) both tell us that circumcision was an object of derision among non-Jews. For reasons of delicacy, neither go into details about the nature of this derision, but Paul does not share their inhibitions: he tells his Gentile converts that circumcision, the rite of entry into the Jewish community, is simply castration, mutilation and phallus worship, and such charges were probably the stock-in-trade of Gentile mockery of

Judaism. There seems to be a deliberate strategy underlying these crude comparisons. Paul is seeking to reinforce stereotyped attitudes towards circumcision and the circumcised, with which his Gentile readers will have been familiar since childhood. His aim in doing so is to create an unbridgeable gulf between his congregations and the Jewish community, together with its Jewish Christian representatives. His own utter alienation from Judaism is evident.

Phil. 3:18f is therefore directed against the same Judaizing missionaries as 3:2ff. There is no evidence that these people were Gnostics or antinomians. Nor have they as yet even appeared among the Philippian congregation;[33] Paul tells the Philippians to be on the lookout for such people and to beware of them (3:2),[34] and 3:18 shows that they know of them only indirectly, through Paul's frequent warnings. He is almost certainly referring to the same people as caused the Galatian crisis. Just as he had warned the Galatians during his first visit to beware of such people (Gal. 1:9), so Phil 3:18 indicates that he had repeatedly warned the Philippians of the possibility of their arrival. Together with the violence of the abuse, this shows how seriously Paul took the threat from James' attempt (cf. Gal. 2:12, 'men *from James*') to break down the barrier he had built up between his congregations and the Jewish community.

C Antithesis in Phil. 3

Because of his intense anxiety about this threat, Paul in Phil. 3 once again seeks to legitimate the separation of the church from the Jewish community. We have already examined two elements of this: denunciation, and the reinterpretation of circumcision in 3:2f. But much the most important element here is antithesis; indeed, 3:2–11 as a whole is a single antithesis, designed to show that any attempt to combine Judaism with the gospel is completely untenable. As in Gal. 1:13f, Paul stresses in Phil. 3:6 that his zeal for the law had once led him to persecute the church; there could hardly be a clearer proof that Judaism and the gospel are irreconcilable.[35] In 3:7–11, he emphasizes the utter worthlessness of his Jewish past from his new perspective: it is 'loss' (vv. 7f), 'rubbish' (σκύβαλα, v. 8). Throughout the passage, his tactic is to argue that his readers have a straight choice between Judaism and 'Christ Jesus';[36] it is impossible to have both at once, and the latter is infinitely preferable.

Like all the other passages in which Paul mentions the law, Phil. 3:2ff has been pressed into the service of the Lutheran interpretation of Paul. V. P. Furnish comments on this passage: 'Putting "confidence in the flesh" means regarding one's own status and achievement as the highest good and the ground of hope. It means regarding oneself as an *achiever* and in effect declaring one's independence of God' (*Ethics*, 137). Furnish evidently has in mind here especially the contrast between 'a righteousness of my own, based on law' and 'that which is through faith in Christ Jesus, the righteousness from God that depends on faith', in v. 9; cf. v. 6, 'as to righteousness under the law blameless'. But the contrast here is not between two abstract principles (achievement and submission to grace), but between two different ways of life in two different communities: the Jewish community, with its allegiance to the law, and the Pauline congregations, with their allegiance to Christ. As soon as one attempts to make this concrete contrast abstract, problems emerge. Thus, the way of life summed up in 3:5f cannot simply be subsumed under the heading of 'achievement', for obedience to the law is here said to take place as a response to the privileges given by God to Israel: 'Circumcised on the eighth day, of the people of Israel, of the tribe of Benjamin, a Hebrew born of Hebrews; as to the law a Pharisee, as to zeal a persecutor of the church, as to righteousness under the law blameless'.[37] What Paul renounces according to Phil. 3.7ff is his whole covenant-status as a Jew, which includes reliance on the divine gifts bestowed uniquely on Israel as well as the confirmation of those gifts by his own obedience.[38] On the other hand, faith in Christ cannot be regarded simply as the renunciation of achievement. If it is, then Paul is contradicting what he said in 2:12, where he exhorts the Philippians, 'Work [or accomplish, or achieve] your own salvation with fear and trembling.'[39] It is true that in 2:13 he goes on to say that 'God is at work in you', but this should not be read as denying the statement of the previous verse; Paul is asserting that both human and divine work are necessary to bring about salvation. Paul was evidently not aware of the Lutheran insistence that it is 'faith alone' which saves, i.e. faith in isolation from the Christian's obedience to the appropriate ethical norms. 'Faith alone' brings salvation only in the sense that for Paul its meaning includes not just 'belief' or 'trust' in the narrow sense, but the acceptance of a new way of life, with all the beliefs, ethical norms and social reorientation which this entails. Thus, there is no problem at all about reconciling the exhortation to accomplish one's own salvation (in response to divine grace and with divine help) with the stress on faith in 3:9. The problem only arises if one insists that faith and works are abstract principles, rather than terms which sum up two different ways of life in two different communities, which Paul hopes will stay different.

It is true that 'righteousness' functions differently in the two ways of life to which 3:9 alludes. In Jewish usage, the 'righteous' are those people of whom God approves, those who are pleasing to him.[40] There is an implicit contrast here with the much larger number of the 'unrighteous', those of whom God disapproves. At its most general, 'righteousness' is therefore that conduct which makes one righteous, i.e. approved by God. In this usage, human activity is in the foreground, although divine grace is also presupposed, understood as the means by which God establishes the possibility of righteousness in the midst of a sinful world − i.e. the gifts of covenant and law. This is a *static* view of the grace of God, typical of a religious community which makes membership dependent on birth. God's activity is essentially confined to the past (although it remains of fundamental significance), and the emphasis is on the present human response of obedience. But a religious community which makes membership dependent on conversion will tend to have a more *dynamic* view of the activity of God, which is now seen as the present reality which has brought the members of the sect from their former life of darkness and sin to their present experience of salvation.[41] Thus, in the phrase, 'the righteousness from God that depends on faith', righteousness is no longer seen as human conduct but as the divine gift which transforms the convert's situation from sin and death to salvation and life.

But this exegesis is by no means the same as the characteristic Lutheran contrast between salvation as a human achievement and salvation as a divine gift. To begin with, this view typically regards this contrast as a profound insight into the existential plight of humanity, whereas in fact it is merely a by-product of two different patterns of religion, which one might perhaps label 'traditional' and 'conversionist' respectively.[42] But more importantly, although divine grace and human activity are differently conceived in the two patterns of religion, both elements are present in both of them. 'Righteousness by the law' presupposes a (static) view of God's grace, to which it is a response; and the (dynamic) view of grace expressed in 'the righteousness from God' is incomplete without the arduous human activity of 'faith' (i.e. the reorientation of one's life according to Christian beliefs and norms), by which grace is appropriated. Paul stresses the active nature of faith in Phil. 3:13b−14: 'One thing I do, forgetting what lies behind and straining forward to what lies ahead,

I press on toward the goal for the prize of the upward call of God in Christ Jesus.' Faith in Christ is seen in this metaphor from athletics as the strenuous human activity which is necessary to gain the prize of salvation, or 'the resurrection from the dead' (3:11). This is in accord with the exhortation of 2:12, 'Accomplish your own salvation' – in response, of course, to God's prior grace in Christ. Thus, Phil. 3 gives no support to the traditional Lutheran contrast between human achievement and divine gift.

It should now be clear that Phil. 3 is to be interpreted against the same background as Galatians. The 'men from James' (Gal. 2:12) had triumphed at Antioch, and had achieved considerable success among Paul's congregations in Galatia. It seems that Paul rectified the situation there by means of his letter, which was followed in due course by a second visit (cf. Acts 18:23, 1 Cor. 16:1). But Phil. 3 shows that even several years later, Paul was still afraid that James' Judaizing missionaries might again infiltrate his congregations; this was the theme of repeated warnings even to the loyal Philippians (cf. 3:18). The issue is the same as in Galatians. It is not: Must one do good works in order to be accepted by God? It is: Should the church be a reform-movement within the Jewish community or a sect outside it? In order to convince the Philippians of the necessity for the latter, Paul legitimates separation, using the same three elements as he used in Galatians: denunciation, reinterpretation and above all antithesis.

2 Judaizers at Corinth?

If it is correct to link Philippians with the crisis referred to in 2 Cor. 1:8ff, then Philippians would have been written towards the end of Paul's three-year stay in Ephesus. 1 Corinthians was written about a year before, as a comparison between 2 Cor. 8:10 and 1 Cor. 16:1ff indicates. The latter passage answers a query in the Corinthians' letter to Paul about his collection for the Jerusalem Christians, and 2 Cor. 8:10 refers to the interest they began to express 'a year ago'. If he has in mind the query in their letter, 1 Corinthians was written about a year before 2 Cor. 1–9,[43] which in turn was written from Macedonia soon after the crisis at Ephesus during which Paul had written Philippians. By analogy with Phil. 3, one might therefore expect that Paul would express an anxiety about possible infiltration of the Corinthian congregation by Judaizers. However, it is by no means clear that he does so. Although 2 Corinthians in particular has often been seen as evidence of Judaizing activity in Corinth, it will be the argument of the following sections that the problems Paul had to deal with at Corinth were unrelated to his controversy with Judaism and Jewish Christianity.

A Judaizers in 1 Corinthians?

1 Cor. 1:12 mentions a Cephas party, and since when we last heard of him Cephas was 'compelling the Gentiles to live like Jews' (Gal. 2:14), one might read this as evidence of Judaizing activity at Corinth. But 1 Corinthians as a whole gives virtually no evidence of this.[44] In 1 Cor. 8:7–13, the 'weak' are not those who take a typically Jewish hostile attitude towards 'food offered to idols'.[45] On the contrary, there is every danger that these people will succumb to participation in idolatrous worship if they see the strong doing so (8:10). Unlike those who are genuinely convinced that 'an idol has no real existence' (8:4), these are people who are likely to be overwhelmed by a sense of the reality of the god in whose honour the sacred meal is held (8:7). Their conscience will be 'defiled' (8:7, 12); that is, they will experience a conflict of loyalties between their new faith in Christ and their old faith in the pagan gods. The result may be that they will give up their Christian faith altogether (8:11, 13). This has nothing to do with Judaizing influence. At most, one might cite 10:28f as evidence that some Christians at Corinth adhered to the synagogue's ban on food offered to idols in any form, but the hypothetical speaker here is probably a pagan.[46] None of the other controversies Paul conducts in 1 Corinthians shows any sign of the presence of Judaizers.

B Paul's opponents in 2 Cor. 10–13

At first sight, 2 Cor. 10–13 tells a different story. The opponents whom Paul first refers to sarcastically as 'superlative apostles' (11:5; cf. 12:11), and then denounces as 'false apostles, deceitful workmen, disguising themselves as apostles of Christ' (11:13),[47] are clearly Jewish Christians: 'Are they Hebrews? So am I. Are they Israelites? So am I. Are they descendants of Abraham? So am I.' It is therefore not surprising that many scholars have held that these people are the same as the Judaizers whom Paul opposed in Galatians (or at least similar to them).[48] However, other scholars have pointed out that nothing is said here about the question of Gentile submission to the law, which is so central to Galatians,[49] and they have therefore suggested that Paul's opponents are representatives of a Jewish

Christian 'enthusiastic' spirituality.[50] A good case can be made out for identifying the false apostles of 2 Cor. 10–13 with Apollos and his (unnamed) companions. It is impossible in the present context to argue this case in detail, as this would take us too far afield; but it may be worthwhile briefly to answer the two most serious objections which might be raised and to note some of the points in its favour.

The first objection is that Paul speaks of 'false apostles' in the plural, whereas nothing is said in 1 Corinthians or Acts about Apollos having had any companions. But we do not know of any early Christian missionary who worked entirely on his own. According to Mk 6:7 and Lk 10:1, Jesus sent out his disciples to preach two by two. Paul was accompanied on his so-called first missionary journey by Barnabas and Mark, according to Acts 13:2, 5, and on his second by Silas and Timothy (Acts 15:40; 16:3; 1 Thes. 1:1; 2 Cor. 1:19). Although in 1 Cor. 2:1–5 he speaks as though he alone had preached the gospel to the Corinthians, in 2 Cor. 1:19 he refers to 'the Son of God, Jesus Christ, whom we preached among you, Silvanus, Timothy and I'.[51] So it is quite possible that Apollos was accompanied by others but that Paul only saw fit to name him. This is perhaps implied by the references in 1 Cor. 4:5 to the Corinthians' 'countless guides in Christ'.[52]

The second objection is more serious: Paul is vehemently opposed to the false apostles of 2 Cor. 10–13, whereas he seems to have had no fundamental disagreement with Apollos.[53] It is true that in several passages in 1 Cor. 1–4, Paul appears to be scrupulously impartial in discussing the claims of the Paul party and the Apollos party: both parties are wrong, because of their 'jealousy and strife' (3:3f); Paul and Apollos should both be accepted as servants of God (3:5–9); Paul, Apollos and Cephas belong to them all, not to separate parties (3:21–3); the Corinthians are not to be 'puffed up in favour of one against another' (4:6). But other passages suggest that Paul was in fact deeply anxious about Apollos' teaching and the effect of his visit.

(i) In 1:17–2:5 he asserts that 'wisdom' and the gospel are fundamentally opposed to each other, and it is likely that this passage is directed against the Apollos party.[54] If it is addressed to all the Corinthians indiscriminately, it is very hard to see what its purpose would be. Paul has just criticized the church for breaking up into parties (1:10–16), and this is followed by an attack on 'wisdom';[55] Paul could perhaps be saying that by attributing too much importance to individual teachers the whole church is shown to be pursuing worldly wisdom, but this seems rather a roundabout way to deal with the problem.[56] The passage is unlikely to have been directed against the supporters of Peter, because according to 1:22 it is Greeks who seek wisdom, and this conflicts with Peter's rather conservative Jewish outlook. 2:1−5 shows that the attack on worldly wisdom is bound up with the need for Paul to defend himself against the charge that his preaching lacks eloquence; the hostile reference to his 'contemptible speech' in 2 Cor. 10:9 and his admission of being 'unskilled in speaking' (2 Cor. 11:6) suggest that in 1 Cor. 1:17−2:5 as well, Paul is replying to criticism. Apollos had a reputation for eloquence, according to Acts 18:24, and so it is likely that this criticism of Paul was made by those who said, 'I belong to Apollos' (cf. 1:12; 3:4).[57] 1:17−2:5 is therefore an attack on Apollos' claim that the gospel is compatible with 'the wisdom of the world'.

(ii) In 1 Cor. 4:14−21, Paul reasserts his authority as founder of the Corinthian church. He distinguishes his unique role as 'father' from the 'countless guides in Christ' (v. 15), who must include Apollos.[58] The Corinthians are therefore to imitate Paul (vv. 16f); those who refuse to do this will be punished (vv. 18−21).[59] This passage indicates that despite the impression of scrupulous impartiality in the passages in which he attacks both the Paul party and the Apollos party (1:13−16; 3:4−9; 4:6), his sympathies are almost entirely with the Paul party. They at least have remained loyal to their 'father', whereas the others are rebels who will be punished if they do not become 'imitators of me'. This passage too indicates that Paul was deeply unhappy about Apollos' influence at Corinth.

(iii) In 1 Cor. 16:12a, Paul writes: 'As for our brother Apollos, I strongly urged him to visit you with the other brethren, but it was not at all his will[60] to come now.' Paul had thus tried to integrate Apollos into his own team of fellow-workers, but Apollos had resisted this attempt to curtail his independence.[61] The emphatic language used (πολλὰ παρεκάλεσα αὐτόν and καὶ πάντως οὐκ ἦν θέλημα) implies that already the relationship between the two men was somewhat tense.[62] This and the other passages suggest that it is quite possible that at a later date and in different circumstances, Paul could have denounced Apollos and his companions as 'false apostles' and 'servants of Satan' (2 Cor. 11:13−15).

With these objections dealt with, we may now turn to the positive evidence in favour of this identification of Paul's opponents in 2 Cor. 10−13.

(i) Paul says in 2 Cor. 3:1 that his opponents need letters of recommendation to and from the Corinthians. Acts 18:27 reports that Christians at Ephesus wrote a letter recommending Apollos to the Corinthian Church.

(ii) Paul describes his opponents in 2 Cor. 11:22 as Jews, but never suggests that they had required Gentile Christians to submit to circumcision and the food-laws, as the Judaizers in Galatia had done.[63] Apollos was a Jew, according to Acts 18:24, but 1 Cor. 1–4 gives no indication that he tried to persuade the Corinthians to submit to the law of Moses. Jewish Christian missionaries with such indifference to the law can hardly have been common.

(iii) Paul writes in 2 Cor. 11:5f: 'I think that I am not in the least inferior to these superlative apostles. Even if I am unskilled in speaking, I am not in knowledge; in every way we have made this plain to you in all things.' It has already been argued that 1 Cor. 1:17–2:5 answers the charge that by comparison with Apollos Paul was a very poor speaker, and 2 Cor. 11:5f reflects exactly the same charge (cf. 2 Cor. 10:10–12).

(iv) In 1 Cor. 16:12, Paul announces Apollos' intention of visiting Corinth in the near future: 'He will come when he has opportunity.' It is clear from 2 Cor. 10–13 that the false apostles had visited Corinth at some time after 1 Corinthians was written, and in the light of 1 Cor. 16:12 that is what we would have expected Apollos to have done.

These points do not constitute a proof that the false apostles of 2 Cor. 10–13 are to be identified with Apollos and his companions. But if this identification is not correct, then the false apostles show remarkable resemblances to Apollos. Like Apollos, they come to Corinth armed with a letter of recommendation from another church. Like Apollos, they were Jewish Christians who do not seem to have been interested in imposing the law on Gentiles. Like Apollos, they were more eloquent speakers than Paul. They visited Corinth at exactly the time when a visit from Apollos might have been expected. This series of coincidences seems somewhat unlikely, and it is therefore plausible to identify the false apostles with Apollos and his companions. This point has important implications for the interpretation of Paul's Corinthian correspondence, but in the present context we are interested only in the negative conclusion that there is therefore no evidence for the presence of Judaizers at Corinth.

C 2 Cor. 3 as evidence for Judaizers?

The contrast in 2 Cor. 3:4ff between Paul's ministry of the new covenant and Moses' ministry of the old covenant is sometimes regarded as evidence of the Judaizing tendencies of Paul's opponents at Corinth.[64] But that is to read too much into it. Paul is asserting the sincerity of his ministry (2:17; 4:1−6), and his main argument for this is his sense of the greatness of the commission entrusted to him, which makes petty, self-seeking aims impossible. Paul's use of the story of Moses' shining face (Ex. 34:29−35) is not directed against Judaizers, but is simply intended to reinforce his point about his own ministry, first by means of an *a fortiori* argument (3:7−11), and secondly by means of a contrast (3:12−18). If the divine glory was manifested in Moses' ministry, although it brought condemnation and was only temporary, how much more will it be manifested in Paul's ministry, which brings the Spirit and righteousness (3:7−11). Thus, Paul is able to speak with complete honesty, unlike Moses, who concealed his face to prevent the Israelites seeing that the glory was only transient,[65] i.e. that the law itself would eventually pass away[66] (3:12−13; this develops into a contrast between the Jewish and Christian communities in 3:14−18).[67] Nothing is said or implied here about the activities of Judaizers.

However, 2 Cor. 3:4ff does provide valuable confirmation of some of the arguments advanced earlier. It indicates that the context of Paul's disparaging statements about the law is the need to distance the church from the Jewish community.[68] Paul speaks in 2 Cor. 3:7−11 of the law as the bringer of death and condemnation, and as being impermanent, and this is no abstract theological speculation, isolated from any significant social context. 3:14f shows that this law is simply the Torah which is read Sabbath by Sabbath in the Jewish synagogues. Those who read it have a veil over their minds; they fail to perceive its true meaning. According to 3:13, the veil is that which prevents the Israelites from seeing that the glory on Moses' face fades, i.e. that the law itself is impermanent (cf. 3:11). Their misunderstanding is therefore not that they fail to perceive that the Scriptures as a whole are to be read as a testimony to Christ, as some exegetes have suggested,[69] but that they fail to perceive that the law is the bringer of death and condemnation, and so must necessarily be impermanent if salvation is to be possible. They regard the law as the gift of God's grace which has salvation as its aim. Becoming a Christian ('turning to the Lord', 3:16) means abandoning this fundamental assumption of the Jewish community, thus separating oneself from that community.[70]

Like other leaders of sectarian groups, Paul insists that the religious tradition which the separated group shares with the parent body must be interpreted esoterically. Only members of the sect truly understand the tradition (in this case, the law), and the tradition thus becomes one of the ways in which the separation between the sect and the parent body is perpetuated. Thus, according to 2 Cor. 3:12–16, the law can only be interpreted correctly from the standpoint of faith in Christ;[71] from that standpoint it is seen as the bringer of death and condemnation, and as impermanent. This point – theologically rather than sociologically understood – is one of the mainstays of Bultmann's interpretation of Paul's view of the law. As we saw in the first chapter, Bultmann opposes the Lutheran *secundus usus legis*, according to which one must first be shown one's sin by the law, and only as the result of this seek mercy in Christ and come to faith in him. He argues that recognition of sin is simultaneous with the revelation of Christ; what is hidden about the law and revealed only through the gospel is that it is being perverted into a means of achieving salvation for oneself.[72] Thus he claims that Paul speaks of the law as 'the letter' in 2 Cor. 3:6 because of the Jewish misuse of the law as a means of earning salvation.[73] But this view is unlikely. τὸ γράμμα in 3:6 is clarified by ἐν γράμμασιν ἐντετυπωμένη λίθοις; the reference is to the Ten Commandments (cf. Ex. 34:38; Dt. 4:13, 10:4), i.e. to the law's character as a demand.[74] In Ex. 34:38f, the story of the glory on Moses' face (which forms the basis for 2 Cor. 3:4ff) is linked with his bringing the Ten Commandments, written by God on stone tablets, to the Israelites, and it is therefore these commandments which are seen in 2 Cor. 3:7–9 as the bringer of death and condemnation.[75] Paul probably understands the law in this way because he regards it from his Christian standpoint as a demand for absolute obedience, offering no possibility of forgiveness, which sinful man cannot fulfil (cf. Gal. 3:10; Rom. 3:10–19); nothing is said here about any Jewish belief that salvation must be earned. However, for Paul the most important thing is the fact that the law brings condemnation, not the question of how it does so, which he does not discuss in 2 Cor. 3.

This view of the law serves to legitimate Paul's belief that his mainly Gentile congregations must be completely separated from the synagogue. However, there is no evidence either in the Corinthian correspondence as a whole or in 2 Cor. 3 in particular that the relationship between the Jewish and Christian communities was a live issue at Corinth. Thus, the placid tone of 2 Cor. 3 contrasts with the vehement polemic of Galatians and Phil. 3. This again suggests that the main purpose of this contrast between the ministries of Moses and of Paul is to reinforce Paul's assertion of his own sincerity and honesty, which he bases on the awe-inspiring greatness of the commission given to him by God. In making this contrast, Paul makes non-polemical use of some of the language and theology he has developed in controversy with Judaizing Christians. This passage is therefore not to be used as evidence of the presence of Judaizers at Corinth; there is no reason to suppose that such people ever went there.

5

THE SITUATION IN ROME

It has been the argument of the previous chapters that there is the closest possible relationship between Paul's theological reflection and the social reality of Gentile Christian congregations separated from the synagogue. He engages in theology in order to legitimate that reality. It will be the purpose of this and the following chapters to apply this principle to Paul's letter to the Romans, which is still often interpreted without any reference to the underlying social situation.

1 The question of the purpose of Romans

F.C. Baur was the first scholar to see Romans as a response to problems within the church at Rome. He writes: 'It is unthinkable that the apostle, without definite circumstances present in the Roman congregation ..., should have felt himself obliged to write a letter with such a content to this congregation' ('Zweck und Veranlassung', 156). Baur argues that the church at Rome was composed mainly of Jewish Christians (202ff) who denied the legitimacy of Paul's Gentile mission. There was thus tension between the Jewish majority and the Gentile minority (149), and to resolve this problem Paul wrote a long defence of Christian universalism over against Jewish particularism. In this way, Baur manages to relate the purpose of Romans very closely to his interpretation of its content.[1]

Subsequent scholarship has largely failed to maintain this unity of purpose and content; the content is related to the purpose only in the most general terms.[2] An exception to this is P.S. Minear, who in his book *The Obedience of Faith* (1971) takes Rom. 14–15 as his starting-point for delineating the situation in Rome. He concludes from this section that there were five groups in the Roman church: the 'weak in faith' who condemned the 'strong in faith'; the strong in faith who despised the weak in faith; the doubters; the weak in faith who did not condemn the strong; and the strong in faith who did not despise the weak. Minear proceeds to relate this hypothesis to the contents of Romans as a whole. For example, he sees 1:18–4:25 as addressed to the weak in faith (46): in Rom. 2, Paul tries 'to prove to Jewish Christians that their prideful condemnations of Gentile culture placed them on the same level in God's eyes and subject to the same penalties as the Gentiles' (51), and in Rom. 4 the weak are told, 'You must accept the strong in faith as children of Abraham and heirs to the promise of Abraham' (53). Even though Minear's case is not always convincing, his insistence that the contents of Romans must be interpreted in the light of the situation of the Roman church is important, as is his use of Rom. 14–15 as the key passage for determining that situation.[3] K. P. Donfried has stated that it is not essential for Minear's case that Rom. 1–4 should be *directly* addressed to Jewish Christians. He writes: 'Is it not very possible that Paul can be dealing with actual problems but in so doing employs rhetorical arguments and theological perspectives of a more general nature which will aid in solving them?' ('False Presuppositions', 126).

W. Wiefel attempts to relate our fragmentary knowledge of the contemporary Jewish community in Rome to the purpose of the letter to the Romans. Acts 18:2 attests both the early existence of Christians in Rome and their expulsion by Claudius, which brought the first congregation to an end ('Jewish Community', 110). Rom. 16 depicts a predominantly Gentile congregation consisting of house-churches independent of the synagogue, and the problem Romans deals with is that of the relationship between this Gentile Christian majority and the returning Jewish Christians (113). Romans 'was written to assist the Gentile Christian majority, who are the primary addressees of the letter, to live together with the Jewish Christians in one congregation, thereby putting to an end their quarrels about status' (113). In a society marked by its hostility towards Jews, Paul aims to raise the status of Jewish Christians in the eyes of Gentile Christians (119).[4] This conclusion is the opposite of Baur's view that Paul's aim is to raise the status of Gentile Christians in the eyes of Jewish Christians.

J. Jervell represents a different approach. He writes: 'The letter itself clearly states that its raison d'être does not stem from the situation of the Roman congregation, but is to be found in Paul himself at the time of writing' ('Jerusalem', 62). Jervell sees Rom. 1:18–11:36 as 'the defense which Paul plans to give before the church in Jerusalem' (64).[5] Here, 'Paul is absorbed by what he is going to say in Jerusalem' (70), and he writes as he does because he wishes to ask the Roman congregation for its solidarity, support and intercession (64). According to 15:15ff, 'Paul wants to represent the whole Gentile world in Jerusalem, including the West' (74).

Jervell is surely right to stress that in all his letters Paul is writing not just for the sake of the congregation but also for his own sake.[6] Although we tend 'to picture Paul more as a theological monument than as a human being', the fact is that 'Paul needs the congregation just as much as they need him' (62). But his own emphasis on Paul's own situation to the exclusion of the situation in Rome is unnecessarily one-sided. As in his other letters, it is probable that Paul is writing both because of factors in the life of the congregation and because of factors in his own life. The present discussion attempts to incorporate the emphases on the close relationship between the purpose of Romans and its content (Baur, Minear), the importance of Rom. 14:1–15:13 for determining its purpose (Minear), the use of information about early Roman Christianity from other sources (Wiefel), and the significance of Paul's own situation (Jervell). It will be argued that Romans presupposes a particular social situation within the Roman church, and that the contents of the theological discussions of Rom. 1–11 are determined by the letter's intended function within that social situation. The contents of Romans cannot be properly understood without an appreciation of the social realities underlying its apparently theoretical discussions.[7]

This view of the purpose of Romans involves the rejection of the view of G. Klein and G. Bornkamm, that in Romans Paul sets out the essence of his gospel in a universally valid way.[8] Klein argues that Paul 'does not regard the local Christian community there [i.e. in Rome] as having an apostolic foundation' ('Purpose', 44), and the purpose of Romans is to remedy this deficiency: 'The fact that Paul writes to the Romans in the form of a theological treatise is indicative of an occasion which calls for the normative message of the apostle and demands that his theological reflections be raised to a new level of general validity' (49). Thus, justification is both the centre of Paul's theology and the only correct foundation for the church, and the task of historical criticism is constantly to rediscover this (49). Bornkamm too thinks that in Romans Paul 'elevates his theology above the moment of different situations and conflicts into the sphere of the eternally and universally valid' ('Testament', 31). What Paul says about the Jews is an example of this universal validity, for according to Paul, 'The Jew represents man in general' (28). Bornkamm continues: 'This man is indeed not somewhere outside, among believers; he is hidden within each Christian, even in Paul himself, and also in those Gentile Christians who now want to pride themselves at the expense of Israel' (29). Thus, even in the discussion of a purely historical problem – the purpose of Romans – traditional Lutheran themes are once again invoked. The overwhelming authority which the Lutheran Paul still possesses is very much in evidence here.[9]

2 The origins of Roman Christianity

In his account of the life of Claudius, Suetonius writes: 'Since the Jews constantly made disturbances at the instigation of Chrestus, he expelled them from Rome ...' (25.4). There can be little doubt that 'Chrestus' is to be identified with 'Christ'.[10] Tertullian complains that 'Christian' is often mispronounced 'Chrestianus', which shows that 'you do not even know accurately the name you hate' (*Apol.* 3.5). Lactantius speaks of 'the error of the ignorant, who by the change of a letter are accustomed to call him Chrestus' (*Inst.* 4.7.5). Suetonius wrongly concluded (perhaps because of the Christian claim that Jesus was still alive) that 'Chrestus' had actually been in Rome in person, stirring up trouble.[11] Suetonius' report is confirmed by Acts 18:2: 'And he [Paul] found a Jew named Aquila, a native of Pontus, lately come from Italy with his wife Priscilla, because Claudius had commanded all the Jews to leave Rome.' Aquila and Priscilla were evidently Christians even before they met Paul, for Luke says nothing about their conversion. Christianity was therefore established in Rome from a very early period.

With regard to the date of the expulsion, there are two main possibilities. Suetonius gives us no clue as to this, and most scholars have relied on the evidence of Luke and Orosius to suggest AD 49. Luke's reference to the expulsion of the Jews from Rome implies that this event took place about two years before Gallio's proconsulship of Asia (Acts 18:11, 12), which probably lasted from July 51 to July 52.[12] This would suggest that the expulsion took place in about AD 49, and this is confirmed by Orosius, who states: 'Josephus reports that the Jews were expelled from the city by Claudius in the ninth year' (*Hist. adv. pag.* 7.6.15). No such report exists in Josephus, but the apparently fortuitous agreement with Luke suggests that the report is reliable nonetheless.[13]

However, G. Lüdemann has recently argued that Orosius should be ignored, that in Acts 18 Luke has combined traditions relating to different visits of Paul to Corinth, and that the expulsion of the Jews from Rome is to be identified with Claudius' decree forbidding the Roman Jews to meet together, which according to Dio Cassius was issued in AD 41 (*Paul*, 158ff).[14] Dio writes: 'As for the Jews, who had again increased so greatly that by reason of their multitude it would have been hard without raising a tumult to bar them from the city, he did not drive them out, but ordered them, while continuing their traditional mode of life, not to hold meetings' (*Hist. Rom.* 60.6.6). Lüdemann claims that Dio is here deliberately contradicting the statement of Suetonius or his source, that the Jews *were* expelled (164ff). This would then mean that the riots which took place 'at the instigation of Chrestus' could be dated to AD 41, which would push back the origins of Roman Christianity almost a decade. However, Lüdemann's hypothesis is very unlikely to be correct. When Dio writes that the Jews 'had again increased so greatly', he implies that a few years earlier there had been many fewer Jews in Rome, and that had indeed been the case, for the Jews were expelled from Rome by Tiberius in AD 19 (Dio Cassius, *Hist. Rom.* 57.18.5a, Tacitus, *Ann.* 2.85, Josephus, *Ant.* 18.81ff, Suetonius, *Vit. Tib.* 36, cf. Seneca, *Epist.* 108.22). When Dio states that in AD 41 Claudius did not expel the Jews from the city, he is therefore not contradicting the statement of Suetonius or his source, but explaining why Claudius did not repeat the action of Tiberius twenty-two years earlier. Combining Dio with Suetonius, Luke and Orosius, we may conclude that Claudius banned Jewish meetings (i.e. synagogue worship) in AD 41, and expelled the Jews after riots 'at the instigation of Chrestus' in AD 49.[15]

It is possible that the two events are linked. In addition to the decree mentioned by Dio, three decrees concerning the Jews, dating from the first year of Claudius' reign, are known; two were sent to Alexandria (Josephus, *Ant.* 19.280–5, P. Lond. 1912)[16] and one to 'the rest of the world' (Josephus, *Ant.* 19.287–91).[17] In each of them, Claudius emphasized that the Jews were to be allowed to practise their distinctive way of life without hindrance; in this way he sought to restore their confidence in Roman rule, which had been dangerously undermined as the result of Caligula's attempt to install a statue of himself within the temple at Jerusalem.[18] There must have been some reason why the Roman Jews had their right to live by the law of Moses confirmed but were not allowed to meet together. At a time when Claudius' policy towards the Jews was in general conciliatory, why were the Roman Jews singled out for punishment? Suetonius may provide us with the answer when he tells us that the Jews were expelled from Rome because they '*constantly* made disturbances at the instigation of Chrestus'. This suggests that disorders among the Roman Jews because of the preaching of the Christian gospel had been going on for some time before Claudius finally lost patience and expelled them in AD 49. His decree forbidding meetings of AD 41 may therefore have been an earlier measure designed to solve the same problem. This would suggest that the origins of Roman Christianity are to be placed at least as far back as the beginning of Claudius' reign.[19]

Suetonius' comment indicates that earliest Roman Christianity was an inner-Jewish phenomenon. The disorders he mentions were caused by controversy within the Jewish community about the truth or falsehood of the Christian message.[20] No doubt the converts to Christianity included a number of proselytes, for Roman Judaism had achieved notable missionary successes (cf. Horace, *Sat.* 1.4.142ff, Tacitus, *Hist.* 5.5), and indeed it was probably mainly for this reason that the expulsion took place in AD 19 (Dio Cassius, *Hist. Rom.* 57.18.5a, cf. Josephus, *Ant.* 18.81ff). But there is no reason to suppose that the status of the law was one of the grounds for conflict between Christian and non-Christian Jews; it is Paul who must take the main credit for first proclaiming freedom from the law to Gentiles.

The Jewish roots of Roman Christianity are stressed in an interesting passage in the prologue of Ambrosiaster's commentary on Romans:

> It is established that there were Jews living in Rome in the times of the apostles, and that those Jews who had believed passed on to the Romans the tradition that they ought to profess Christ but keep the law ... One ought not to condemn the Romans, but to praise their faith; because without seeing any signs or miracles and without seeing any of the apostles, they nevertheless accepted faith in Christ, although according to a Jewish rite.[21]

It is uncertain whether or not this passage derives from genuine historical tradition. According to Cranfield (*Romans*, I, 20), it is more likely that Ambrosiaster's statements reflect 'either his own inferences from the epistle or the influence of Marcion's preconceptions'. The Marcionite prologue to Romans speaks of false apostles who taught the Romans to accept the law and the prophets as well as faith in Jesus Christ (Cranfield, *Romans*, I, 20n). But it is noteworthy that Ambrosiaster is much more positive than this about the Romans' Jewish tendencies, and that he does not make use of the standard theory (present also in the Marcionite prologue to Romans) that heresy is always a falling away from the true faith which was initially held.[22] It is perhaps more likely that Ambrosiaster's comments represent inferences from Romans itself. But Romans can hardly be said to have compelled him to such a view; for example, Rom. 14 shows that there were Gentile Christians in Rome who practised freedom from the law. Ambrosiaster clearly found the Romans' Jewish tendencies somewhat embarrassing, and it is therefore hard to see why he should have stressed this if the passage does not represent genuine tradition; it is thus at least possible that Ambrosiaster gives us authentic information about the origins of Roman Christianity. But even if his statements are mere inferences from Paul or the Marcionite prologue, the view of Roman Christian origins which they present is probably correct, since we know from Suetonius that Christian preaching caused controversy initially only within the Jewish community. That community contained a large number of proselytes, and it is highly probable that some of these were converted to Christianity while continuing to observe the law.

But this raises an important problem. When Paul wrote to the Romans about seven or eight years after Claudius' expulsion of the Jews from Rome in AD 49, he assumed the presence of Gentile Christians who did not observe the law (Rom. 11:13ff; 14:1–15:13), as well as Jewish Christians. What was the origin of Gentile Christianity without the law in Rome? To answer this question, we must examine the evidence about the situation in Rome provided especially by Rom. 14–16.

3 The two Roman congregations: Rom. 14:1–15:13

The legitimacy of using Rom. 14:1–15:13 as evidence about the situation of the Roman church has been strongly disputed by R.J. Karris. He argues that the identification of the 'weak' and 'strong' parties has been conjectural and unproductive ('Romans 14:1–15:13', 82), and that this section is rather to be interpreted as a generalized rewriting of 1 Cor. 8–10 (83ff), eliminating everything which has reference only to a concrete situation (i.e. food offered to idols).[23] The present argument aims to show that Rom. 14:1–15:13 should not be understood as mere general paraenesis, but gives clear evidence of the situation in the Roman church.[24] First, it must be shown that there is no real problem identifying the 'weak' and the 'strong': the former are Christians who observe the Mosaic law, while the latter are Christians who do not.[25] For convenience, one may refer to these two groups as 'Jewish Christians' and 'Gentile Christians', so long as it is remembered that the former group may well have included proselytes,[26] whereas the latter group may well have included Jews who like Paul himself did not observe the law.

The main difficulty in identifying the 'weak' with straightforward Jewish Christians who observed the law is that according to 14:2 they abstained not simply from pork, from the meat of animals that had been incorrectly slaughtered and from meat offered to idols, but from meat in general: 'The weak man eats only vegetables.'[27] The difficulty is increased when Paul refers to abstention from wine as well as meat (14:21; cf. 14:17).[28] Some scholars have concluded from these statements that the 'weak' have been influenced by syncretistic ascetic ideas.[29] But Jewish abstention from meat and wine is mentioned several times in other texts. In Dn. 1:8–16, Daniel and his companions obtain permission to abstain from meat and wine, which would defile them (v. 8), and to live off vegetables and water. Judith refuses to eat and drink the food and wine provided by Holofernes (Jud. 12:1–4). Esther tells how she has not eaten at Haman's table or at the king's feast, and how she has not drunk 'the wine of the libations' (Esth. 14:17, LXX). Josephus commends the priests who were taken captive to Rome in AD 61, and who did not forget their religion and so 'supported themselves on figs and nuts' (*Vit.* 14).[30] In all these examples, Jews are in a Gentile environment, cut off from their community, in which ceremonially pure meat and wine might be obtained, and this suggests a plausible interpretation of the 'weak' in Rom. 14. Suetonius tells us that there was constant unrest in the Jewish quarter of Rome[31] because of Christian preaching, and even before the expulsion of AD 49 it must have been hard for the Jewish Christian minority to live alongside the non-Christian Jewish majority. The situation would have been exacerbated by the expulsion. Non-Christian Jews would blame the Christians for what had happened, and the ill-feeling might well have been sufficient to prevent the Christians resettling in the Jewish quarter when the return to Rome took place. They would therefore be forced to live in another part of Rome, where they would be unable to obtain the ceremonially pure meat and wine which was available only in the Jewish quarter.[32] They therefore did what Daniel, Judith, Esther and the priests did when in a Gentile environment: they abstained from meat and wine.[33] The fact that they did so is therefore not evidence of syncretistic or ascetic tendencies, but is fully compatible with the situation of Jewish Christians who wished to remain faithful to the law in difficult circumstances.[34]

There are several further indications in Rom. 14:1–15:13 that show that the weak are to be identified as Jewish Christians.[35] First, in 14:14 Paul mentions the belief of the weak that certain food is κοινόν, and elsewhere in the New Testament this term refers to food which is unclean according to the Jewish law (Acts 10:14, 28; 11:8). In Rom. 14:20, πάντα μὲν καθαρά is equivalent to οὐδὲν κοινόν in v. 14,[36] and this recalls Acts 10:15 and 11:9, ἃ ὁ θεὸς ἐκαθάρισεν, σὺ μὴ κοίνου; cf. Mk. 7:19, καθαρίζων πάντα τὰ βρώματα. Secondly, Rom. 14:5 tells us that 'one man esteems one day as better than another', and speaks of 'he who observes the day'. This seems to refer to Jewish Sabbaths, feasts and fasts.[37] Thirdly, 15:7–13 speaks unambiguously of the duty of Jews and Gentiles to welcome one another as Christ has welcomed them. There is no break between 14:1–15:6 and this passage, and it is therefore natural to conclude that the whole passage concerns the relationship between Jewish and Gentile Christians. Indeed, this final point puts this identification virtually beyond doubt.

The purpose of Rom. 14:1–15:13 is indicated in 14:1: 'As for the man who is weak in the faith, welcome him, but not for disputes over opinions.' We have here two separable injunctions: (i) Welcome him; (ii) Do not argue with him. In 14:1, Paul adopts the standpoint of the strong, but elsewhere he is more even-handed. Thus, the second injunction is applied both to the strong and to the weak in 14:3–9: those who eat and who esteem all days alike are not to despise those who abstain and who esteem one day as better than another, but nor are the latter to pass judgment on the former. For Gentile and Jewish Christians to be able to meet together in harmony, both sides must make concessions. Gentiles must not regard observance of the Jewish law as incompatible with Christian faith (indeed, according to 14:13ff, it may be wise for them to make concessions as regards what they eat),[38] and Jews must not regard it as essential to Christian faith. By far the greater concession is demanded of the Jews. They are required to abandon the idea that the law is the authoritative, binding law of God, to which all must submit, and to regard it instead as purely optional, a matter of individual choice and of private piety. In the light of this, it is not surprising that their present tendency is to 'pass judgment' on Gentile Christians who ignore important aspects of the Mosaic law.

The fact that the two sides differed so fundamentally about the law makes it extremely unlikely that they shared common worship. *Paul's argument does not presuppose a single congregation in which members disagree about the law; it presupposes two congregations, separated by mutual hostility and suspicion over the question of the law, which he wishes to bring together into one congregation.* This is the significance of the injunction of 14:1, 'Welcome him', or, applying it to both sides impartially, 'Welcome one another, therefore, as Christ has welcomed you' (15:7).[39] The purpose of welcoming or receiving one another is common worship: 'that *together* you may *with one voice* glorify the God and Father of our Lord Jesus Christ' (15:6).[40] Because Christ came to save both Jews and Gentiles, Jews are exhorted to join with the Gentiles in common worship: 'Therefore I will praise thee *among the Gentiles*' (15:8f).[41] Likewise, Gentiles are exhorted to join with Jews for worship: 'Rejoice, O Gentiles, *with his people*' (15:10). Then the Jews are again reminded that Scripture speaks of the Gentiles praising God (15:11), and of the salvation which the 'root of Jesse' will bring to the Gentiles (15:12). There is therefore no need for them to continue to separate themselves from the life and worship of the Gentile Christian community.[42]

Thus, Rom. 14:1–15:13 addresses itself not to tensions between Jewish and Gentile Christians within a single congregation (the usual view), but to the problem of two separate congregations who regard each other with suspicion and who hold no common worship. 15:7–13 seems to put this interpretation beyond doubt: why should Paul exhort Jewish and Gentile Christians to worship together if they are already doing so? It is probable that the Jewish Christian congregation is the remnant of the first Roman congregation which was dispersed in AD 49; Rom. 14:1–15:13 thus confirms the essentially Jewish nature of that congregation.[43] Paul exhorts them to recognize the legitimacy of a Gentile Christianity which does not require submission to the law. They are to regard the law, and especially its commandments about food, Sabbaths and feast days, as purely optional, matters between the individual and God rather than authoritative divine commands. Conversely, Gentile Christians are to regard these practices as permissible, and are not to despise those who observe them; but in their case nothing of fundamental importance has been sacrificed, whereas for the Jewish Christians a radical change of outlook is required. Paul's aim is thus to create a single 'Paulinist' congregation in Rome — 'Paulinist' in the sense that the Pauline principle of freedom from the law is accepted. To put it another way, he wishes to convert the Jewish Christian congregation to Paulinism – to the theory of freedom from the law, if not to the practice.

If this view of the purpose of Rom. 14:1–15:13 is correct, it has considerable importance for the interpretation of the rest of Romans, which may be interpreted in a similar way: Paul's purpose in writing Romans was to defend and explain his view of freedom from the law (i.e. separation from the Jewish community and its way of life), with the aim of converting Jewish Christians to his point of view so as to create a single 'Pauline' congregation in Rome.[44] At the same time, he encourages Gentiles to be conciliatory towards their Jewish fellow-Christians, since the union for which Paul hopes will not be possible without a degree of tact and understanding on the part of the Gentile Christians. But before attempting to interpret Rom. 1–11 in the light of these conclusions, a discussion of Rom. 16 is necessary. This will confirm the conclusions already reached, and provide a possible answer to the historical riddle of the origins of Gentile Christianity in Rome.

4 Gentile Christianity in Rome: Rom. 16

It has often been suggested that Rom. 16 is addressed not to the church of Rome but of Ephesus, and that it is either an independent letter (in whole or in part)[45] or an appendix to a copy of Romans which was sent to Ephesus.[46] The main reason for this hypothesis is that it is thought unlikely that Paul should have known as many individuals in the Roman church as are mentioned in vv. 3–16. Ephesus is suggested because Prisca and Aquila were last heard of in connection with that city (Acts 18:19, 26), and because of the reference in v. 5 to 'my beloved Epaenetus, who was the first convert in Asia for Christ'. But Prisca and Aquila were only ever in Corinth (Acts 18:2f; cf. 1 Cor. 16:19) and Ephesus (Acts 18:18f, 26; 1 Cor. 16:19) because they had been expelled from Rome along with other Jews by Claudius (Acts 18:2). It is therefore by no means unlikely that they should have returned to Rome by the time Romans was written. Some of the others who are named in Rom. 16 may also have been refugees from Rome, whom Paul met in the East as he had met Prisca and Aquila, and who have also now been able to return to Rome.[47] Even if one still finds it surprising that Paul should have known so many individuals in the Roman church, the view that Rom. 16 like Rom. 1–15 is addressed to Rome is preferable to the cumbersome theory that without any break or explanation Paul suddenly addresses not Rome but Ephesus, and to the view that an entirely unrelated letter-fragment has un-accountably been attached by a later editor to the letter to the Romans.[48] If Rom. 16 can be satisfactorily explained as an integral part of the letter to the Romans, the Ephesian theory collapses automatically.

It is in fact by no means certain that Paul knew personally all the individuals who are named in Rom. 16.[49] He clearly knew Prisca, Aquila and Epaenetus (vv. 3–5), and he must also have known those who are described as 'beloved': Ampliatus (v. 8), Stachys (v. 9) and Persis (v. 12). The fact that he describes Rufus' mother in v. 13 as 'his mother and mine' suggests that he knew them both. Urbanus is described as 'our fellow-worker in Christ' (v. 9, cf. v. 3); but Mary, whose work only in the Roman congregation (and not alongside Paul) is mentioned (v. 6), may never have met him personally. It is not certain whether 'those workers in the Lord, Tryphaena and Tryphosa' (v. 12) have worked alongside Paul or solely in Rome. Paul refers to Andronicus and Junias as 'fellow-prisoners' (v. 7), but he also describes them as 'fellow-countrymen', and it may be that in both expressions he is simply wishing to assert his solidarity with people he has never met:[50] like him, they are Jews, and like him, they have suffered imprisonment for the sake of Christ.[51] Paul may or may not have known 'Apelles, who is approved in Christ' (v. 10). There is nothing in vv. 10f to show that Paul knew personally the family of Aristobulus, or Herodion, or the family of Narcissus, and this is true also of the ten individuals who are listed in vv. 14f, about whom nothing is said other than the instruction that they are to be greeted. This leaves only nine people who are certain to have been known personally by Paul: Prisca, Aquila, Epaenetus, Ampliatus, Urbanus, Stachys, Persis, and Rufus and his mother.[52] Some of the others were no doubt also known to him; but when one bears in mind the possibility that some may have come from Rome in the first place, as Prisca and Aquila had done, the evidence of Rom. 16 is hardly sufficient to suggest that it must have been sent to Ephesus. In answer to the obvious question of why Paul should have bothered to greet people who were known to him by name and reputation only, one may point out that Romans as a whole is addressed to such people. Having written at great length to people most of whom he has never met, it is not at all surprising that he should send individual greetings to some of the more eminent of them.

In discussing Rom. 14:1–15:13, it was suggested that this section gives evidence of two separate groups within the Roman church:

Gentile Christians, who like Paul himself had abandoned many of the ceremonial prescriptions of the law of Moses, and Jewish Christians for whom the whole law was still in force. Paul exhorts them to worship God *together* (15:7ff), and this suggests that at the time of writing the two groups did not share common worship. Rom. 16 sheds further light on these two groups. We may assume that most or all of the people named there whom Paul knew personally were associated with the Gentile group. This is certainly the case with Prisca and Aquila, who are mentioned in connection with 'the churches of the Gentiles' (v. 4). Since they had once been members of the original Roman congregation (for Acts 18 never suggests that they were converted by Paul) their association with 'the churches of the Gentiles' who did not observe the law must have been due to Paul's influence.[53] If our interpretation of Rom. 14:1 – 15:13 is correct, they would have been regarded with great suspicion by other Jewish Christian members of the original congregation. As regards the others, Epaenetus and probably Ampliatus were Paul's own converts, Urbanus and perhaps Persis had worked alongside him, and Rufus and his mother had shown him hospitality (hence 'his mother and mine') − these people too were perhaps Paul's converts. Such people may be described as 'Paulinists' − i.e. Christians who shared Paul's practice of freedom from the law and separation from the Jewish community. The fact that they were known to Paul personally suggests a solution to the riddle of the origin of Gentile Christianity in Rome: the Gentile group addressed especially in Rom. 14:1 – 15:13 and in 11:13ff may well have been founded by Paul's own converts and associates: *Gentile Christianity at Rome is therefore Pauline Christianity*. In encouraging Jewish Christians to worship together with Gentiles, Paul is encouraging them to recognize the legitimacy of his own work.[54] He wishes to convert the Jewish Christian congregation in Rome to Paulinism.[55] They are to regard observance or non-observance of the law as a matter of purely private piety, and the obstacle to worshipping together with Paul's Gentile Christian friends (and Paul himself, when he comes to Rome) is thus to be removed.

Rom. 16 also seems to confirm the existence of a (separate) Jewish Christian congregation at Rome. In v. 7, Paul writes: 'Greet Andronicus and Junias, my fellow-countrymen and my fellow-prisoners; they are men of note among the apostles, and they were in Christ before me.' Andronicus and Junias (or Junia)[56] are thus linked with earliest Jewish Christianity. As apostles, they will therefore have shared in the Jewish church's mission 'to the circumcision' (cf. Gal. 2:7–9), for Paul knows of no apostle other than himself (and perhaps Barnabas) who is sent to the Gentiles.[57] We may therefore assume that Andronicus and Junias shared the Jerusalem church's deep suspicion of Pauline 'freedom from the law' — a suspicion to which Paul alludes in Rom. 15:31, and which is evident above all from Gal. 2. For Paul, being an apostle implies first that one has seen the risen Lord, and secondly that one has founded a congregation (cf. 1 Cor. 9:1f), and it is therefore probable that these two people were the founders of the Roman congregation.[58] In any case, their status as apostles must have made them the most important and influential members of the Jewish Christian congregation, whose favour Paul had to gain if he was to persuade that congregation to unite with the Paulinists.

Another member of that congregation may have been 'my fellow-countryman Herodion' (v. 11). As with Andronicus and Junias, Paul stresses the link of Jewish birth between himself and the recipient of the greeting, and in this way tries to bridge the gap between himself and Jewish Christianity; cf. Rom. 9:3; 11:1. (In the case of Prisca and Aquila, who were also Jews, according to Acts 18:2, this was not necessary, since they were already Paulinists.) If it is correct to identify Aristobulus in v. 10 with the member of the Jewish royal family who had died in Rome probably between AD 45 and 48,[59] then the members of his family whom Paul greets in v. 10 may also have been prominent members of the Jewish Christian congregation.

Thus, Rom. 16 confirms the hypothesis about the purpose of Romans derived from 14:1–15:13. The purpose of Romans is to encourage Jewish and Gentile Christians in Rome, divided over the question of the law, to set aside their differences and to worship together. The latter group are Paulinists, and it is converts and associates of Paul who have brought his message of freedom from the law and separation from the Jewish community to Rome, and established a congregation there. The former group represents the remnants of the original Roman Jewish Christian congregation, which regards Paulinism with deep suspicion.[60] The chief purpose of Romans is to overcome this suspicion. One of the means by which Paul attempts to do this is to include greetings for members of both congregations in the final part of his letter.

Two other features of Rom. 16 support this interpretation. First, in vv. 3ff Paul does not greet the individuals named directly; rather, he commands his readers to greet them, for the verbs are all in the imperative. Paul is in effect requesting his readers in both groups to introduce themselves to one another.[61] Thus, Gentile Christians are not to 'despise' (cf. 14:3) Andronicus and Junias, the most important members of the Jewish Christian group. They are to regard them as 'men of note among the apostles', and to bring them their greetings. Conversely, Jewish Christians are not to 'pass judgment' (cf. 14:3) on Prisca and Aquila; they are to be greeted as people who have greatly assisted the spread of the gospel. The function of these commands to greet the individuals named is thus similar to the general command to Jewish and Gentile Christians to welcome one another (15:7).

Secondly, the reason for Paul's polemic in 16:17–20 becomes clear. On the whole, Paul has tried to keep his letter to the Romans as tactful as possible, and until 16:17–20 it is free of the violent polemic that characterizes Galatians and Phil. 3.[62] In Rom. 16:17, Paul writes: 'I appeal to you, brethren, to take note of those who create dissensions and difficulties, in opposition to the doctrine which you have been taught; avoid them.'[63] The best explanation for this is that Paul knows that there will be opposition to his attempt to persuade Jewish Christians to accept the legitimacy of the Paulinists and to join with them for worship. Not all of the Jewish Christians will be convinced even by Romans that observance of the law is a matter of personal taste, and Paul here anticipates their objections and denounces them in advance for creating, or rather perpetuating, 'divisions'. As in the case of Gal. 6:13 and Phil. 3:19, the view that Paul's language implies that his opponents were antinomians[64] takes his violent polemic much too literally. When Paul denounces people, he does not do so with scrupulous fairness; the idea that one should be fair to one's opponents was not widespread in antiquity.

5 The evidence of Rom. 1:1–17 and 15:14–33

The hypothesis developed above has suggested that there were two main groups in Rome: Jewish Christians, who comprised the remnants of the original Roman congregation, and Gentile Christians who were Paulinists – converts and associates of Paul. The former observed the law, whereas the latter did not, and for this reason the two groups were separated from each other. Paul is writing chiefly to persuade the Jewish group to recognize the legitimacy of the Gentile group, and thus of his own Gentile mission; this would mean in effect a final break with the Jewish community. The real test for this hypothesis is whether or not it sheds light on the doctrinal core of Romans (1:18–11:36); that will be the subject of the following chapters. But it is important to ask whether the hypothesis is consistent with the two passages in which Paul speaks directly of the Roman Christians and of his aim in writing to them, 1:1–17 and 15:14–33. If it is not, then there is little point in trying to apply it to 1:18–11:36. But in fact, it does appear to be consistent with 1:1–17 and 15:14–33, and indeed suggests possible solutions to one or two of the exegetical problems of those passages. Rom. 1:1–17 and 15:14–33 provide support for the following three aspects of the hypothesis developed above: (i) Romans was addressed primarily to Jewish Christians; (ii) Gentile Christianity in Rome was Pauline in origin; (iii) Paul wrote Romans to persuade the former group to accept the legitimacy of the latter.

(i) 1:5f is a crucial passage for determining whether or not the primary addressees of Romans were Jewish Christians.[65] Apostleship has been entrusted to Paul εἰς ὑπακοὴν πίστεως ἐν πᾶσιν τοῖς ἔθνεσιν ὑπὲρ τοῦ ὀνόματος αὐτοῦ, ἐν οἷς ἐστε καὶ ὑμεῖς κλητοὶ Ἰησοῦ Χριστοῦ. Here, ἐν οἷς must mean 'among whom' either in the sense that the addressees are themselves Gentiles,[66] or in the sense that they live in the midst of Gentiles.[67] If the former is the meaning, the Roman Gentile Christians are being seen as the objects of Paul's missionary activity, just like any other Gentiles. But this seems unlikely, for the addressees are *already* 'called by Jesus Christ' (1:6). The key to the verse is the phrase, καὶ ὑμεῖς: '... among whom *you too* are called by Jesus Christ'.[68] 'You too' probably means 'you as well as me', for Paul has spoken of himself in 1:1 as having been 'called', and in 1:5 he states that his call has taken him among the Gentiles. Paul is saying: 'You too are called by Jesus Christ in the midst of Gentiles, just as I am.' Already a hint is given that the relationship of the Jewish Christian addressees to the Gentiles is to be the main theme of the letter.[69]

(ii) In 1:13–15, Paul expresses his desire to undertake a mission to the Gentiles in Rome. He wishes to come to Rome 'so that I may reap some fruit among you just as among the rest of the Gentiles' (1:13; cf. 1:15). In 1:13 and 1:15, καὶ ἐν ὑμῖν and καὶ ὑμῖν are used somewhat loosely: Paul does not mean that his readers are themselves to be the objects of his missionary activity (cf. 1:8),[70] but is simply addressing them as inhabitants of Rome − hence, 'to you who are in Rome' (1:15). But the real problem of 1:13–15 is that Paul announces his intention of conducting a Gentile mission in a place where there are already Gentile Christians (cf. 14:1–15:13; 11:13), thus apparently contradicting the principle expressed in 15:20, not to build on another man's foundation (cf. also 2 Cor. 10:13ff).[71] The problem is solved if the Roman Gentile Christians are converts and fellow-workers of Paul:[72] his Gentile mission in Rome will therefore not involve building on another man's foundation.

(iii) Romans was not addressed exclusively to Jewish Christians, even though its content suggests that they are the primary addressees.[73] 1:6 does not exclude Gentile Christians, and 1:7 addresses the letter 'to *all* in Rome who are beloved by God, called to be saints'. It may be significant that, contrary to his normal practice at the beginning of his letters, Paul does not address the recipients as an ἐκκλησία.[74] This need not be of any great importance, since the same is true of Phil. 1:1.[75] But Rom. 1:7 is at least consistent with the view that there was no single Roman congregation, but two opposing groups. This is apparently confirmed by 1:16. Paul has just spoken of his own apostleship in 1:13–15: he is apostle to the Gentiles, so he wishes to preach the gospel in Rome. But in 1:16, he unexpectedly states that the gospel is 'for the Jew first, and also for the Greek'. This sudden reference to the Jews is comprehensible if 1:16 is still referring to the Roman situation, like 1:8–15: 'For the Jew first' expresses Paul's acknowledgment of the priority and the pre-eminence of the Roman Jewish Christian congregation,[76] whereas 'and also for the Greek' asserts the legitimacy of the group of Pauline Gentile Christians in Rome. Paul wishes to persuade the Roman Jewish Christians that salvation is not for them alone but 'for *everyone* who believes' – including Gentiles.

If Paul is primarily addressing Jewish Christians, why does he do this so explicitly as apostle to the Gentiles (1:4, 15:15–21)? The situation is perhaps somewhat similar to Gal. 2:2, where Paul tells how he 'set forth the gospel which I preach among the Gentiles' to Jewish Christians, in an attempt to secure recognition of the legitimacy of his work. This is also the case in Romans, whose primary aim is that the Roman Jewish Christians should unite with the Roman Paulinists.

Rom. 1:11ff and 15:23ff also provide hints of a longer-term aim: having won over the Roman Jewish Christians by means of this letter, he would be able to use the Roman church as a base for mission in Rome (1:13ff) and in Spain (15:24, 28). The collection (15:25ff) is to be seen as another attempt to secure recognition from Jerusalem of the legitimacy of his Gentile Christian congregations in Asia Minor and Greece (see the Excursus to Chapter 9). This would then stop the Judaizing interference he had experienced in the Galatian churches and which he feared would take place at Philippi, and free him for a new stage of his universal mission, using Rome as a base. The conversion of the churches of Jerusalem and of Rome to his way of thinking was essential to the accomplishment of these grandiose plans, and Paul sought to secure the former through the collection and the latter through the letter to the Romans.

It is possible to speculate further. Had these plans been devised in consultation with Prisca and Aquila, who knew the Roman church and who had a particularly close relationship with Paul (cf. Rom. 16:3f)? Had they, and others to whom greetings are sent in Rom. 16, volunteered to go to Rome to prepare the way for Paul? But at this point, we can only guess.

Contrary to the picture given in Acts (cf. 20:22−5, 37; 21:4, 10−14), Paul did not go up to Jerusalem with the sombre sense that the end of his apostolic labours was near. In Romans, he manifests an extraordinary self-confidence, a sense that he stands on the threshold of new worlds to conquer.[77] The desire to do so was present some months before at the time of the 'severe letter' to the Corinthians (2 Cor. 10−13),[78] in which Paul complains that unnecessary problems are holding him back from breaking new ground (2 Cor. 10:15f). By the time of Romans, he feels that such obstacles have at last been overcome; now at last he can bring to fruition his plans in connection with the Roman Christians (Rom. 1:9f; 15:22f). The letter itself was an essential part of these plans. Its function was preliminary: to persuade the Roman Jewish Christians to accept the Paulinists, in preparation for Paul's longer-term plans.

Yet this view of the function of Romans must be regarded as a mere hypothesis until it can be shown that it makes sense of the letter as a whole. The following chapters address themselves to this task.

6

THE SOCIAL FUNCTION OF ROMANS: ROM. 2

1 A sociological approach to Rom. 1–11

The two sociological models developed earlier shed light on the situation in Rome, as outlined in the previous chapter.

(i) The Roman Jewish Christian congregation had begun as a reform-movement within the Roman Jewish community, as is implied by Suetonius' statement about the riots among Roman Jews caused by 'Chrestus'. The evidence in Rom. 14 about the Jewish Christians' diet (abstention from all meat and wine) suggests that after the return to Rome which followed the expulsion by Claudius, they were forced to accept a certain degree of separation from the Roman Jewish community as a whole. It is not clear, however, that this separation can properly be regarded as 'sectarian'. One of the key features of sectarianism is that the religious traditions of the wider community are reinterpreted by the sect in the light of the belief that its members are the sole legitimate possessors of these traditions; the wider community is thus deprived of its heritage. In Rom. 9–11, as we shall see, Paul defends himself against the charge that his gospel involves the complete repudiation of the Jewish people, and it seems likely that this hostile view of Paul was held by the Roman Jewish Christians, among others. We may therefore suppose that the Roman Jewish Christian congregation had not yet adopted an attitude of sectarian separation from non-Christian fellow-Jews. By encouraging them to abandon their belief in the vital importance of observing the law of Moses, and to recognize the legitimacy of the Gentile Christians, Paul is trying to persuade them to make a final break with the Jewish community. He wishes to turn a failed reform-movement into a sect. It is thus to follow in his own footsteps, for he himself had earlier abandoned his unsuccessful preaching to the Jews and turned to the Gentiles instead.[1]

(ii) If the argument so far is correct, this provides us with the key for interpreting the great theological argument of Rom. 1–11. Scholars have on the whole assumed that Rom. 1–11 belongs to the realm of pure theory.[2] Here, if anywhere, Paul rises above particular circumstances and presents his profound understanding of the gospel on a general plane.[3] Few of the scholars who are critical of this assumption have themselves succeeded in showing in detail how their perception of the situation in Rome sheds light on the argument of Romans as a whole.[4] But if Paul is indeed trying to persuade the Roman Jewish Christian congregation to turn its back on the Jewish community and to accept the legitimacy of the Paulinists, thereby transforming itself from a failed reform-movement into a sect, then we would expect this to be apparent in Rom. 1–11 as well as in Rom. 14:1–15:13. *Rom. 1–11 should therefore be seen as the theoretical legitimation for the social reorientation called for in Rom. 14:1–15:13.*[5] It is not pure theory; it does not abandon concrete circumstances in order to attain a more universal significance. It has a clear social function, explaining to the Roman Jewish Christians why it is that a social reorientation is necessary.

When writing earlier to the Galatians, Paul had to defend himself against certain Jewish Christian charges. It was claimed that although he had once been an accredited emissary of the Jerusalem church, he had now forfeited that status because of the insubordination towards Peter and James which he showed at Antioch, when he rejected the imposition of the law on Gentile converts (cf. Gal. 1–2). His motive was that he wished to 'please men' (cf. 1:10), by setting aside some of the law's more rigorous demands in order to make it easier to gain Gentile converts. He preached a gospel of 'cheap grace'; he made Christ an agent of sin (cf. 2:17) through his claim that faith in Christ involved setting aside the divine commandments of the law; his message of freedom from the law encouraged licentiousness (cf. 5:13), and taught people, 'Do whatever you want' (cf. 5:17).[6] Such charges were the inevitable Jewish Christian reaction to Paul's understanding of his mission to the Gentiles as involving freedom from the law.

For this reason, Paul is again acutely aware of these charges while developing his legitimation of separation in Rom. 1–11; he anticipates the obvious objections to his outlook which he knows that the Roman Jewish Christians will put forward.[7] He acknowledges that he may be accused of trying to overthrow the law through his understanding of faith (Rom. 3:31). His opponents claim that he teaches, 'Let us do evil that good may come' (3:8), since that is what the belief that 'we are not under law but under grace' (6:14f, cf. 6:1) amounts to. By teaching that obedience to the law is incompatible with faith in

Christ (cf. Gal. 5:2–4), he is, according to his opponents, clearly asserting that 'the law is sin' (Rom. 7:7) – i.e. that the conduct prescribed by the law is sinful. This irresponsible attitude towards the divine commandments also involves the repudiation of Israel's heritage. He teaches that being a Jew and being circumcised is of no avail for salvation (cf. 3:1, 9f); the same is true of descent from Abraham (cf. 4:1). Paul, it is claimed, is obviously not in the least interested in the salvation of the Jewish people (9:1–5; 10:1 and 11:11ff should be read as denials of this charge), for he teaches that God has forsaken his people (cf. 11:1, 11) and installed Gentiles in their place (cf. 11:11ff). For these reasons, the Roman Jewish Christians 'pass judgment' on Paul and on the Paulinists in Rome (cf. 14:3f, 10f, 13).[8] In attempting in Rom. 1–11 to legitimate separation from the synagogue, Paul therefore has to defend himself against such accusations. If he is to persuade the Roman Jewish Christians to turn their backs on the synagogue and to identify themselves with the Paulinists, he must convince them that the obvious Jewish objections to his standpoint are not valid.

According to his opponents, Paul's doctrine of freedom from the law is a recipe for moral chaos. Rom. 1:18–32 may be read as an attempt to reassure the Roman Jewish Christians on this point. There is nothing distinctively Pauline or even distinctively Christian in this passage – in this respect it is unique in the Pauline corpus. Paul adopts precisely the stereotyped view of Gentile life that was held by many Jews; close parallels between this section and Jewish anti-Gentile polemic abound.[9] Paul denounces Gentile idolatry as a perversion of the true knowledge of God (1:18–23), and then attacks Gentile sexual perversion (1:24–7)[10] and moral anarchy in general (1:28–32). The doctrine of freedom from the law has created the impression among Christian and non-Christian Jews that Paul is positively in favour of such typically Gentile abominations, and Paul assures his readers that this is by no means the case. He too regards the conduct of the Gentiles as utterly reprehensible, and his doctrine of freedom from the law does not compromise this standpoint in any way. The Jewish Christians in Rome need not fear that the Paulinists there hold a lax attitude towards such vices as idolatry and sexual perversion. Paul's own attitude towards such things is exactly the same as that of the Roman Jewish Christians.

The function of such anti-Gentile polemic in Jewish sources is to reinforce the barrier which separates the Jewish community from the Gentile world. But in Romans, it serves as the prelude to an argument for separation from the Jewish community (as well as from non-Christian Gentiles), and for identification with Gentile Christians. That is the function of Rom. 2–4, whose argument may be summed up under the three headings of denunciation, antithesis and reinterpretation, which apply to each of the three chapters respectively. There is a certain amount of overlap; antithesis is used in Rom. 4 as well as in Rom. 3, and Rom. 3 also contains some reinterpretation. Nevertheless, these three headings are a convenient way of summarizing Paul's argument in this section of Romans. Throughout the following discussion, the aim will be to stress the social function of Paul's argument in the light of the view of the purpose of Romans developed above.[11] In the course of this discussion, serious weaknesses in the typical Lutheran interpretation of this section will be exposed. Interpretation from the Lutheran standpoint characteristically ignores the social function of these chapters, and so misunderstands them.

Rom. 2 has always been a particular stumbling-block for the Lutheran interpretation of Paul, and the rest of this chapter will be devoted to a detailed discussion of it, which aims to show how an emphasis on its social function solves many of its interpretative problems.

2 Rom. 2: denunciation

Each of the three chapters, Rom. 2, 3 and 4, contains both an argument against continuing membership of the Jewish community, and an argument in favour of the union of Jewish and Gentile Christians. In the light of Rom. 14:1–15:13, the social function of these arguments is clear. The argument in Rom. 2 for separation from the Jewish community will be discussed first, followed by the argument for union with Gentile Christians.

A Denunciation of the Jewish view of the covenant

One preliminary point must be settled. While most scholars have held that Paul is addressing Jews throughout the chapter, a minority has held that he only turns to the Jew in 2:17, and that 2:1–16 is therefore addressed to anyone, whether a Jew or a pagan moralist, who judges the sins of his neighbour.[12] The indefinite expression, ὦ ἄνθρωπε πᾶς ὁ κρίνων in 2:1 might give some support to this idea, but it is nevertheless unlikely. This phrase is probably to be understood in the light of ὦ ἄνθρωπε in 9:20, i.e. in terms of the gulf between the creature and the Creator. In 9:20, this phrase shows up the presumption of the creature in answering back to the Creator, whereas in 2:1 it suggests that sinful man is trying to usurp the function of judgment which belongs to God.[13] Thus, the word ἄνθρωπε does not exclude the possibility that 2:1ff is addressed solely to Jews, and this is likely on other grounds. The main reason for this is that it is wrong to assume that there is a real break in the thought in 2:17, when the Jew is explicitly addressed. In fact, 2:12−24 is a single section,[14] discussing the Jew's claim to superiority over the Gentiles on the basis of possession of the law of Moses. Paul argues (i) that the Gentile also has some knowledge of the law, and (ii) that the Jews, who undoubtedly know the law, fail to obey it. The phrase, σὺ Ἰουδαῖος in 2:17 is introduced to emphasize the contrast with the Gentiles of 2:14f, and not to indicate that Paul is suddenly turning to a new group of people who have not been previously addressed. A similar contrast between Gentiles and disobedient Jews is found in 2:25−9; indeed, this passage builds on the earlier contrast.[15]

Several other points confirm this interpretation.

(i) As the second person singular is used throughout 2:1−6, and is resumed in 2:17ff, it is most likely that the same person is being addressed throughout.

(ii) 2:1−6 argues, 'Do not think that you will escape God's judgment, for you yourself do the same things'; 2:17−24 argues that the Jew does the same things as the Gentiles. Neither argument is complete without the other,[16] and both must therefore be addressed to the same person.

(iii) Paul distinguishes between 'Jews and Greeks' (1:16; 2:9, 10; 3:9), between those who sin ἀνόμως and those who sin ἐν νόμῳ (2.12), and between 'Gentiles' and 'You, a Jew' (2:14, 17), and this suggests that this twofold division of the human race applies throughout 1:18−3.20.[17]

Rom. 2 falls into three main sections: vv. 1−11 deal in general terms with the Jew who falsely relies on his covenant status, and vv. 12−24 and 25−9 deal with the two components of this privileged status which distinguish Israel from the Gentiles: possession of the law and circumcision, respectively.[18] The Jew whom Paul is addressing condemns the behaviour of the Gentiles (v.1), and believes that God will ultimately confirm his opinion by passing judgment on them (v.2). Yet the extraordinary thing is that the judge does exactly the same things himself.[19] He believes that despite this he will be exempted from God's condemnation (v. 3), because as a member of the covenant community he can rely on 'the riches of God's kindness and forbearance and patience' (v. 4).[20] At the judgment, God will bestow eternal life on the Jews (cf. vv. 7, 10, in opposition to this view), whereas Gentiles who do not have the law and circumcision will be condemned (opposed in vv. 8f). At present, Jews must live in the world alongside Gentiles, but on the day when God's righteous judgment is revealed he will destroy his enemies and vindicate Israel. All this springs from the fact that he has chosen Israel out of all of the nations in order to bestow his love uniquely upon her (the view opposed by v. 11). Paul's argument is that God's judgment is impartial, and that he therefore takes account only of people's deeds, not of whether they are Jews or Gentiles, and he is clearly opposing the view (which he attributes to the non-Christian Jewish community) that the mere fact of being a Jew guarantees one salvation, irrespective of one's deeds. It is this false reliance on the grace of God expressed in the covenant which enables the Jew of vv. 1–5 to 'sin boldly'.

What are the marks of this privileged status which distinguishes Israel from the Gentiles? The first is the possession of the law (vv. 12–24).[21] The Jew regards himself as a 'hearer of the law' and as such 'righteous before God' (opposed in v. 13). He has been taught the law since childhood, in the synagogue[22] and in the home, and pities the miserable state of the Gentiles who 'do not have the law' (v. 14). At the same time, their existence causes him to rejoice all the more in that which separates him from them. Conscious of this privileged status, he is proud to call himself a Jew, and regards the law as the charter of that status (v. 17). He rejoices[23] in his unique relationship to God (v. 17), and in God's full and complete revelation through Moses.[24] Through having been instructed in the law, he is privileged to know God's will, that is, to be able to distinguish between good and evil (v. 18). In the law, he has that full embodiment of knowledge and truth for which others search in vain (v. 20b), and for this reason he is conscious of his responsibility to enlighten them (vv. 19–20a). Yet, as in vv. 1–5, his pride in his privileged status is matched by a complete disregard for the prescriptions of the law in his actual conduct.[25] The Jewish teacher of righteousness to the Gentiles is himself guilty of robbery, adultery and sacrilege (vv. 21f).[26] Thus he dishonours God and causes a scandal among Gentiles, to whom his hypocrisy is all too obvious (vv. 23f).

The other characteristic which distinguishes the Jews from the Gentiles is circumcision (vv. 25–9). This is understood in the view

Paul is opposing as the sign of membership of the people of the covenant, originally given to Abraham and handed down to his descendants. Through circumcision, the Jewish child (or Gentile proselyte) receives a share in all the privileges and promises given to Israel alone.[27] Circumcision thus guarantees salvation, even if the other commandments of the law are not kept (cf. vv. 25, 27 — here, of course, Paul is parodying the Jewish position). As Gentiles are to be pitied for being without the law (cf. vv. 12, 14, 19), so they are to be pitied for being uncircumcised (cf. vv. 26f), for salvation is dependent on being a Jew and being circumcised (cf. vv. 28f).

Throughout the chapter, Paul's argument is that the Jewish reliance on the covenant as a guarantee of salvation leads to a failure to observe the law. To put it in the language of the Reformation, the Jews teach a doctrine of *sola gratia*, and this leads them to live by the maxim, *pecca fortiter*. This is the exact opposite of the Reformation view of the relationship between Paul and Judaism.[28] On that view, it is Paul who teaches salvation by grace alone, and Judaism which teaches salvation solely through one's own achievements. But in Rom. 2, it is Judaism which teaches salvation by grace alone, and Paul who (as we shall see) teaches salvation by one's own achievements (i.e. by obedience to the law).[29] F. Kuhr is therefore wrong when he comments on vv. 5–11: 'Paul speaks from a Jewish standpoint, according to which men are justified on the basis of their works' ('Römer 2, 14f', 253). This is a good example of the distorting effect which the Reformation tradition has on the exegesis of Paul, for in fact it is the 'Jewish standpoint' which Paul is attacking for its over-emphasis on God's grace, while the theology of salvation by keeping the law is his own.[30] Admittedly, Rom. 2 is not typical, for elsewhere Paul acknowledges the Jews' pursuit of works of the law (Gal. 2:16; Phil. 3:6; Rom. 3:20; 9:13f; 10:2f). But the fact that in Rom. 2 Paul can accuse the Jews of putting too much emphasis on divine grace suggests that, when he does speak of 'works of the law', he is not referring to the belief that salvation comes solely through one's own efforts; rather, he understands 'works of the law' as the loyal Jew's response to the grace of God manifested in the covenant. This point has already been made in earlier chapters in connection with Galatians and Phil. 3, and Rom. 2 suggests that it must also apply to Romans, unless Paul is being utterly self-contradictory, one moment accusing the Jews of too great an emphasis on divine grace, the next moment accusing them of ignoring grace and relying on their own achievements. Paul does not attack Judaism because of any theoretical incompatibility between his own emphasis on grace and the alleged Jewish emphasis on achievement. He attacks it because Jewish failure to respond to the gospel had led him to proclaim a law-free gospel to the Gentiles, and to form congregations living in sectarian separation from the Jewish community. His attack on Judaism serves to establish and maintain that sectarian separation.

The fact remains that, while Paul everywhere stresses the importance of the divine gift of the covenant to the Jewish theology which he opposes, Rom. 2 is unique in claiming that the Jews emphasize grace to such an extent that they are completely oblivious to the need to obey the law in practice. The reason for this appears to be that Paul is seeking to answer his Jewish Christian critics. They accuse him of teaching, 'Let us do evil that good may come' (3:8; cf. 6:1, 14f; Gal. 2:17), while themselves trying to maintain their membership of the Jewish community as a whole. Paul replies that it is not he who teaches, 'Let us do evil that good may come', but the leaders of the Jewish community, who stress the divine gift of the covenant as the guarantee of salvation to such an extent that obedience to the law becomes superfluous. The first part of Paul's plea for sectarian separation from the Jewish community thus takes the form of denunciation.[31]

Would this argument have been convincing to the Roman Jewish Christians? This is an important point, because if the argument could be shown to be utterly unsuitable to such an audience, it would cast doubt on the present view of the purpose of Romans. It might be suggested that Rom. 2 presents such a travesty of the authentic Jewish view of the covenant that it cannot have been intended as a serious argument for Jewish Christians.[32] But there are two points which may be put forward in answer to this objection.

First, it should be noted that Rom. 2 is an attack not primarily on the Jewish community as a whole but on its teachers – i.e. its leaders.[33] The Jew who is addressed condemns the behaviour of the Gentiles (vv. 1–3), and seeks to instruct them about 'the embodiment of knowledge and truth' which is to be found in the law (vv. 19f). It is characteristic of a reform-movement that it encounters opposition first of all from the traditional religious authorities, and it is they who are initially perceived as the movement's chief enemies, and not the people as a whole. Thus, in the synoptics, Jesus' enemies are not 'the Jews' (as in John, which thus betrays a sectarian standpoint), but the Pharisees, Sadducees and Herodians. We have seen that Roman Christianity began as a reform-movement within the Roman Jewish community, and it is likely that it was the leaders of that community who were the most implacably opposed to the Christian gospel, which would have represented a threat to their authority. Jewish Christian bitterness would therefore have been directed especially against the leaders of the non-Christian Jewish community, and they might therefore have been willing to accept Paul's denunciation of those leaders.

Secondly, there are several features of Paul's argument which seem particularly applicable to the Roman Jewish leaders. Proselytizing activity is emphasized (vv. 19f), and we know from other sources that proselytizing was vigorous in Rome.[34] Josephus tells us in *Ant.* 18.81−4 of a notorious incident in AD 19 in which a Jew who 'played the part of an interpreter of the Mosaic law and its wisdom' (cf. Rom. 2:19f) misappropriated the money of a female proselyte (cf. 'Do you steal?', Rom. 2:21) which was intended for the temple in Jerusalem[35] (cf. 'Are you a temple-robber?', Rom. 2:22).[36] This led to the expulsion of the entire Jewish community from Rome. As regards the further question, 'Do you commit adultery?', this may also relate to proselytizing activity. Jewish teachers of the law were male, whereas many proselytes were female. In the passage referred to above, Josephus tells how the proselyte Fulvia began to meet regularly with the Jewish teacher and his companions, and it is easy to see how the charge of adultery could arise from such meetings as these.[37] Paul does not state in Rom. 2:21ff that all Jewish teachers of the law are immoral.[38] But his questions imply that many of them are, and he adds significantly that it is for this reason that the Gentiles are so hostile to the Jews and their religion: 'As it is written, "The name of God is blasphemed among the Gentiles because of you"' (v. 24). This is again directly relevant to the Roman Jewish Christians. Together with non-Christian Jews, they had endured expulsion from Rome in AD 49 by order of Claudius. As Suetonius informs us, the reason for this was the disruption caused by the arrival of the Christian gospel, and the Christians would therefore have been blamed for the economic and social catastrophe of banishment which, it was claimed, they had brought on the whole community. One of the functions of Rom. 2:17−24 is therefore to suggest an alternative explanation of the Gentile hostility towards the Jewish community which resulted in the expulsion: it was not the fault of the Christians but of Jewish teachers who had brought disrepute upon the whole community by their immoral conduct. The fact that this had clearly been the case in the earlier expulsion under Tiberius would have given some weight to Paul's argument. Such an explanation of Gentile hostility would have been welcomed by the Roman Jewish Chistians, and it is therefore probable that Rom. 2 was written primarily for their benefit.[39]

There are therefore grounds for thinking that the Roman Jewish Christians would have welcomed Paul's denunciation of the leaders of the non-Christian Roman Jewish community in Rom. 2. These leaders had probably been the most implacable opponents of the preaching of the gospel; and the view that it was their moral depravity which led to the Gentile hostility underlying the expulsion from Rome would have seemed greatly preferable to the view that the Jewish Christians were themselves to blame. But Paul's purpose in this denunciation is not simply to express his solidarity with the Roman Jewish Christians in their opposition to the leaders of the non-Christian Jewish community, but to increase the sense of distance between Christian and non-Christian Jews. He hopes that separation from the rest of the Jewish community will facilitate unity with the Gentile Christian community.

B The obedient Gentiles

In Rom. 2 Paul thus attacks the view that salvation is certain for all who are within God's covenant with Israel, and that obedience is therefore unimportant. In place of this false view, he argues for a judgment according to one's works, not according to whether one is a Jew or not. Everyone will be judged by their works, so that those who have done good receive eternal life whereas those who have done evil are condemned (vv. 6–8). This notion of judgment according to works is commonplace in the Jewish literature of the time, especially apocalyptic.[40] But Paul uses this time-honoured idea in a remarkable way: to abolish the essential difference between Jew and Gentile.[41] In Jewish usage, judgment by works distinguishes those within the covenant who have sought to confirm their covenant membership by obedience from those within the covenant who have in effect denied their covenant membership by disobedience.[42] But in Paul's usage, the point is that Gentiles have just as good a chance as Jews of doing good and receiving salvation, and that Jews have just as good a chance as Gentiles of doing evil and being condemned.[43] It first becomes clear in vv. 9f that this is the unique Pauline understanding of judgment by works:[44]

> There will be tribulation and distress for every human being who does evil, *the Jew first and also the Greek*, but glory and honour and peace for everyone who does good, *the Jew first and also the Greek*.

Paul defends this novel interpretation of judgment by works and divine impartiality in vv. 12–15. In vv. 12f, he defends the idea that Jews who possess the law may be condemned: those who sinned under the law will be judged by it, for God does not accept mere hearers of the law but doers of it. In vv. 14f, he defends the idea that Gentiles may obey the law and so be saved; vv. 12f and vv. 14f thus elaborate the points made in vv.9 and 10 respectively – i.e. that Jews may be condemned as well as Greeks, and that Greeks may be saved as well as Jews.[45] Vv. 14f uses Stoic language which had already been taken over by Hellenistic Judaism to affirm that lack of knowledge of the written law does not make obedience completely impossible. It is possible to obey the law by nature, since the law is written on the heart. The actual deeds of some Gentiles bear witness to this, together with conscience and their discussions with one another about the meaning of good and evil (καὶ μεταξὺ ἀλλήλων τῶν λογισμῶν κατηγορούντων ἢ καὶ ἀπολογουμένων, v. 15).[46] Thus, the difference between those who have the written law and those who do not is relativized, and Paul's claim that Greeks as well as Jews may do good and receive salvation is confirmed.

V. 16 is a problem. As the text of vv. 15f stands, it is stated, 'They show that what the law requires is written on their hearts ... on that day when ... God judges the secrets of men through Christ Jesus.'[47] The present tense of v. 15 clashes with the future reference of v. 16. If, as seems probable, v. 15 is related to v. 14, the meaning is that the Gentiles 'show the work of the law written on their hearts' when they 'do by nature what the law requires', i.e. in the present and not at the judgment.[48] The witness of conscience and ethical debates (v. 15b) to the existence of the law in their hearts is likewise best understood as a present witness. There are three witnesses to Gentile knowledge of the law: their deeds, their conscience and their ethical debates (cf. the Jewish law of evidence in Dt. 19:15, which Paul also alludes to in 2 Cor. 13:1f). This threefold witness seems to relate to the present rather than to the day of judgment,[49] and (with all due deference to the correct principle that one should do one's best to interpret the text as it stands), it therefore seems likely that v. 16 is a gloss.[50] It contains the phrase, 'according to my gospel', which is elsewhere found only in deutero-Pauline passages (Rom. 16:25; 2 Tim. 2:6), and if one is prepared to accept that 16:25–7 is a deutero-Pauline addition (as most scholars do),[51] there should be no objection in principle to seeing another such addition in 2:16.[52] Thus, vv.14f has no reference to the day of judgment, but defends the view that Gentiles without the law may do good and be saved (cf. v.10) by reference to their inward knowledge of what the law requires, manifested by their deeds, their conscience and their ethical debates.[53]

Vv.25–9 has the negative function of denying that circumcision is a guarantee of salvation. But it also has a positive function as an answer to a further objection that might be made to the claim of vv.10, 14f, that Gentiles may do good and so be saved, as well as Jews: How can it be said that the Gentiles may obey the law when they do not obey the fundamental commandment to be circumcised? Paul writes in v.26: 'If a man who is uncircumcised keeps the precepts of the law, will not his uncircumcision be reckoned as circumcision?' In vv.28f, he argues that being circumcised and therefore being a Jew is not a matter of an external rite but of an inward disposition of the heart. It is therefore possible for Gentiles as well as Jews to do good and be saved, even without being physically circumcised.

In arguing in Rom. 2 against the notion that being a Jew in itself makes salvation certain, Paul makes use of themes that are drawn from Jewish tradition: the ideas of judgment according to works and of divine impartiality, which involve the condemnation of disobedient Jews alongside Gentiles. There is nothing in this part of the argument which would be controversial to Paul's Jewish Christian readers. But where he is controversial is in his emphatic claim that Gentiles may do good and be saved alongside obedient Jews (vv.10, 14f, 26ff), even though they are not physically circumcised. Commentators are in general so concerned to find Paul in this passage apparently arguing for justification by obeying the law that they fail to do justice to the theme of Gentile obedience in Rom. 2. The interpretation of the purpose of Romans which is being developed here suggests an obvious interpretation of the significance of this theme: the Roman Jewish Christians are being encouraged not only to distance themselves from the Jewish community but also *to recognize the possibility and reality of genuine obedience to the law even among the uncircumcised Gentile Christians.* Paul argues cautiously here, in apparently theoretical and general terms; but in the light of 14:1–15:13, his meaning is unmistakable. But in order to establish this interpretation, a more detailed discussion is required of the problem of salvation by obedience to the law which Rom. 2 poses.

Most commentators have abandoned the attempt to find a single explanation of 2:6–15, 25–9, and interpret these passages in a piecemeal way.[54] Thus, Käsemann argues that v. 6 does not contradict justification by faith because of the 'power-character' of the gift of righteousness: 'If the gift is finally the sign and content of Christ's lordship on earth, we can no longer live by our own will and right but constantly stand in responsibility and accountability' (*Romans*, 58).[55] Thus, justification involves a judgment according to works. And yet Käsemann does not interpret the notoriously difficult v. 13 in this way – indeed, he has virtually nothing to say about it (62). As regards vv. 25ff, he writes: 'There can no more be a Gentile who as such fulfils the Torah than there can be anyone else who of himself does what the law specifically requires. Is Paul losing himself in hypotheses?' (74). His answer is that what had been a mere hypothesis in vv. 26f becomes concrete in vv. 28f, which refers to Gentile Christians (74–7).[56] Käsemann does not explain the function of these references to Christians. Neither does he explain the purpose of the 'hypothesis' that Gentiles may keep the law (vv. 26f), nor how and in what sense the hypothesis becomes reality in vv. 28f. As with other commentators in the Reformation tradition, one senses that Rom. 2 is an enigma and an embarrassment to Käsemann.

Another attempt at a solution is to be found in Cranfield's commentary; he argues that all these passages are about Christians.[57] Thus, 'works' in v. 6 refers to 'each man's conduct as the expression either of faith or of unbelief' (I, 151). But v. 6 is not to be understood in a legalistic way as referring to requital according to deserts, and the people in vv. 7, 10 do not *earn* eternal life (146). The doing of the law in v. 13 is likewise explained as 'that beginning of grateful obedience to be found in those who believe in Christ' (155), and it is this to which vv. 14f refers – a view which, as Cranfield notes, is already to be found in Ambrosiaster and Augustine (155f).[58] This means that γραπτὸν ἐν ταῖς καρδίαις αὐτῶν may be taken as a reminiscence of Jer. 31:31 (158f).[59] In v. 26, ἐὰν οὖν ἡ ἀκροβυστία τὰ δικαιώματα τοῦ νόμου φυλάσσῃ means 'not a perfect fulfilment of the law's demands ... but a grateful and humble faith in God and the life turned in the direction of obedience which is its fruit'; Paul again has the Gentile Christian in mind (173).[60] There is thus no contradiction in Rom. 2 to the doctrine of justification by faith (153).

The problem with Cranfield's exposition is that he has to keep introducing glosses, derived from Reformed piety: for example, Rom. 2:6ff may *appear* to be about the obnoxious notions of 'merit' and 'earning salvation', but the commentator must exclude such notions even though the text itself does not. With the interpretations of both Cranfield and Käsemann, one suspects that the main problem is not so much Rom. 2 as the Reformation doctrine of justification by faith as the presupposition with which the commentator approaches the text.[61] One might indeed say that the hallmark of a correct interpretation of Paul's doctrine of justification by faith must be its ability to give a satisfactory interpretation not only of Rom. 3–4 but also of Rom. 2.

The problem of Rom. 2 can be most clearly seen by comparing v. 13b ('The doers of the law will be justified') with 3:20a ('No human being will be justified in his sight by works of the law'). There is certainly a verbal contradiction here; Paul must be working with two different concepts of law. The main lines of an explanation of this contradiction have already been established in previous chapters. When in 3:20–2, 27f, 4:2–8 Paul contrasts 'faith' with 'works', 'works' does not refer to human moral activity in general but specifically to the Jewish way of life. By claiming that salvation is through faith in Christ rather than through works of the law, Paul is asserting that salvation is to be found in the Christian community rather than in the Jewish community, and that the two communities are essentially separate. Thus, Bultmann is wrong to define faith as 'the radical renunciation of achievement' (*Theology*, I, 316). It is in fact the radical renunciation of membership of the Jewish community – ideally, where faith is strong, to the extent of abandoning the practice of the law; thus, in 14:1 the man who adheres to the law is 'weak in faith', whereas true faith recognizes that 'everything is indeed clean' (14:20, 22f). Faith may therefore be seen as thoroughly active, once one has ceased to define it by a misinterpretation of the term, 'works'.[62] It involves a life of heroic trust in God and in his promises, despite adverse circumstances (4:18ff). The link between faith and the baptismal confession in 10:9 indicates that faith is not a private, internal decision, but the public renunciation of one way of life and the adoption of another.[63] This new way of life involves being 'obedient from the heart to the standard of teaching to which you were committed' (6:17) – i.e. a complete moral reorientation. It is faith in this comprehensive sense which is the condition of salvation.[64] To say that such faith *earns* or *merits* salvation would be misleading, for faith is a response to God's prior grace in Christ.

But it should certainly be stated that human achievement or action as well as divine grace is for Paul an essential condition of salvation, and that final salvation is in part a reward for such achievement or action.

For this reason, belief in judgment by works is an integral part of Paul's theology, and not simply an unfortunate remnant of a Jewish outlook which the apostle has carelessly omitted to harmonize with his essential outlook.[65] He actually believes that even for Christians it is true that 'if you live according to the flesh you will die' (Rom. 8:13), that 'he who sows to his own flesh will from the flesh reap corruption' (Gal. 6:8), and that 'those who do such things [i.e. the works of the flesh] will not inherit the kingdom of God' (Gal. 5:21).[66] He also believes that 'if by the Spirit you put to death the deeds of the body you will live' (Rom. 8:13), that 'he who sows to the Spirit will from the Spirit reap eternal life' (Gal. 6:8), and that Christians must 'work [or accomplish, or achieve] your own salvation with fear and trembling' (Phil. 2:12). Salvation or condemnation will be decided at a judgment according to works – i.e. according to whether people have lived satisfactorily as Christians, or whether they have denied their Christian confession by failing to live by Christian teaching (Rom. 14:10–12, 1 Cor. 4:3–5, 2 Cor. 5:10, Gal. 6:5, etc.).[67] To this extent, salvation is a reward for the appropriate human activity. The term 'reward' is only inapplicable (Rom. 4:4) in the sense that the idea of conversion from a sinful way of life to the Christian way is integral to Paul's gospel. When one recalls that salvation from the moral depravity of one's previous life is only possible because of the grace of God in Christ (cf. Rom. 3:23f; 4:5; 5:6–10), one cannot understand salvation as a 'reward' in the strict sense, κατὰ ὀφείλημα (Rom. 4:4). But the fact that a strenuous response to grace is necessary if salvation is to be attained means that, with the qualification mentioned above, the notion of 'reward' is appropriate (1 Cor. 3:8, 14). To put this point in a thoroughly controversial form: *the idea that salvation occurs solely through God's grace represents a deep misunderstanding of Paul.* The view that salvation by grace alone is the essence of true religion, and that it is taught especially by Paul, is so deeply entrenched, particularly among Protestant scholars, that any different interpretation of Paul may seem inconceivable. But the vast amount of Pauline material which qualifies his stress on divine grace cannot be overlooked, or explained away by exegetical sleight-of-hand.[68]

This means that there is no tension at all between the teaching of

Rom. 2:6–11 that salvation depends on 'patience in well-doing' (v. 7) or 'doing good' (v. 10), and the teaching of Rom. 3–4 that justification is by faith.[69] Where the two passages do differ is in their understanding of the law. In Rom. 2, the law is evaluated thoroughly positively. The obedience of those who will receive eternal life is seen as obedience to the law (v. 13), and the fact that Gentiles can be said to 'do by nature what the law requires' (v. 14) and to 'keep the precepts of the law' even without being circumcised (v. 26) shows that living by the law is here separated from membership of the Jewish community. In general, however, these two things are inseparable for Paul. Those who produce 'works of the law' (3:28) are Jews (cf. 3:29). Because being 'under law' (6:14f) means being a member of the Jewish community, Christian obedience is not defined by reference to the law (6:15ff). However, in other contexts, Paul is able to see Christian living as the fulfilment of the essence of the law (8:4; 13:8–10; Gal. 5:14),[70] and this is also the case in Rom. 2. The main difference between Rom. 2 and Rom. 3 is thus that in Rom. 2 the law transcends the Jewish community, whereas in Rom. 3 and generally the law is inseparable from the Jewish community. This difference is only surprising if one thinks that Rom. 2 and 3 form a single tightly-knit argument, which they do not.[71]

There is therefore no obstacle in the way of the view that the Gentiles of Rom. 2 are Christians. Paul affirms that these Gentiles do good and will receive eternal life, no less than Jewish Christians (vv. 9f, cf. vv. 6–8).[72] He defends the possibility of Gentile obedience to the law on general anthropological grounds in vv. 14f, and argues that uncircumcised Gentile Christians who obey the law are true Jews and truly circumcised, in a spiritual sense (vv. 25ff).[73] There is a twofold message for the Jewish Christian readers of Rom. 2. First, they must recognize the moral depravity into which a false understanding of the covenant has led the leaders of the non-Christian Jewish community, and therefore distance themselves from that community. Secondly, they must acknowledge the genuine obedience to God and his law of the uncircumcised Gentile Christians on whom they have tended to 'pass judgment' (14:3f, 10), and identify themselves with these people in place of the corrupt Jewish community. Again, the charge against Paul and the Paulinists that they teach that one should do evil so that good might come (3:8) is in the background here. Paul claims that this is in fact precisely the error into which the leaders of the Jewish community have fallen, whereas it is he and his Gentile Christian followers who are truly concerned with obedience to God.[74] Paul does not spell out the practical implications of his argument at this point; they will only be made fully explicit in 14:1–15:13. But when one reads Rom. 2 in the light of the later passage, its purpose becomes clear.

Reading Rom. 2 with an eye to its social function has produced a very different interpretation to one in which the Reformation's view of justification by faith is the presupposition. The Jewish leaders are accused not of trying to earn salvation, but, on the contrary, of teaching that for the members of the covenant people salvation is by grace alone, so that one may 'sin boldly'. The Pauline Gentile Christians are presented as people who are truly concerned to obey God, and who will through their obedience gain the reward of eternal life when their works are judged. They are the 'true Jews' (2:28f), in contrast to those who are Jews in name but who because of their disobedience are reckoned by God to be uncircumcised (2:25). We see here once again the sectarian claim to sole legitimate possession of the religious traditions of the community as a whole. Paul is trying to persuade the Roman Jewish Christians to abandon the remaining ties that bind them as a (failed) reform-movement to the Jewish community, and to join with his own followers in sectarian separation.

7

THE SOCIAL FUNCTION OF ROMANS:
ROM. 3–4

In Chapter 5, it was argued that exegesis of Rom. 14:1–15:13 provides the key to the purpose of Paul's letter to the Romans. There were two congregations in Rome: one was Jewish Christian, the other Gentile Christian. The former represented the remnant of the original Roman Christian congregation, whereas the latter was composed mainly of converts and associates of Paul. Paul's purpose in writing Romans was to bring the two together. This would involve persuading the Jewish congregation to separate themselves finally from the non-Christian Jewish community, and to recognize the legitimacy of the Pauline congregation, which based itself on the premises of freedom from the law and separation from the synagogue. In Chapter 6, this hypothesis was applied to Rom. 2, in which Paul denounces the leaders of the Jewish community and so tacitly encourages the Jewish Christians to distance themselves from that community, and commends the obedience of uncircumcised Gentile Christians, with whom the Jewish Christians should now identify themselves. Nowhere in Rom. 2 is this social function made explicit, but the view that it was intended to have such a function has resolved problems of exegesis which have proved intractable for other views.

In the present chapter, the hypothesis about the social function of Romans will be applied to Rom. 3 and 4. Paul's attempt to legitimate separation from the synagogue in these chapters will be considered under the headings of antithesis and reinterpretation respectively. The same two features – arguments for separation from the Jewish community and for association with the Gentiles – are very much in evidence in these chapters.

1 Rom. 3: antithesis

Rom. 3 is based on the antithesis between law and faith. In vv. 1—20, Paul argues that being a Jew and obeying the law (i.e. living within the covenant) is not the presupposition for salvation. It does not create an absolute separation from the Gentile world, for the law when rightly understood places the Jew in exactly the same position of guilt before God as the Gentile. In vv. 21—31, Paul argues that faith in Christ is God's means of salvation, and that one of the chief characteristics of this faith is that Jews and Gentiles are treated in exactly the same way. Jewish Christians are told that the law places the Jewish community in the same position of guilt as the Gentiles, whereas faith unites Jewish and Gentile Christians in the possession of salvation. This argument should not be understood as purely theoretical; the aim is once again to persuade the Jewish Christians to separate themselves from the Jewish community (vv. 1—20) and to identify themselves with the Pauline Gentile Christians (vv. 21—31).

A Jewish privilege and the law (Rom. 3:1—20)

This interpretation involves regarding 3:1—20 as a single, unified argument. Particular attention must be given to vv. 1—8, a section often regarded as an obscure digression from the main argument, yet which makes perfectly good sense when one realizes that the subject throughout is *God's covenant with Israel*.[1] The passage begins with the questions, 'Then what advantage has the Jew? Or what is the value of circumcision?' (3:1), which obviously arise from Rom. 2.[2] Paul replies that the Jew's advantage over the Gentile is 'much in every way', in that to the Jews were entrusted the oracles of God (3:2). But he raises the question of the Jew's advantage again in v. 9, and this time denies any such advantage: the Jew cannot claim exemption from the judgment, for he stands in the same position of guilt before God as the Gentile (3:9—20). V. 9 is clearly linked to the preceding by the question, τί οὖν; τί οὖν (cf. Rom. 3:1, 11:7) or τί οὖν ἐροῦμεν (Rom. 4:1, 6:1, 7:7, 8:31, 9:14, 30) never marks a completely new train of thought, but raises the question of the deductions to be made from the point just established.[3] As v. 9 is concerned with the question of the advantage of the Jew over the Gentile as regards salvation, this suggests that not just vv. 1—3 but the whole of vv. 1—8 is concerned with the same point.

This indicates that the general tendency to regard vv. 5—8 as concerned with mankind as a whole, and not simply with the Jewish people, leads to misunderstanding. On that view, the problem raised in v. 5 and repeated in v. 7 becomes utterly trivial: our unrighteousness causes God's righteousness to shine forth all the more brightly, and is he not therefore unjust to punish us for the sin which serves to exalt him?[4] It is as if the prisoner in the dock, having been found guilty, should argue that as his trial has manifested the judge's justice, the judge ought in gratitude to set him free. Such an argument is not only 'unexpected' in this context (Cranfield, I, 183),[5] and not only 'strange' (Lagrange, 65); it is obviously completely absurd, and it is inconceivable that Paul should have thought it worth mentioning, let alone repeating (v. 7). The 'objector' in Romans always raises genuine problems (cf. 3:1, 3; 6:1, 15; 7:7, 13; 9:14, 19); Paul does not parody his opponents by suggesting that they are mere quibbling sophists.[6] Furthermore, on this view of 3:5, v. 6 is not a genuine answer to the question at all, but an evasion.[7] The questioner asks whether, in the circumstances, God would be unjust in punishing men, and Paul answers: How could God judge the world if he were unjust? In other words, the questioner claims that God cannot punish men (who by their sin have caused his justice to be manifested) because that would make him unjust, and Paul answers that God cannot be unjust because that would make it impossible for him to punish men. The reply simply assumes the very thing that is being questioned. The usual view of this passage is thus open to the insuperable objections that the question of vv. 5, 7 is absurd, and that Paul is quite unable to answer it effectively.

The reason why it is widely held that in vv. 5–8 Paul is discussing God's relationship with the world (and not merely with Israel) is that v. 4 refers to the falseness of 'every man'.[8] But πᾶς ἄνθρωπος plays a very subordinate role in v. 4a, merely serving to emphasize the unchangeable truthfulness of God. The statement, 'Let God be true and every man be false!' pictures a courtroom scene (cf. v. 4b) in which God and man are opposing one another.[9] Even if the whole human race testifies against him, it is they who are false and not God. This is vivid language used to assert God's truthfulness, and not a sign that Paul's discussion is no longer confined to Israel and the covenant. On the contrary, the context shows that the latter must still be the subject in v. 4. V. 3 asks whether Israel's unfaithfulness has led God to abandon his covenant with her, and Paul answers his own question in v. 4 with his characteristic μὴ γένοιτο, followed by an assertion of God's unfailing truthfulness. In this context, God's truthfulness must refer to his maintaining of his covenant with Israel (as it does in 15:8); it is synonymous with 'faithfulness' in v. 3, for only so does v. 4 answer the question raised in v. 3. V. 4b (a quotation from Ps. 50:6, LXX) introduces a new synonym into the discussion: when God's conduct towards Israel is examined, it will be found to be *righteous*. God's faithfulness, truthfulness and righteousness all refer to his keeping his covenant with Israel.[10] 3:1—4 thus makes the simple point that no faithlessness on the part of the Jews can cause God to annul his covenant with them.

The problems discussed in vv. 5—8 arise from the fact that Paul and his opponent have different views about the nature of this saving covenant-faithfulness. Paul is able to affirm this faithfulness because he sees it fulfilled in the revelation of God in Jesus Christ (3:21ff). The promise fulfilled in Christ is intended not for the salvation of the Jews alone, but for Jew and Gentile alike (cf. 3:29f; 4:16f). However, in 3:1—8 he does not yet explain his own reasons for affirming God's covenant-faithfulness, and is concerned only to refute his opponent's view that this must involve the salvation of Israel and the condemnation of the Gentiles.

In v. 5, a question is posed: 'But if our wickedness shows forth the righteousness of God, what shall we say? That God is unjust to inflict wrath on us?' The question may be paraphrased as follows: 'You have just affirmed that Israel's guilt in no way annuls God's covenant-promise of salvation. Would you not agree that God would therefore be unfaithful to his covenant if he inflicted punishment on the Jews?'[11] For the questioner,[12] God's 'righteousness' — his faithfulness to his covenant and his promise of salvation — can only mean that salvation is guaranteed for Israel, and this is obviously inconsistent with the view that the Jews will be judged with the same degree of strictness as the Gentiles (cf. Rom. 2).[13] This is not really a problem for Paul, who believes that the promise of salvation was intended for Jew and Gentile alike, and that one participates in it through faith in Christ (3:21ff). However, instead of explaining this at this stage, he points in v. 6 to a weakness in his opponent's position: 'How then could God judge *the world*?' In other words: How can God give preferential treatment to the Jew in the judgment, and yet remain the just and impartial judge of all mankind?[14] V. 6 thus repeats the argument against the Jewish theology of the covenant established in 2:6—11.[15]

V. 7 confirms the correctness of this interpretation of vv. 5f: 'If, despite my falsehood with regard to the covenant, God still remains true to his covenant promise of salvation, how is it that *I too* (κἀγώ) am condemned as a sinner?' It is important to note the significance of κἀγώ here:[16] the Jew regards himself as through the covenant quite distinct from 'Gentile sinners', but realizes that on Paul's view *he too* is a sinner. Thus the problem of v. 7 is that on the one hand Paul claims that God remains true to his covenant-promise of salvation, despite Israel's guilt, whereas on the other hand he claims that disobedient Jews will be condemned as guilty sinners alongside Gentiles. The objector argues in vv. 5, 7 that Paul cannot have it both ways: he may argue *either* that Israel's sin does not affect the fulfilment of God's covenant-promise, *or* that Israel's sin means that Jews will be condemned alongside Gentiles, but not *both*.[17] Once again, the questioner is handicapped by the fact that Paul has not yet explained his unique interpretation of the idea of God's faithfulness to the covenant-promise of salvation. He is concerned at this stage only to exclude the false interpretation of this, according to which it must involve salvation for the Jews and condemnation for the Gentiles, and thus an absolute advantage of the Jew over the Gentile.

In v. 6, Paul responded to the objector with a counter-question, and it seems likely that in v. 8 he is doing the same thing; v. 8 is thus not a further objection to Paul's own teaching, which Paul merely dismisses with the words, 'Their condemnation is just.'[18] V. 8 may be paraphrased: 'My opponent claims that if Israel's guilt does not affect the fulfilment of God's covenant-promise of salvation, then Israel must be saved and not condemned alongside the Gentiles. But is not this in effect to say, "Let us do evil that good may come"? Thus my opponents are guilty of precisely the blasphemy which they wrongly attribute to me.' Here, part of the motivation for the argument of 2:1 – 3:8 is revealed. Paul turns the tables on opponents who accuse him of teaching, 'Let us do evil that good may come',[19] by asserting that this is precisely the position of his opponents themselves, as adherents of the Jewish theology of the covenant which asserts that God will save Jews simply because they are Jews. Paul concludes, 'Their condemnation is just' (v. 8), and this is not a vindictive pronouncement about those who criticize his teaching, but derives from the whole argument so far: those who presume upon the grace of God because they are within the covenant, and yet do not fulfil the law, are justly condemned, and are in the same position of guilt before God as the Gentiles (3:9, 19).

Throughout 3:1 – 8, Paul is therefore discussing 'the advantage of the Jew' (v. 1). He accepts that God's covenant-promise of salvation, given to Israel, remains valid, despite Israel's guilt (vv. 1 – 4). But he opposes the view that this fact guarantees salvation for the Jewish people, on the grounds that God could not be the just judge of the whole world if he gave Israel preferential treatment (vv. 5f), and that this view makes obedience to the law superfluous (vv. 7f). 3:5—8 thus recapitulates the argument about the impartiality of God in 2:1—11. Although he states with remarkable emphasis that 'the advantage of the Jew' (3:1) is 'much in every way' (3:2a), he actually concedes very little to his opponent, for his opponent wishes to claim an advantage *as regards salvation*, and it is this that Paul will not admit. God must judge all people alike, and so the Jew can have no advantage over the Gentile as regards salvation.

This is precisely what is said in v. 9. On the other view of 3:1—8, according to which vv. 4—8 refers not to the Jews alone but to the whole of humanity, the return of the question of the Jewish advantage in v. 9a disrupts the flow of the argument (if, on this view, the argument of vv. 4—8 can be said to have a flow). But on the view outlined above, v. 9 fits perfectly. If the Jew sins, he is liable to judgment just like the Gentile (vv. 5—8), and so the question is again raised (cf. v. 1), 'Are we Jews *really* any better off, as regards salvation?'[20] When Paul answers with a negative, this is again in agreement with vv. 5—8. He proceeds to assert that 'both Jews and Gentiles are under the power of sin' (v. 9b), and in its context as an answer to the question of v. 9a, the emphasis must be on the former group: Jews will have no advantage over Gentiles in the judgment, for all alike are in the same position of guilt and accountability to God. Indeed, the aim of 3:9—20 is not simply to show that sin is universal, but to show that Scripture puts Jews on the same level as Gentiles, and thus to deny again the claim that salvation is to be found through membership of the Jewish community.[21]

This explains the train of thought in vv. 19f:

> We know that whatever the law says, it says to those who are under the law, so that every mouth may be stopped, and the whole world may be held accountable to God. For no human being will be justified in his sight by works of the law, since through the law comes knowledge of sin.

Why is it that the proof from Scripture[22] that Israel is held by God to be unrighteous means that the whole world is guilty? It can hardly be said that τοῖς ἐν τῷ νόμῳ refers not just to Jews but to the whole human race, who are therefore seeking salvation by works of the law (v. 20).[23] Throughout Rom. 2—3, possession of the written law is

Israel's prerogative (cf. 2:12, 17–20; 3:2). The phrase ἐν τῷ νόμῳ in 3:19 is paralleled by ἐν νόμῳ in 2:12, where the reference is obviously to Jews. The meaning of 3:19 is rather that the law places Israel in exactly the same position as the Gentiles before God.[24] The Jew thinks that the law differentiates him from 'Gentile sinners' (Gal. 2:15) who are without the law (Rom. 2:12, 14). Paul shares the assumption that the Gentile is a sinner, but argues that the law reveals this to be true also of the Jew. Thus, the fact that the law condemns the Jew too shows that 'the whole world' is 'accountable to God'. The law itself finally 'stops the mouth' (cf. v. 19) of the Jew who has insisted in 3:1–8 on the absolute advantage of the Jew over the Gentile. Salvation through the law is excluded, because the real significance of the law is not that it demarcates the righteous Jew from the unrighteous Gentile, but that it places the Jew in the same position of guilt before God as the Gentile. This must also be the meaning of 3:20b, 'For through the law comes knowledge of sin.' If this statement simply means, 'The law makes sin conscious',[25] it is banal and commonplace; its meaning must be that the law reveals that the Jew, like the Gentile, stands as a sinner before God, liable to his judgment (cf. vv. 9–19, of which v. 20b is a summary).[26] The Jew is placed on the level of the Gentile by the very law which he believes differentiates him from the Gentile. The message for the Roman Jewish Christians is therefore that membership of the synagogue and adherence to its way of life is of no avail for salvation.

In 3:20, Paul writes: 'By works of the law shall no flesh be justified before him.' Despite Rom. 2, he is not really concerned to argue that the Jews in general show no interest in obeying their law, and the point of 3:20a is therefore that the law is powerless to save not only the Jew of 2:21f who steals, commits adultery and robs temples, but also the Jew who seeks to confirm his membership of the covenant people by obeying the law (cf. Phil. 3:4–6). But what one must not do is to remove 3:20a from its context and regard it as a reference to the supposed Jewish belief that one gains salvation purely by one's own efforts. The idea of God's covenant with Israel as the pledge of his grace dominates 3:1–20 just as it dominates Rom. 2. It is apparent in the question about the advantage of the Jew and the value of circumcision in 3:1. The objector wishes to claim not that the Jews are able to earn salvation by fulfilling the law, but that God's faithfulness, truthfulness and righteousness with regard to the covenant mean that the final salvation of the Jewish people is guaranteed. Unlike the Jew of ch. 2, the objector of ch. 3 thinks that 'works of the law' are also important (v. 20a), but only as the Jews' response to their elect status (vv. 1–8), and not as a means of earning salvation solely by one's own efforts.

Käsemann interprets Rom. 3:20a as follows:

> The actual law as it has been handed down does not bring about genuine obedience for the apostle since the religious seize it and make it not only the ground of their attainment but also of their boasting. However, that is simply sacrilege. Because Paul sees this sacrilege constantly in progress in the works of the law, he can only sharply reject it.   (89)

This passage perfectly exemplifies the Lutheran tendency to ignore Paul's view of 'works of the law' as the Jew's response to the grace of God manifested in the covenant (cf. 3:1–8), and to regard the Jews as representatives of a more general phenomenon, 'religion', which involves human achievement and boasting before God.[27] But this completely misunderstands Paul's meaning. He does not reject 'works of the law' because they represent the principle of achievement which is incompatible with the principle of submission to the free grace of God. He understands 'works of the law' solely as the way of life of the Jewish people, those who are within God's covenant with Israel, and rejects this because of his view that the church should be entirely separated from the synagogue and its way of life. The view that 'works' represents 'achievement' in general fails to recognize the social context and function of Paul's teaching. It is unable to reach a genuinely historical interpretation of Paul because it remains trapped in the theological categories of the Reformation.

In Rom. 3:1–20, Paul is therefore telling his Jewish Christian readers that membership of the Jewish community and adherence to its way of life is not a *sine qua non* of salvation. God is indeed faithful to his promise of salvation (vv. 1–4 – this will be developed in vv. 21ff), but not in such a way that the salvation of the Jewish community is guaranteed, for that view is incompatible with the impartiality of God (vv. 5f) and encourages moral indifference (vv. 7f). In fact, far from separating the Jews from the ungodly Gentiles, the law places the Jews in exactly the same position of guilt before God as Gentiles (vv. 9ff), which makes the way of life based on the law vain (v. 20).[28] This is not a purely theoretical argument, but involves an implicit call for social reorientation. The law itself paradoxically becomes an argument for separation from the Jewish community. By means of this negative argument for separation, Paul prepares the way for his positive argument for the union of Jewish Christians with Gentile Christians, which begins in 3:21.

B Jews, Gentiles and the righteousness of God (Rom. 3:21–31)

In 3:1–8 Paul shares with the Jewish objector the idea of 'the righteousness of God' − i.e. God's faithfulness to his covenant-promise to bring salvation. For the Jew, this means that salvation is guaranteed for the Jewish community, the adherents of the law. Paul contests this view of the righteousness of God in 3:5–20, and explains how he himself understands it in 3:21ff.[29] Perhaps the best starting-point for the interpretation of this passage is v. 25, where it is widely recognized that Paul is using Jewish Christian tradition.[30] The sacrificial death of Jesus is understood here as 'a sign of his [i.e. God's] righteousness'. Using 3:1–8 as the key to the meaning of 'the righteousness of God' in this context, the Jewish Christian tradition underlying v. 25 is therefore stating that through the death of Christ God fulfilled his covenant-promise of salvation for the Jewish people.[31] The death of Christ is seen as a sign of God's faithfulness to his covenant.[32] It has as its goal 'the passing over of former sins' − that is, the forgiveness of sins committed in one's pre-Christian life, not of those who died before the coming of the Messiah.[33] Thus, in the Jewish Christian understanding of the death of Christ preserved in v. 25, membership of the Jewish people is essential; the original covenant-promise of salvation was given to them alone, and its fulfilment is also for their benefit alone. This expresses the standpoint of the reform-movement, for whom membership of the wider religious community is still vitally important, and not of the sect, which is characterized by separation from the community as a whole.

But in vv. 21–6, Paul sets this traditional view in a new context which radically alters its meaning. The righteousness of God − his faithfulness in Christ to the covenant-promise of salvation − now requires not membership of the Jewish community but faith in order for one to benefit from it. Faith is interpreted here not as passive submission to the grace of God, as the renunciation of all achievement, but as the attitude which is common to both Jewish and Gentile Christians. In vv. 21–22a, Paul announces that the righteousness of God is 'apart from the law' and 'through faith in Jesus Christ'. In the light of the previous discussion of 3:1–20, it should be clear that 'apart from the law' must mean 'without the necessity for membership of the Jewish community and adherence to its way of life'.[34] In contrast to this, faith is defined in vv. 22b–4 as the bond of unity between Jewish and Gentile Christians.[35] According to v. 22b, 'There is no distinction' (διαστολή), and this must be understood in the light of 10:12: 'There is no distinction *between Jew and Greek*' (διαστολή again). Jew and Greek are in the same position because they have sinned in the same way (3:23) and because they are justified in the same way, by God's grace (3:24).[36] Jewish Christians are therefore wrong if they hold that one has to be a member of the Jewish community in order to enjoy the benefits of the sacrificial death of Christ, which is the manifestation of God's 'righteousness', his faithfulness to his covenant with Israel. Faith is the condition for benefiting from God's righteousness, and faith sets aside the barrier between Jew and Gentile.[37] Jewish Christians should therefore identify themselves not with the Jewish community as a whole, but with their Gentile fellow-Christians. Faith requires the Roman Jewish Christian congregation to abandon its remaining ties with the wider Jewish community and to join with the Gentile Christian congregation which does not observe the law. The Jewish Christians are thus to praise God *among the Gentiles* (cf. 15:9).[38]

According to v. 27, boasting is excluded not διὰ νόμου τῶν ἔργων, but διὰ νόμου πίστεως. In this context, νόμος must mean 'principle'.[39] V. 28 has the function of explaining how it is that boasting is excluded through the νόμος πίστεως (NB γάρ); and as v. 28 simply refers to πίστις (and not, for example, to the law's testimony to faith), it seems best to regard v. 28 as a succinct statement of the νόμος πίστεως, the 'principle of faith':[40] 'For we hold that a man is justified by faith apart from works of the law.' This view of νόμος here accords with the indefiniteness of the question, διὰ ποίου νόμου; ('Through what kind of law?'), which is not at all the same as, 'Through what interpretation of the law?'[41] Paul's argument in vv. 27f is therefore that boasting is excluded, not by 'works' but by 'faith'.[42]

With this point dealt with, we may turn to more important issues. Rom. 3:27f may be regarded as the *locus classicus* of the modern Lutheran interpretation of Paul. Käsemann may again serve as the spokesman for this standpoint. Commenting on v. 27, he writes:

> Faith and self-boasting are incompatible, for the believer no longer lives out of or for himself. The eschatological end of the world proclaims itself anthropologically as the end of

one's own ways of salvation, whereas the law in fact throws
a person back upon himself and therefore into the existing
world of anxiety about oneself, self-confidence, and unceasing self-assurance. (102)

Käsemann does not explain how 'self-confidence and unceasing self-
assurance' are compatible with 'anxiety about oneself'; his meaning
is perhaps that the apparent self-confidence of the religious on the
basis of their achievements masks a deep and hidden anxiety. But the
main point is that the antithesis between works and faith in Rom. 3:27f
is interpreted here as a conflict between the religious person's pursuit
of achievement, of which one may boast, and the true believer's
renunciation of achievement. Once again, the fact is ignored that
'works' refers to the way of life of the Jewish community, and to that
alone.[43]

'Boasting' in v. 27 is in fact the attitude of the Jew who relies on
a uniquely privileged position,[44] an attitude which has already been
attacked in vv. 1–20. It is characterized by the claim that being a Jew
and being circumcised guarantee one salvation (v. 1), that God's
faithfulness to his covenant-promise means that the Jewish community
as a whole will be saved (cf. vv. 5–8), and that an indispensable
hallmark of that community is its acceptance of the way of life set
forth in the law of Moses (cf. v. 20, 'works of the law'). It is also
characterized by a strong sense of the distinction between Jews and
the ungodly Gentiles (cf. v. 9). This standpoint clearly involves the
claim that divine grace (election and the promise of salvation) and
the human response of obedience to the law are both necessary for
salvation. Thus, as v. 27 puts it, the 'principle of works' does not
exclude boasting; 'works' are a constituent element in 'boasting'. But
'the principle of faith' does not exclude boasting in the sense that
boasting emphasizes obedience too strongly. Paul is not saying in
vv. 27f that we are justified by faith because faith is the renunciation
of all achievement. Faith has already been defined in vv. 21–4 as the
principle which abolishes the distinction between Jews and Gentiles:
Jews and Gentiles are the same in their guilt before God (v. 23) and
as the recipients of his grace in Christ (v. 24). Justification is therefore
'by faith apart from works of the law' (v. 28) because 'faith' unites
Jew and Gentile whereas 'works of the law' separates them. If Paul's
Jewish Christian readers accept the νόμος πίστεως, they will abandon
their 'boasting' (their belief in the uniquely privileged status of the
Jew), separate themselves from the Jewish community as a whole,

in which belief in this special status is maintained, and unite themselves with the Pauline Gentile Christians on the grounds of their common faith (cf. 15:7ff). *Faith is incompatible with works because participation in the life of a Pauline Gentile Christian congregation is incompatible with continuing membership of the Jewish community.* The Gentile Christian congregation does not observe the law, and to accept its legitimacy is to abandon the cardinal belief of the Jewish community, the absolute divine authority of the law of Moses, even if one continues to observe it oneself. The antithesis between faith and works is thus not a clash between two great opposing theological principles. It must instead be interpreted sociologically: it expresses the sectarian separation of Pauline congregations from the Jewish community, and in the context of Rom. 3 it constitutes an appeal to the Roman Jewish Christians to throw in their lot with the former and to turn their backs on the latter.

This interpretation is strikingly confirmed by vv. 29f: 'Or is God the God of Jews only? Is he not the God of Gentiles also? Yes, of Gentiles also, since God is one; and he will justify the circumcised on the ground of their faith and the uncircumcised through their faith.' This passage makes clear the sociological basis of the assertion of v. 28 that 'a man is justified by faith apart from works of the law'. 'Works of the law' is linked with the belief that God is the God of the Jews only, i.e. that membership of the Jewish community is a *sine qua non* for salvation. 'Faith' means that the distinction between Jews and Gentiles is abolished;[45] Jews who believe should therefore separate themselves from the community which believes that God is the God of the Jews only, and identify themselves with Gentile fellow-believers.

Paul has set aside the law in so far as it functions as the central element of the Jewish community's identity, its consciousness of being set apart from the Gentiles. In v. 31a, he is thus anticipating the anxious or angry question of his Jewish Christian readers: Does he do away with the law altogether? He replies in v. 31b that, on the contrary, he upholds the law. Dodd finds this assertion 'confusing and misleading' (86),[46] but in fact it points to an important factor in sectarian self-definition, the tendency to reinterpret the religious traditions of the wider community in a sense favourable to the sect, rather than rejecting those traditions altogether.[47] Paul has argued in 3:9–20 that the law when correctly understood places the Jews in the same position of guilt before God as the Gentiles, and this is the presupposition for his proclamation of the unity of Jews and Gentiles in vv. 21ff; this is probably the sense in which, according to 3:31, faith upholds the law.[48]

This interpretation of 3:27−31 has stressed the coherence of the passage, a coherence which according to many commentators is lacking.[49] Thus, Cranfield writes: 'This short section is specially difficult. While its general sense and its function in the overall structure of the main division ... are clear enough, it is extraordinarily difficult to define the internal articulation of its argument precisely' (I, 218). But there is only a problem in this respect if one fails to note that the contrast between boasting and works on the one hand and faith on the other (vv. 27f) is identical with the contrast between the Jewish view of the uniquely privileged position of Israel and the Pauline view of the unity of Jewish and Gentile Christians (vv. 29f).[50] Failure to understand the link between vv. 27f and vv. 29f is the fault of the continuing influence of the Reformation's interpretation of the faith−works antithesis. If one holds that vv. 27f contrasts the principle of achievement intended to establish a claim on God with the principle of receiving God's grace as a gift and renouncing achievement, then the link with vv. 29f will seem problematic. But if one interprets the passage sociologically rather than theologically, the problem disappears. 'Faith' is the principle which unites Jewish and Gentile Christians in sectarian separation from the Jewish community, whereas 'works' is the hallmark of membership of the Jewish community. This interpretation is also in agreement with the reinterpretation in vv. 21−4, 26 of the traditional view of the atonement in v. 25.

2 Rom. 4: reinterpretation

Rom. 4 is often understood as a proof from Scripture of the doctrine of justification by faith outlined in 3:21−31.[51] Thus, according to Dodd, Rom. 4 is 'a long digression or excursus, in which Paul illustrates and confirms his doctrine of justification "apart from the law" by a reference to Abraham' (87).[52] Conzelmann thinks that Abraham is chosen to illustrate justification by faith as a random example (*Outline*, 169, 190). According to Käsemann, 'Paul's thesis is now shown to be vindicated by the OT' (105). Cranfield writes: 'The function of this section is to confirm the truth of what was said in the first part of 3:27. (At the same time it also adds an independent contribution of its own, particularly in vv. 17b−22, to the exposition of "by faith".)' (I, 224). This approach does not do justice to the fundamental importance of the figure of Abraham for the Judaism which Paul is opposing, nor does it recognize the profound social implications of Paul's reinterpretation of Abraham in Rom. 4, where he denies the legitimacy of the Jewish community's view of Abraham as justifying its own way of life and beliefs, and asserts that Abraham in fact justifies the way of life and beliefs of 'Pauline' Jewish and Gentile congregations.[53] The assertion that the sectarian group is the sole legitimate possessor of the religious traditions of the wider community is an essential part of the theoretical rationale for separation which any sectarian group requires.

A The Jewish view of Abraham

Abraham has a twofold significance in the Judaism which Paul opposes. First, he is seen as a model of obedience to God; secondly, he is seen as the original recipient of the promise of salvation for himself and his descendants. He is thus an essential element in Jewish self-definition, legitimating the Jews' distinctive way of life and their hope of ultimate vindication. This twofold understanding of Abraham is remarkably constant throughout the post-exilic and inter-testamental literature, and only a few representative examples of it will be given.

1. Abraham is seen as a model of obedience to God above all because he kept the law. According to Sir. 44:20, 'He kept the law of the Most High.'[54] 2 Bar. 57:2 says of the time of Abraham, 'At that time the unwritten law was named among them, and the works of the commandments were then fulfilled.'[55] This is worked out in great detail in the book of Jubilees.[56] Abraham's emigration to Canaan is seen as the final stage of his long conflict with the idolatry and superstition of the Chaldeans (Jub. 11–12). Negatively, obedience to the law means separation from the ways of the Gentiles, and so Abraham warns Isaac:

> I see, my son, that all the works of the children of men are sin and wickedness, and all their deeds are uncleanness and an abomination and a pollution, and there is no righteousness with them. Beware lest thou shouldest walk in their ways.
> (21:21f)[57]

Positively, obedience to the law is seen above all in Abraham's observance of the feasts of weeks or first-fruits (6:19; 14:20; 15:1f; 22:1ff), and of booths (16:20–31).[58]

Perhaps as the result of experiences in the time of Antiochus Epiphanes, Jewish writers of the period emphasize that Abraham's obedience to the law and to God involved serious difficulties; it was thus seen as faithfulness and loyalty to God in testing times. In 1 Macc. 2:52, Mattathias asks his sons: 'Was not Abraham found faithful when tested, and it was reckoned to him as righteousness?' Here, Gen. 15:6 is interpreted as a reference to Abraham's whole life.[59] In Jud. 8:25–7, Judith exhorts her fellow-citizens to realize that God is 'putting us to the test, as he did our forefathers'. They should 'remember what he did with Abraham' and the other patriarchs, how he tried them with fire in order to search their hearts. In 4 Macc. 16:19f, the mother of the seven martyrs reminds her sons that for God's sake 'our father Abraham made haste to sacrifice his son Isaac, the ancestor of our nation; and Isaac, seeing his father's hand lifting the knife against him, did not shrink'. Jub. 17:17f sees Abraham's faithfulness in times of trial as the theme which binds together his whole life; it was manifested in his leaving his home, through famine, through 'the wealth of kings', through the abduction of his wife, through circumcision, and through Ishmael and Hagar. The greatest trial of all was the command to sacrifice Isaac, and here again Abraham was found faithful.[60]

Abraham is thus seen in inter-testamental Judaism as a model of obedience to God. His function is to reflect and legitimate the self-understanding of the pious and loyal Jew of the present. He too, like Abraham, must separate himself from the ways of the Gentiles and devote himself wholly to the law of God, whatever the suffering this entails. The figure of Abraham symbolizes this sense of a unique status, privilege and responsibility.

2. But Abraham is also seen as the original recipient of the promise of salvation for himself and his descendants; he is thus a source of hope. According to Sir. 44:21, because Abraham was faithful, 'The Lord assured him by an oath that the nations would be blessed through his posterity, that he would multiply him like the dust of the earth, and exalt his posterity like the stars, and cause them to inherit from sea to sea and from the River to the ends of the earth.'[61] It is perhaps these scriptural promises which enable the author to pray: 'Crush the heads of the rulers of the enemy, who say, "There is no-one but ourselves". Gather all the tribes of Jacob, and give them their inheritance as at the beginning' (36:10f). Test. Ash. 7:7 is similar: 'But the Lord will gather you together in faith through his tender mercy,

and for the sake of Abraham, Isaac, and Jacob.' This understanding of the promises to the patriarchs as the ground for the hope of salvation is also expressed in Pr. Az. 11–14:[62]

> For thy name's sake do not give us up utterly
> and do not break thy covenant,
> and do not withdraw thy mercy from us,
> for the sake of Abraham thy beloved
> and for the sake of Isaac thy servant and Israel thy holy one,
> to whom thou didst promise
> to make their descendants as many as the stars of heaven
> and as the sand on the shore of the sea.
> For we, Lord, have become fewer than any nation,
> and are brought low this day in all the world because of our
>   sins.

The Jews of Jerusalem greet their brethren in Egypt with the words, 'May God do good to you, and may he remember his covenant with Abraham, and Isaac and Jacob, his faithful servants' (2 Macc. 1:2). 2 Bar. 57:2 states that in the time of Abraham, 'The hope of the world that was to be renewed was then built up, and the promise of the life that should come hereafter was then implanted.' In all of these examples, it is said in different ways that God will do good to the Jewish people in fulfilment of his promise to Abraham, and that the present sufferings are merely the dark prelude to a glorious future. Thus Abraham inspires hope as well as obedience.[63]

B Paul's reinterpretation of Abraham

It is this twofold view of Abraham as a model of obedience and the recipient of the promise of salvation which Paul attacks in Rom. 4: he opposes the view that Abraham legitimates the way of life of the loyal and faithful Jew who observes the law, and he opposes the view that the promise to Abraham gives grounds for the hope of salvation for those who are his physical descendants.[64] He thus attacks vital elements in the self-understanding of the Jewish community. But he does not simply dispense with the figure of Abraham, but reinterprets this twofold Jewish view of him.[65] Abraham becomes a model of a different kind of obedience, the obedience which consists in faith (cf. 1:5).[66] This is established polemically against the Jewish view in 4:1–12 and 4:18–25.[67] Abraham also becomes the recipient of a different kind of promise, entirely separate from the law and intended for Jewish and Gentile Christians (4:13–17). In both cases, Paul sees Abraham as legitimating a particular community in this twofold way: not the Jewish community, whose appeal to Abraham is rejected, but the church as he envisages it, consisting of Gentile Christians who do not observe the law and the Jewish Christians who identify with them.[68] Once again, the social function of this chapter is vitally important. The Roman Jewish Christians appeal to 'Abraham, our forefather according to the flesh' (v.1), perhaps in response to Paul's setting of Jews and Gentiles on the same level (Rom. 3). But Paul argues that instead of continuing to regard Abraham as a bond joining them to the non-Christian Jewish community, they should regard him as a model legitimating the conduct of Gentile Christians who do not observe the law, and as the ground for their hope of salvation. It is therefore these Gentile Christians with whom they should identify themselves.[69] Understood in this way, Rom. 4 becomes much more than a scriptural proof of some aspect or other of 3:21–31. It is a far-reaching reinterpretation of the figure of Abraham with important social implications, and not a purely theoretical argument opposing salvation by one's own achievements with salvation by grace alone. Following the analysis of the Jewish view of Abraham outlined above, we may consider Paul's reinterpretation of Abraham first as a model of obedience, and secondly as the recipient of the promise of salvation.

1. In 4:1–8, Paul contrasts two different views of Abraham as a model of obedience. The first is the Jewish view, which held that Abraham lived by the law ('works') and that he therefore had grounds for boasting (v.2). On this view, his 'reward' (v.4) – i.e. 'righteousness', v.3 – would be κατὰ ὀφείλημα, commensurate with what he had done. On the other view, Abraham was initially 'ungodly' (v.5),[70] but was reckoned as righteous (vv.3, 5, 6) and had his sins forgiven (vv.7, 8) by means of God's grace and his own faith (vv.3–5).

Once again, Paul is here contrasting two different patterns of religion. The pattern which Paul commends emphasizes the necessity of conversion. Prior to conversion, people are 'ungodly' (v.5). The powerful working of divine grace is needed to deliver them from this plight, and 'righteousness' – the state of being accepted by God, and no longer at enmity with him – is therefore a divine gift. The pattern which Paul opposes emphasizes the continuity of a traditional religious community. Its members do not feel the need for a radical transformation, and the emphasis is instead placed on constant loyalty to the community's norms. But this contrast between two patterns of religion is by no means the same as the Lutheran tradition's under-standing of faith and works, since the difference between the two patterns is relative and not absolute. In 3:1–8, Paul attributes to Judaism not only an emphasis on 'works' (cf. 3:20) but also an emphasis on God's covenant-faithfulness. The beginning and end of salvation-history is therefore the gift of God's grace, even though Israel's obedience must also play a part. Obedience to the law ('works') takes place as Israel's response to grace.[71] Conversely, Paul does not hold that salvation is by grace *alone*, i.e. that it is entirely the work of God with no need for human co-operation. The divine initiative ('grace') requires a response ('faith'), and this response is seen in Rom. 4 as a human activity which is absolutely necessary for salvation.[72] It has been argued earlier that faith in Paul does not mean 'the renunciation of achievement'. Faith is incompatible with works only because for Paul faith is bound up with the legitimacy of Gentile Christians who do not observe the law and are separated from the synagogue, whereas works stands for the way of life of the Jewish community. Once this is recognized, one may see that, on Paul's view, faith is a human activity which is absolutely necessary for salvation.

This view of faith is especially clear in 4:18ff, where Abraham's faith is seen as a steadfast and heroic trust in God to fulfil his promises, despite unfavourable outward circumstances. According to v. 22, it was because Abraham had this kind of faith that righteousness was reckoned to him. 4:18ff is thus incompatible with the view that for Paul salvation is by grace alone. Grace is presupposed here in the form of the promise, but a strenuous human response, encompassing one's whole life, is required. Thus, the contrast between the two patterns of religion in 4:1–8 is relative and not absolute. It is absolute only in the sense that membership of a Pauline congre-gation is incompatible with membership of the Jewish community. That is the antithesis on which Paul insists above all else.

The sociological implications of Paul's discussion of Abraham are particularly clear in 4:9–12. According to U. Luz, 4:1–8 is to be regarded as an exposition of 'by faith', and 4:9–16 as an exposition of 'by faith *alone*' (*Geschichtsverständnis*, 175).[73] But Paul does not regard circumcision as a mere example of a meritorious 'work', as this suggests, but as the rite of entry into the Jewish community.[74] V. 9 asks which is the community in which the blessing of righteousness and forgiveness is to be found. Is it to be found only within the περιτομή, the Jewish community? Or is it also to be found among the ἀκροβυστία, the Pauline Gentile Christian congregations? Paul claims that since Abraham enjoyed righteousness by faith both before and after he was circumcised, he aptly symbolizes the union of Gentile and Jewish Christians (vv. 10–12).[75] In v. 12, it becomes clear that righteousness is not to be found among the περιτομή as such, as v. 9 seemed to imply, but only among those Jews who like Abraham have faith.[76] The message to the Roman Jewish Christians is that they should therefore recognize the legitimacy of the uncircumcised Gentile Christians, and identify themselves with them, rather than with the Jewish community.[77] The old view of Abraham as the ideal Jew is destroyed, and a new view of him as the ideal Pauline Christian takes its place.[78]

2. In the Jewish view, Abraham is also the recipient of the promise of salvation for the community of the law which comprises his descendants. Paul claims in vv. 13–15 that this cannot be the case, and he does so on the basis of the view of the law which he has set forth in 3:9–20. There he argued that the law, when correctly understood, does not separate Israel from the Gentiles, but places Israel in exactly the same position of guilt before God as the Gentiles. Thus, it can be said in 4:14b–15 that the promise of salvation cannot be fulfilled through the law, since the law merely accentuates condemnation.[79] In other words, membership of the Jewish community is neither necessary nor desirable. οἱ ἐκ νόμου (v. 14) are not the true seed of Abraham which is heir to the promise of salvation; the true seed consists of Jewish and Gentile Christians (vv. 16f).[80] The wording of vv. 16f makes it clear that once again Paul is defending the legitimacy of the Gentile congregation to Jewish Christians. He states that it is not only Jewish Christians who are heirs to the promise, but Gentiles too, who do not observe the law but who still share Abraham's faith.[81] He wishes them to regard Abraham no longer merely as 'our forefather according to the flesh' (v. 1), but as 'the father of us all ... before God in whom he believed'[82] – i.e. as the father of Gentiles as well as Jews (vv. 16f); as Scripture says, 'I have appointed you the father of many Gentiles' (v. 17). The Jewish Christians' old solidarity with the Jewish community as a whole must be replaced by a new solidarity with the Gentiles whom at present they 'condemn' (cf. 14:3f, 10, 13).

This discussion of Rom. 4 has emphasized the same point as the earlier discussions of Rom. 2 and 3: Paul is seeking to persuade members of the Roman Jewish Christian congregation to separate themselves from the Jewish community and to recognize and unite with the Pauline Gentile Christian congregation.[83] In other words, he asks them finally to abandon their old conception of themselves as a reform-movement within the Jewish community, and to adopt a new social position of sectarian separation, alongside the Gentile Christians. For this reason, he constructs in Rom. 2–4 a theoretical rationale for separation. In Rom. 2, he denounces the Jewish community (and especially its leaders) for failing to recognize the importance of obeying the law, and suggests that true obedience is to be found among Gentiles. Rom. 3 consists of an antithesis between 'law' (i.e. the Jewish community, its view of its relationship to God and its way of life) and 'faith' (i.e. the separate existence of Pauline congregations, in which Jews are united with Gentiles who do not observe the law). In Rom. 4, he reinterprets the figure of Abraham, denying the view that he legitimates the way of life and the hope of the Jewish community, and using him instead to legitimate his understanding of the church and its hope.

8

THE SOCIAL FUNCTION OF ROMANS: ROM. 5–8

In the previous two chapters, Paul's exposition of 'justification by faith' in Rom. 1–4 has been interpreted as an appeal to the Roman Jewish Christian congregation to unite with the Gentile congregation, thereby separating itself from the Jewish community as a whole. For this reason, these chapters contain a number of references to Jewish and Gentile Christians.[1] According to 1:16, the gospel is 'the power of God for salvation to everyone who believes, to the Jew first and also to the Greek'. 2:10 promises salvation to everyone who does good, 'the Jew first and also the Greek'. 3:22b–24 proclaims that there is no distinction between Jew and Gentile in that both are guilty before God and both are redeemed through his grace. In 3:29f, Paul argues that since God is the God of Gentiles as well as Jews, he justifies Jews and Gentiles in exactly the same way, through faith. 4:9–12 argues that Abraham is the father of both Jewish and Gentile Christians, and it is these two groups who are identified in 4:16f with 'the seed of Abraham' who are heirs to the promised salvation. The emphasis on Jewish Christians as well as on Gentiles is very striking when one compares Romans to Galatians, in which the former play virtually no part (except as opponents). This new emphasis seems, in the light of 14:1–15:13, to be accounted for by the situation in Rome and Paul's purpose in writing Romans.[2]

That situation and that purpose also shed light on the rest of the argument of Rom. 1–11, and the present chapter will discuss this with reference to Rom. 5–8.

1 The social significance of hope (Rom. 5)

There is some disagreement about the theme which binds together Rom. 5:1–11. It is recognized that v. 1 indicates that Paul is about to draw further conclusions from the fact of justification by faith, which he has established in the previous chapter: 'Therefore, since we are justified by faith ...' Since Paul goes on to say, 'We have peace with God through our Lord Jesus Christ',[3] it could be argued that 'peace with God' is the theme of vv.1–11 as a whole, and this would receive some support from the emphasis on reconciliation in vv.10f.[4] But a comparison between vv.9 and 10, which have a very similar structure, suggests that being 'reconciled to God by the death of his Son' (v.10) is not so much a consequence of being 'justified by his blood' (v.9) as another way of expressing the same thing.[5] In any case, despite vv.1, 10 and 11, 'peace' does not seem to be prominent enough in vv.1–11 to be seen as the theme of the whole passage.

It is better to interpret the passage as a meditation on hope; although the word ἐλπίς occurs only in vv.2, 4 and 5, the idea is expressed throughout the passage, and also links it to the discussion of 'the promise' in 4:13ff, towards which the correct attitude is 'hope' (4:18). According to 5:1f, the consequence of justification, peace and grace is that 'we rejoice in hope of the glory of God'. Suffering too gives rise to hope, in that it produces 'steadfastness' and δοκιμή (vv.3f). The love of God[6] poured into our hearts by the Holy Spirit means that hope will not disappoint us (v.5). The death of Christ for our sins shows God's love for us (vv.6–8) and assures us that, being justified and reconciled, we shall finally be saved (vv.9f), and this is a cause for joy (v.11). Thus, the various themes of the passage – justification, reconciliation, suffering, the Holy Spirit, the death of Christ – are all mentioned in order to encourage hope. Hope is the theme which binds all these subordinate subjects together.[7]

How is this meditation on hope related to the situation of the Roman Christians and Paul's purpose in writing to them? Rom. 15 seems to provide the answer. In v.4, Paul mentions parenthetically that it is the purpose of the Scriptures to kindle hope, and then prays in vv.5f that the Jewish and Gentile Christians of Rome may live in harmony with one another so as to be able to worship together. In vv.7–12, Paul uses texts from the Psalms and from Isaiah to show that it is God's purpose that Jews should worship God alongside Gentiles, that Gentiles should worship together with Jews, and that the Messiah should come for the salvation of Gentiles as well as Jews. After this appeal to the Jewish and Gentile groups to join together for worship, Paul writes in v.13: 'May the God of hope fill you with all joy and peace in believing, so that by the power of the Holy Spirit you may abound in hope.' V.13 is surely not unrelated to vv.7–12.[8] Paul is not simply expressing pious aspiration, but is implying that one of the consequences of the union of the Jewish and Gentile congregations for worship will be that through the Spirit they will abound in hope.

Why should this shared worship lead them to abound in hope? A sociological interpretation of hope suggests a possible answer. 'Hope' refers to the subjective confidence of the community and its individual members of the reality of the future salvation in which they believe and for which they long. That salvation is 'unseen' (Rom. 8:24f), and its reality is explicitly or implicitly denied by society at large; this makes hope peculiarly vulnerable. The massive, visible reality of everyday life makes subjective confidence in an unseen, greater, future reality hard to maintain[9] (cf. Rom. 4:19ff, where Abraham is praised because he overcame this difficulty). The problem becomes particularly acute in 'suffering', i.e. the sectarian group's experience of hostility from society as a whole, which resents the existence of a group which rejects its norms and beliefs and adheres to alien norms and beliefs of its own. Although suffering can enhance hope (cf. Rom. 5:3f), it also threatens it, for there is a danger that some of the group's members will decide that the price of separation is too great and so 'fall away' (cf. Mk 4:17, 1 Thes. 3:5).[10] Nothing is so damaging to the group's confidence as the defection of its own members, and 'suffering' is one of the main causes of such defections. Thus, 'hope' (the feeling of subjective confidence in the reality of the future salvation) is constantly under threat, and since it is precisely 'hope' that gives the group its *raison d'être* and its cohesion, its maintenance is a matter of great importance.

How is hope to be maintained? Above all, *hope requires social support*. If hope is threatened by everyday reality and by the hostility of society, the group's meetings become all the more important as the place at which hope is rekindled. This takes place through the group's constantly renewed articulation of its beliefs and aspirations in hymns, prayers, readings from Scripture (cf. Rom. 15:4), teaching and exhortations.[11] Through participation in these various elements of the group's worship, the individual is able to reappropriate the norms and beliefs of the group and to defy the threat to his confidence posed by everyday reality. When Paul attributes increase in hope to 'the power of the Holy Spirit' (Rom. 15:13), he is indicating that hope is dependent on social support, for the idea of the Holy Spirit in Paul is very closely related to the emotional experience generated by communal worship (cf. Rom. 8:15f).

If hope is dependent on social support, this explains why Paul in Rom. 15:7 – 13 believes that the union of Jews and Gentiles in worship will lead them all to 'abound in hope'. In isolation from one another, each group represents part of the threat to the 'hope' of the other. When they 'despise' or 'pass judgment on' one another (cf. Rom. 14:3f, 10–13), they each betray in their hostility their anxiety about their own standing. Indeed, the hostility of those who to a large extent share one's own religious traditions and outlook and yet deny one's legitimacy represents a particularly significant threat to hope. Thus, the antipathy between the Jewish and Gentile congregations in Rome is damaging to both, and conversely the union of the two is likely to increase hope by providing the additional social support which will enable it to flourish. It is for this reason that in Rom. 15:7–13 Paul expresses his belief that the union of the two congregations will lead hope to abound.

This seems to provide the key to the social function of Rom. 5:1–11 in its context. In Rom. 1–4, Paul's exposition of justification by faith has involved a tacit appeal to Jewish Christians to recognize the legitimacy of their Gentile counterparts, and to unite with them. Rom. 5:1–11 describes the greatly increased 'hope' which will be the outcome of that unity; increased social support will enable hope to flourish. By presenting hope in this attractive light, Paul is attempting to bring unity nearer.

5:1–11 discusses the hope which arises from justification by faith (involving union of Jew and Gentile), and 5:12–21 discusses the same subject in a different way. Those who receive the gift of righteousness will reign in life (v. 17). Jesus Christ's act of righteousness brings justification which leads to life (v. 18). Christ has established a reign of grace 'through righteousness to eternal life' (v. 21). The free gift of grace leads initially to justification (vv. 16, 19) and ultimately to eternal life (vv. 17, 18, 21). In vv. 1–11, Paul has described hope as it is or should be experienced within the congregation. In vv. 12–21, he gives a broader description of the grounds for hope by means of a portrayal of salvation history[12] in terms of two antithetical realms: the realm of Adam, sin, death, law and condemnation, and the realm of Christ, grace, righteousness and life. He thus universalizes the concept of salvation; Jesus Christ is no longer merely the Messiah of Israel but the Saviour of Jews and Gentiles alike. The situation he came to remedy is not the oppression of Israel but the fallen state of the world, which has succumbed to sin, death and condemnation. Those who are under the law (i.e. the Jewish community) are merely a part of that fallen world;[13] indeed, the law has intensified the reign of sin (vv. 20f). In this portrayal of two antithetical realms, there is no question of any significant difference between Jew and Gentile. Paul is in effect appealing to his Jewish Christian readers to abandon their restricted view of Jesus as the Messiah of Israel,[14] a view which would make it impossible for them to separate themselves finally from the Jewish community and to unite with the Gentile congregation.[15] Thus, even in this apparently purely theoretical passage, the situation at Rome and Paul's purpose in writing Romans are of the greatest importance for interpretation.[16]

2 'Grace alone' as a misunderstanding (Rom. 6)

If the restricted Jewish Christian interpretation of Jesus as the Messiah of Israel constituted one obstacle to unity, their continuing loyalty to the law constituted another, and the whole of Rom. 6:1–8:17 is concerned with this problem. Rom. 6 poses the question, 'Are we to continue in sin that grace may abound?' (v. 1), or, as v. 15 puts it, 'Are we to continue in sin because we are not under law but under grace?'. In 3:8, Paul states that he was falsely accused of teaching, 'Let us do evil that good may come'; in that context, he is concerned not so much to defend himself against this charge as to make precisely the same accusation against his Jewish opponents, who believe that God's faithfulness to his covenant guarantees the salvation of Israel. But in Rom. 6, he does defend himself.[17] The origins of this Jewish charge may be deduced from Gal. 2:11ff. The Christians of Antioch have neglected the food laws and circumcision, and so, according to the men from James, they have made Christ a servant of sin (Gal. 2:17). They hold that the law may be disregarded and yet that salvation through Christ is still assured. Similarly, in Gal. 5:13ff Paul defends his understanding of Christian freedom against his opponents' claim that it in effect amounts to 'an opportunity for the flesh' (v. 13), 'gratifying the desires of the flesh' (v. 16), 'doing whatever you want' (v. 18). The Jewish Christians may well have thought that if any of the commandments were disregarded, all of them might be. Paul assures his readers that this is not what he teaches; those who transgress Christian ethical norms will not receive salvation (Gal. 5:21, 6:7f).

From the Jewish standpoint, the behaviour of those who dissociate themselves from the Jewish community and its way of life could only be seen as 'sin' (Gal. 2:17). That was no doubt the attitude of the Roman Jewish Christians towards Paul and his followers in Rome. They neglected circumcision, the food-laws, the Sabbaths and the feasts, and many of the other commandments. Their behaviour was quite simply sin. Their reliance on Christ for salvation amounted to the claim that no matter how much one sinned, salvation was sure.[18] For this reason, they 'judge' or 'condemn' the Gentile Christians (14:3, 10, 13). Paul's argument in Rom. 6 is therefore that, despite the fact that he and his followers have set aside the Jewish law (vv. 14f), his gospel is utterly opposed to sin. Christians, like Christ, have 'died to sin'; they have left the realm in which sin holds sway, and this prevents them from succumbing to their passions (v. 12) and from yielding their members to sin as instruments of wickedness (vv. 15ff).

In other words, Paul defends himself against the charge that he preaches a gospel of *sola gratia* and *pecca fortiter*. The obedience of which he speaks in Rom. 6 is not something which is in the last resort unnecessary for salvation. On the contrary, sin leads inevitably to 'death' (vv. 21, 23a), whereas obedience leads to 'eternal life' (v. 22). Eternal life is indeed τὸ χάρισμα τοῦ θεοῦ (v. 23), in that it would be unattainable without Jesus Christ. But the condition for receiving this χάρισμα is that one should be a 'slave of obedience' (v. 16), 'obedient from the heart to the standard of teaching to which you were committed' (v. 17), a 'slave of righteousness' (v. 18), and a 'slave of God' (v. 22). Grace alone – i.e. the activity of God alone – is insufficient for salvation. Grace must meet with the human response of obedience in order to lead to salvation.[19] The Lutheran view of Paul has turned the slogan, *sola gratia* into the touchstone of his theology and of any true theology. But it is clear to anyone who approaches Rom. 6 without Lutheran presuppositions that it is precisely the notion of *sola gratia* that Paul excludes here with his characteristic μὴ γένοιτο (vv. 1, 15).[20] Obedience is not merely desirable; it is necessary, for there can be no salvation without it.[21] Grace alone is as insufficient for salvation as obedience alone.

Paul thus assures his Jewish Christian readers that to abandon the Jewish community and its way of life does not mean that one casts off all ethical restraints. They need not fear that they will find all the typically Gentile vices (cf. 1:18ff) among the Roman Gentile Christians. They should find no obstacle to union here.[22]

3 The dire consequences of the law (Rom. 7:1–8:17)

In Rom. 6, Paul thus answers a Jewish Christian objection to his proclamation of freedom from the law. In answer to the claim that it must lead inevitably to moral anarchy, he insists on the vital importance of whole-hearted obedience to God. His opponents believe that only those under the discipline of the law (and therefore members of the Jewish community) are free from the dominion of sin, and so in 6:14f Paul claims that precisely the opposite is the case: 'Sin will have no dominion over you, since you are not under law but under grace.' The implication is that where the law is, there sin reigns, and this is confirmed by 5:20: 'Law came in, to increase the trespass.' Far from freeing people from sin, the law makes their situation still worse. In other words, Paul is once again turning the tables on his detractors. They claim: the law leads to obedience to God, whereas Pauline freedom from the law leads to disobedience. Paul replies: freedom from the law leads to obedience, whereas the law leads to disobedience. The first part of this reply is to be found in Rom. 6, the second in Rom. 7. Paul's polemical tactic is exactly the same as in 2:1–3:8, where he argues that his opponents are themselves guilty of precisely the theological error which they impute to him.

How is Paul able to make such negative statements about the law as he makes in 5:20, 6:14f and 7:1ff? It is often claimed that he does so for theological reasons; so, for example, Cranfield comments on 6:14b that 'the meaning of this sentence is that believers are not under God's condemnation pronounced by the law but under His undeserved favour' (I, 320). This comment is inadequate because it fails to recognize that in Paul the law is only very rarely isolated from the Jewish community which practises the law as its way of life.[23] When Paul claims that the law increases the trespass (5:20), he means that this has taken place within the Jewish community; and when he proclaims that his readers are free from the law (6:14f; 7:1–6), he means that they are free from, or separated from, the Jewish community which practises the law. In other words, his negative statements about the law can only be understood if one bears in mind the main social function of Romans: to persuade the Roman Jewish Christians to break the ties that still bind them to the non-Christian Jewish community and to unite with the Pauline Gentile Christians.[24] If he can convince his Jewish Christian readers that the effect of the law in the Jewish community is to intensify disastrously the dominion of sin, an important part of his purpose will have been achieved.[25]

In Rom. 7:1–6, Paul spells out his notion of freedom from the law, drawing on the idea outlined in 6:3–13, that baptism is to be equated with 'death'. The law is binding on people only during their lifetimes – this is true of any law. Since Paul's readers have 'died' in baptism, the Jewish law no longer applies to them (7:4–6). In v. 3, Paul, using the image of the woman who is bound to her husband as long as he lives (v. 2), argues that the woman is not an adulteress if she remarries after the death of her husband. The details of this argument are somewhat obscure,[26] but it seems that v. 3 and the argument in general is intended to allay the Jewish Christian anxiety that freedom from the law is quite simply apostasy. Paul claims that this would only be the case if the 'death' of baptism had not taken place; in fact, it marks such a radical break with the old life (i.e. life as a member of the Jewish community) that the law itself has become a thing of the past, no longer binding. As in 5:20 and 6:14, the law is seen as merely intensifying the dominion of sin: 'While we were living in the flesh, our sinful passions, *aroused by the law*, were at work in our members to bear fruit for death' (7:5).[27] If such a view of the law is correct, then salvation must involve salvation from the law itself and thus separation from the Jewish community.

The law increases the trespass and it arouses sinful passions. The obvious conclusion would be that the law is sin (v. 7) – i.e. that the law arouses sin in the sense that the conduct prescribed by the law is sinful, so that obedience to the law is disobedience to God. Nevertheless, Paul repudiates this conclusion in vv. 7ff, drawing a distinction between the content of the law – which is of divine origin and therefore good – and the effect of the law – which through the machinations of Sin (here regarded as a quasi-demonic power) gives rise to sin and death.[28] The argument of vv. 7–12 is not simply that the law reveals sin, but that in some mysterious way the effect of the law is to arouse sin; the whole passage thus elaborates the reference in v. 5 to 'our sinful passions, aroused by the law'. When in v. 7 Paul says that without the law 'I should not have known sin' and 'I should not have known what it is to desire', he means not that he would not have *understood* sin or desire without the law, but that he would not have *experienced* sin or desire.[29] This is clear from the sequel: 'But sin, finding opportunity in the commandment, wrought in me every kind of desire' (v. 8). Without the law, he would not have known desire (v. 7), whereas with the coming of the law desire was created in him (v. 8), and in order for these two statements to balance one another, the 'knowledge' of v. 7 must be experiential rather than theoretical.

Exactly the same view is presented in vv. 8b–12, except that here a new element is added, the fact that in the hands of Sin the law becomes the instrument producing not only sin but also its penalty, death. Thus, 'Sin worked death in me through what is good', i.e. through the law (v. 13).

However this strange argument is to be interpreted, Paul's strategy seems reasonably clear. The 'sin' he concentrates on is that of 'desire' (ἐπιθυμία), and in the light of the parallel phrase in v. 5, 'sinful passions' (παθήματα τῶν ἁμαρτιῶν), the reference is probably at least primarily to sexual lust.[30] That is the case in 1 Thes. 4:4f, where Paul exhorts each of his readers to take a wife for himself, μὴ ἐν πάθει ἐπιθυμίας καθάπερ καὶ τὰ ἔθνη τὰ μὴ εἰδότα τὸν θεόν. Sexual desire is here seen as a sin; cf. Rom. 1:24; 6:12; 13:14; Gal. 5:16ff, in each of which ἐπιθυμία has a primarily sexual sense.[31] Paul's starting-point is therefore a phenomenon which will be familiar to his Jewish Christian readers, which even the law is unable to eradicate completely. He then makes an astonishing claim about the origins of this 'desire': it was the law itself which aroused it. He hastens to add that the law is good in itself and only had this appalling effect because it fell into the hands of Sin; but this qualification does little to mitigate the radical nature of Paul's claim. His strategy is clear: he wishes to evoke in his readers a horror of the law. They may retain their belief in its essential goodness, but they must also recognize that its effect in practice has been to arouse lust – that notorious thorn-in-the-flesh even of the righteous. This is therefore yet another argument intended to persuade the Jewish Christians at Rome to separate themselves from the law and from the community which practises it.

But how can Paul make such a claim about the law and expect it to be credible? It has been argued that he is referring to the tendency of any authoritative commandment to provoke resentment and rebellion,[32] or to the way in which the law leads to the sin of 'legalism', seeking to establish one's own righteousness.[33] Neither view is very plausible. Throughout 7:7ff, sin is seen as a cruel fate against which the subject protests, rather than as a deliberate act of rebellion springing from resentment. The view that 'desire' here means the desire to earn salvation is based on the misunderstanding of Paul's faith–works antithesis which it has been one of the main aims of the present work to expose; in addition, the identification of ἐπιθυμία with 'legalism' is utterly arbitrary and receives no support from Pauline usage elsewhere.[34] Many interpreters have correctly noted that the narrative of Gen. 2–3 is alluded to in Rom. 7:7ff,[35] and it is this fact which may provide the key to Paul's strange argument. Detailed correspondences between the two passages are as follows.

(i) 'I was once alive apart from the law' (Rom. 7:9). In Gen. 2:7–9, the Lord God forms man out of the dust and places him in Eden, where he is able to partake of 'the tree of life in the midst of the garden'.[36]

(ii) 'But when the commandment came ...' (Rom. 7:9). According to Gen. 2:16f, 'the Lord God commanded (ἐνετείλατο) the man, saying, "You may freely eat of every tree of the garden"', and so on. The commandment (ἐντολή, Rom. 7:8, 9, 10, 11, 12, 13) was 'unto life' (Rom. 7:10)[37] in that its aim was the preservation of access to the tree of life, just as its contravention meant separation from the tree of life (cf. Gen. 3:22ff).

(iii) The result of the coming of the commandment was that 'sin revived and I died' (Rom. 7:9). This is a highly compressed statement. The first stage is that sin 'found opportunity in the commandment' (Rom. 7:8, 11). In Gen. 3:1–5, the serpent uses the commandment to further his ends.

(iv) Through the commandment, 'sin ... deceived me' (ἐξηπάτησεν με, Rom. 7:11). Eve too complains that the serpent, using the commandment, 'deceived me' (ἠπάτησεν με, Gen. 3:13).

(v) The serpent's use of the commandment to deceive leads to sin: 'Sin ... wrought in me every kind of desire' (Rom. 7:8).[38] As argued above, 'desire' means primarily sexual desire, and this may be linked with Gen. 3:7: 'Then the eyes of both were opened, and they knew that they were naked; and they sewed fig leaves together and made themselves aprons.' This verse suggests that the 'sin' of v. 6 was sexual in nature, and for this reason Paul can identify the commandment of Gen. 2:17 with the commandment, 'You shall not desire',[39] just as he can identify the transgression of the commandment in Gen. 3:6f with the awakening of 'every kind of desire' (Rom. 7:7f). Thus, Sin has used the commandment to arouse sinful desire.

(vi) The result of this is death: 'I died' (Rom. 7:9); 'the commandment ... proved to be death to me' (7:10, cf. v. 13); 'Sin, finding opportunity in the commandment, ... by it killed me' (7:11). In Genesis, the effect of the sin which has arisen through the commandment is mortality rather than immediate death (cf. 3:19, 22ff). But the statement, 'In the day that you eat of it you shall die' (Gen. 2:17) may have led Paul to a spiritualized understanding of 'death', which would then be identified with the expulsion from Eden.

These correspondences are so close that there can be little doubt that Paul has the Genesis story in mind throughout.[40] This is confirmed by 5:13f, which suggests that there is an analogy between Adam's sin and Israel's sin under the law.[41] It is the Genesis story alone which accounts for Paul's claim that the good commandment of God had the effect of arousing the sin of desire and so leading to death. He reaches this conclusion not from psychological observation but from Scriptural exegesis. As has already been stated, his purpose is to distance his Jewish Christian readers still further from the law and from the community in which it is observed. When they realize that the law was involved in the origins of sexual lust, its prestige will be greatly diminished.

It is true that Paul here emphasizes the goodness of the law (Rom. 7:12, 13, 14, 16, 22) as well as its evil effects. This has led some scholars to regard the whole section as an 'apologia for the law'.[42] But that is surely an exaggerated claim, since there is a far greater emphasis on the evil results of the law's coming than on its essential goodness.[43] It is also frequently claimed that Paul's appreciation here of the goodness of the law shows that his thought has developed and matured since the angry and intemperate discussions of the law in Galatians.[44] But as with other differences between Galatians and Romans, the explanation is to be found in the different audiences addressed rather than in development of thought. Galatians is addressed to Gentiles who have in many cases only recently become acquainted with the law, whereas Rom. 7 is addressed primarily to Jewish Christians ('Those who know the law', v. 1), for whom the goodness and holiness of the law is second nature. One might indeed argue that Paul's argument is pragmatic and opportunist, rather than being the result of profounder theological reflection than he was capable of when he wrote Galatians.[45] He wishes to persuade the Roman Jewish Christians to separate themselves from the Jewish community and its way of life, and he knows that he stands a greater chance of success if he adds a theoretical acknowledgement of the essential goodness of the law to his devastating description of its actual effects, rather than repeating the denial in Gal. 3:19f of its divine origin. To those who hold that Paul was a radical theologian concerned only to explore the profound existential implications of the gospel (and who thereby make Paul in their own self-image), this will appear too cynical a view of the apostle. But he himself admits, or rather boasts, that he becomes all things to all men (1 Cor. 9:22) and that he tries to please all men in everything that he does (1 Cor. 10:33), in order that they may accept the gospel as he preaches it. At least this view has the merit of recognizing that Paul was actually trying to *achieve* something by writing Rom. 7. He was no disembodied theorizer.[46]

In Rom. 7:13, Paul again uses his standard rhetorical device of suggesting a false conclusion from what has just been said and then rejecting it with a μὴ γένοιτο. He has already done this in v. 7, and this suggests that v. 13 is intended as the beginning of a new paragraph. This is confirmed by the fact that v. 14 must function as an explanation of some aspect of v. 13, since it is linked to that verse with a γάρ. And yet it has proved extremely difficult to explain how the two verses are linked. V. 13 does not seem to progress beyond what has already been said: we have here once again the claim that sin uses the good law in order to bring forth death (cf. vv. 8−11). But vv. 14ff appears to have nothing further to say on that subject, and to be discussing a new subject, inability to obey the law in the present. Scholars frequently refer to Rom. 7:14−25 as a self-contained paragraph, and so ignore the structural necessity of accounting for the link with v. 13 and thus with the previous paragraph. This isolation of vv. 14ff from the context influences exegesis, as in the still-widespread view that Paul has suddenly switched from a discussion of life under the law to a discussion of Christian existence and its moral difficulties.[47]

But v. 13 does add something to the thought of the previous paragraph, and this provides the key to the connection with vv. 14ff.[48] It is not only said in v. 13 that sin worked death through the commandment; there are also two comments about sin's purpose or strategy in doing this which have no parallel in vv. 7−12. Sin worked in this way ἵνα φανῇ ἁμαρτία and ἵνα γένηται καθ᾽ ὑπερβολὴν ἁμαρτωλός.[49] The meaning of these phrases is at first sight obscure. But in Paul's preceding interpretation of Gen. 2−3, Sin is identified both with the serpent, seen as an active quasi-demonic power which makes use of the divine commandment to further its own ends, and with the result of its actions, sexual desire. Sin, as an external power, has as its goal actual human sin or transgression. This explains the first phrase from v. 13: Sin (the external power) used the commandment to produce death, so that sin (actual human transgression) might appear as a constant feature of human life. It is in this way that Sin (the power) becomes 'exceedingly sinful', i.e. by as it were reproducing itself within human beings. The difference between v. 13 and vv. 7−12 is that vv. 7−12 has described a primal event in which Sin used the commandment to produce desire and death, whereas v. 13 is referring to the present reality which has sprung from that primal event: the presence of indwelling Sin (the power) and its constant manifestation in the form of actual human sin.[50] That is precisely the point which vv. 14–25 develops: it is repeatedly stated there that actual transgression (doing what one does not want) is the work of 'sin which dwells within me' (vv. 17, 20), or 'the law of sin which is in my members' (v. 23; cf. v. 25).[51] Sin as a power originally, in the primal event, made use of the law in order to establish itself within the human frame, to produce actual transgressions; it is still there, producing actual transgressions unchecked. It was the law which initially gave Sin the opportunity of establishing itself in this way, and now it proves unable to rectify the situation.

7:14–25 is therefore not a separate argument; it is to be linked with v. 13 and thus with the passage as a whole. The present tense merely indicates that Paul is now discussing the enduring effects of the primal event described in vv. 7–12; it does not mean that he is now discussing the Christian experience of sin.[52] V. 25a ('Thanks be to God through Jesus Christ our Lord!') is not a valid argument in favour of identifying the speaker as a Christian, since it is merely an interjection anticipating the description of liberation from the law of sin in 8:1ff.[53] The claim that the delight in the law portrayed in 7:22 is incompatible with Paul's view of 'unredeemed humanity'[54] is another example of the distorting influence of presuppositions derived from the Reformation, since Paul is quite capable of ascribing to the Jews a genuine zeal for the law (Rom. 10:2; cf. Phil. 3:6). The speaker here should not be seen as a Christian but as a Jew[55] – an imaginary Jew who has become aware of his desperate plight as one who lives under the law (a view first advocated by W. G. Kümmel).[56] However, Rom. 7:14ff is 'a description of man under the Law from the perspective of faith' (Hübner, *Law*, 76f) only in the sense that 'faith' for Paul involves separation from the non-Christian Jewish community, and must therefore view that community and its way of life in a very negative way in order to justify its own separate existence.

Exegesis thus confirms the previous reconstruction of the purpose of Rom. 7: to persuade the Roman Jewish Christians to accept the Pauline notion of freedom from the law (with its corollary of separation from the synagogue), on the grounds that the law was instrumental in the origin of sexual lust, and that having once allowed Sin to enter the human frame, the law is powerless to prevent it carrying on its evil work of producing actual transgressions. Once again, Paul stresses the goodness of the law (vv. 14, 16, 22, 25). But as 8:3 shows, the real point of the section is the law's *weakness*: it is unable to rectify the situation which it has unwittingly made possible. Paul does not wish to deprive his readers of the dogma of the law's essential goodness, so long as they accept that in practice its effects have been disastrous. In insisting that the law is good, Paul is in fact damning it with faint praise.

For the purposes of his argument, Paul has in vv. 7–13 virtually identified 'the law' with 'the commandment', i.e. the commandment, 'You shall not desire' (v. 7). That is probably the reason why he is able to claim in vv. 14ff that obedience to the law is impossible, even though one wishes to obey it. He is not claiming that absolute moral anarchy reigns within the Jewish community; that claim would disregard the empirical facts (not to mention Paul's teaching elsewhere) so completely that he could not possibly have hoped to persuade his readers of it.[57] But the idea that sexual desire (itself seen as a sin) cannot be eradicated by the mind and the law in which the mind delights is much more plausible; that seems to be Paul's meaning. He is therefore arguing that the sin of sexual desire was first made possible by the law, and that it is still a reality in the community which delights in the law, a reality which leads to the death and condemnation of its members.[58]

Conversely, Paul proclaims in 8:1ff that freedom from this situation is to be found 'in Christ Jesus' – the community of Gentile as well as Jewish Christians. This freedom has been accomplished by the Spirit, the power at work in the Christian community and specifically in its worship. The Spirit brings 'life' (8:2, 7, 10), and deliverance from 'the law of sin and death' (8:2) – i.e. from 'sin which dwells within me' (7:17, 20), 'the law of sin which dwells in my members' (7:23; cf. v. 25),[59] the indwelling power which is responsible for sexual desire. The Spirit thus restores the primal condition before the coming of the commandment gave Sin its opportunity: 'I was once alive apart from the law' (7:9). There is a new creation; paradise is regained. Freedom from the power of indwelling sin (8:2) means that 'the decree of the law' (τὸ δικαίωμα τοῦ νόμου) is 'fulfilled in us' (8:4). The closest parallel to this phrase is in Rom. 2:26, which refers to τὰ δικαιώματα τοῦ νόμου – i.e. the sum of the individual commandments of the law, and in the light of this, τὸ δικαίωμα τοῦ νόμου in 8:4 must refer to a specific commandment of the law, and not to 'the just requirement of the law' (RSV), seen as a vague general entity. The specific commandment that is often mentioned in connection with 8:4 is, 'Love your neighbour as yourself' (13:8–10).[60] But this has not been referred to in the present context; the one commandment which has been repeatedly mentioned is, 'You shall not desire' (7:7ff). The probable meaning of 8:4 is therefore that freedom from 'sin which dwells within me' (8:2) means freedom from the sin of desire and so the fulfilment of the law's prohibition of sexual desire.[61] The Spirit gives life and eradicates sexual desire, and this is the result of the atonement which the law was not able to achieve (8:3). The ecstatic experience of the Spirit (8:14–16) enables people to 'set their minds on the things of the Spirit' rather than on 'the things of the flesh' (8:5).

But Paul does not regard this as an automatic process for Christians. He has already rejected one form of *sola gratia* in Rom. 6 (the view that links it with *pecca fortiter*), and in Rom. 8 he implicitly rejects another form, according to which human obedience is entirely the work of the Spirit. Paul signifies his rejection of this possibility by his use of the active verb, 'walk', in 8:4, by his warning about the continuing possibility of setting the mind on the flesh in 8:5–8, and above all by the statement of 8:12f: 'So then, brethren, we are debtors, not to the flesh, to live according to the flesh – for if you live according to the flesh you will die, but if by the Spirit you put to death the deeds of the body you will live'. Salvation is not by divine activity ('grace') alone; grace must lead to human cooperation, if there is to be salvation.

In 8:18, Paul returns to the subject of hope which he earlier discussed in ch. 5, and so there are grounds for regarding 6:1–8:17 as a single argument in which Paul continues his debate about the law with his Jewish Christian readers. Paul's rejection of certain of the commandments of the law of Moses, his separation from the synagogue, and his view of the law as the bringer of death have led his critics to claim that he is indifferent to all moral standards, that he teaches that since salvation is certain one may behave as one wishes. This suspicion is one of the many obstacles which separate the Roman Jewish Christians from the Gentile followers of Paul, and Paul tries to remove it in Rom. 6 by arguing that obedience to 'the standard of teaching to which you were committed' (v. 17) is a necessary condition of salvation, as well as the divine grace which precedes obedience. But Paul also argues that it is not his teaching which leads to an increase of sin, but the law itself. In order to persuade the Jewish Christians of Rome to separate themselves finally from the Jewish community and to unite with his own followers, he must demonstrate not only the stress on obedience among the latter, but also the disastrous effects of the law among the former. He therefore claims that 'our sinful passions' (i.e. 'desire') were 'aroused by the law' (7:5); the law, although good in itself, was instrumental in producing sexual desire, as Gen. 2–3 indicates. The law is powerless to overcome this sexual desire and to liberate its adherents from death; but life and the eradication of desire are possible through the power of the Spirit, who is to be experienced within the Christian community, 'in Christ Jesus', where Jew and Gentile are one. Christian hope (5:1–21; 8:18–39) is independent of the law (5:20f), but this does not mean that it is based on the false doctrine of salvation by grace alone; on the contrary, true obedience to God which is a necessary condition for salvation is only possible in the community of those who are free from the law, the community of the Spirit.

Thus, the argument of Rom. 5–8 as a whole might be summed up in the sentence: Christian hope is independent of the law and therefore of membership of the Jewish community, because the law leads to sin, and the true obedience which is necessary for salvation is possible only in Christ.[62] This is no purely theoretical argument, but like the rest of Romans contains an implicit call for social reorientation.[63] When one bears in mind the situation of the Roman Christians and Paul's purpose in writing to them, the coherence of the difficult argument of Rom. 5–8 becomes apparent.[64]

Hope and predestination (Rom. 8:18–39)

The general function of 8:18–39 in the overall argument has been mentioned above. To this one might add that, as in 5:12ff, Paul in 8:18–27 sets the doctrine of salvation not within the narrow horizon provided by the Jewish view of election, but within a universal and cosmic horizon. He removes the division between Jews and Gentiles by regarding both as representatives of fallen humanity (Rom. 5:12ff) and fallen creation (Rom. 8:18ff), and so removes an obstacle to their unity in Rome.

But there is another feature of the argument of 8:18–39 which is relevant in this context: the manner in which the ultimate ground for hope is seen as divine predestination, explicitly in 8:28–30, and implicitly throughout the passage. It has been argued above that Paul rejects the view that he proclaims salvation by grace alone as a perversion of his teaching. But a doctrine of salvation based on divine predestination seems to have 'grace alone' as its inevitable corollary. Does 8:28–30 therefore give any grounds for the Reformation tradition's view that *sola gratia* is at the heart of Paul's theology?

It must be conceded that 8:28–30 does imply salvation by grace alone. The fact that certain people are called, justified and glorified is in this passage ascribed entirely to the will of God, who predestined these people to be 'conformed to the image of his Son, in order that he might be the first-born among many brethren' (v. 29). But it is an entirely different matter whether salvation by grace alone ought therefore to be regarded as determinative of Paul's theology as a whole. In practice, he only allows predestination (or election) a very limited role in his thought. He writes to the Thessalonians: 'We know, brethren beloved by God, that he has chosen you' (1 Thes. 1:4), and indicates that the reason for his confidence is the manner in which they received the gospel (1:5) and endured suffering (1:6). And yet this knowledge of their election is not unassailable, for in 3:5 he refers to his fear that persecution might have led them to abandon their new-found faith. Knowledge of predestination is therefore dependent on continuing commitment to the Christian community with its norms and beliefs, and it is the latter and not the former which is fundamental for Paul's thinking. Predestination (or election) cannot be harmonized in a rationally consistent way with Paul's constant emphasis on the need for particular forms of human behaviour in response to the divine grace. Its function is not to be part of a comprehensive *Weltanschauung*, but to be an element of Paul's *paraklesis*: his converts are assured that their somewhat anomalous position with regard to society as a whole is not the result of their own (perhaps arbitrary and misguided) decisions, but the result of divine activity.[65] The notion of predestination thus legitimates the community's separation from the world and its sense of an elite, privileged status. On other occasions, Paul places the emphasis on the urgent need to obey Christian norms in one's everyday conduct, and supports this with the threat of judgment according to works. From a rationalistic standpoint, these two things are incompatible, but they correspond to real needs in sectarian groups, and so both are found alongside one another in Paul. Thus, the fact that Rom. 8:28–30 implies that salvation is by grace alone does not mean that this is true elsewhere in Rom. 1–8, where the emphasis is on the human response of obedience to God as well as on the grace of God which precedes it. The triumphant proclamation of the certainty of salvation in 8:31–9 is still subject to the caveat of 8:13: 'If you live according to the flesh, you will die, but if by the Spirit you put to death the deeds of the body, you will live.'

9

THE SOCIAL FUNCTION OF ROMANS: ROM. 9–11

1 The purpose of Rom. 9–11

There are very few passages in Romans without major exegetical problems. Whether one regards this as a sign of the apostle's theological profundity or of a tortuous and confused mode of thought, the fact remains that Romans is one of the most difficult texts in the New Testament. Perhaps this accounts in part for the fascination which this epistle has held for countless exegetes down the centuries; of all the New Testament writings, this one poses the most obvious intellectual challenge. No interpretation can hope to solve all of its problems, but it has been the claim of the previous chapters that close attention to the situation of the Roman Christians and to Paul's purpose in writing to them is much more important for the interpretation of the epistle than is commonly thought. The supposition that Romans presupposes an existing social situation, and was intended to function in particular ways within that situation, seems more profitable than the common view that in Romans Paul the theologian rises above the concrete situations which he has had to deal with in Corinth, Galatia and so on, and at last sets forth his gospel in a definitive and universally valid manner. The survival of the latter view shows how difficult it has proved to set aside theological presuppositions in order to interpret the text in a genuinely historical way.

Can the method of interpretation developed in the previous chapters help us to understand Rom. 9–11? It will be the argument of this chapter that this is indeed the case. The starting-point must be an examination of the precise nature of the problem or problems which Rom. 9–11 attempts to solve: the common view that the subject here is simply 'Israel's failure to accept the gospel'[1] is too superficial to be of much use.

The subjects discussed in Rom. 1–8 are many and various, but they are held together by a single purpose: to persuade Jewish Christian readers to accept the legitimacy of Pauline Gentile Christianity and to deny legitimacy to the claims of the synagogue. The Jewish leaders are corrupt, and true obedience to God is rather to be found among uncircumcised Gentiles (Rom. 2). Far from separating Israel from the Gentiles, the law places Israel in exactly the same position of guilt before God as the Gentiles, whereas faith unites Jewish and Gentile believers who are the beneficiaries of salvation in Christ (Rom. 3). The church, composed of Jewish and Gentile believers, is the true seed of Abraham, to whom the promise of salvation was given, rather than the members of the Jewish community (Rom. 4). Christian hope is independent of the law and the Jewish community (Rom. 5; 8:18ff), for the law led to sinful desire and death for its adherents (Rom. 7), and God can only be truly served in the community of those who are free from the law (Rom. 6; 8:1–17).

What would Paul's Jewish Christian readers have made of these arguments? Paul was quite capable of converting Jewish Christians to his standpoint, as the case of Prisca and Aquila probably shows, and some of his readers in Rome may likewise have been willing to accept the arguments of Rom. 1–8. But what would have aroused the anger or perplexity of many of them would have been the fact that in Rom. 1–8 and in his general conduct, Paul seemed to have turned his back on his own people in his concern for the Gentiles. He had denied the validity of the unique God-given privileges of his own people, claiming that they belonged by right to the small break-away groups founded by himself, composed mainly of Gentiles who did not even observe the law. He showed thereby (so it would have been asserted) not the slightest trace of loyalty towards his own people.[2] In order to justify his conduct, he claimed that God himself had transferred his favour from Israel to the Gentiles, thus apparently ascribing gross inconsistency to the God who promises in Scripture that he is Israel's God for ever. It is not difficult to imagine the indignation which Rom. 1–8 and Paul's missionary activity would have aroused among many of the Jewish Christians in Rome.

The function of Rom. 9–11 is to answer these two interconnected charges: that Paul himself is utterly indifferent to his own people, and that the view of God which corresponds to Paul's activity among the Gentiles makes God inconsistent.[3] The charge of indifference must underlie the strangely emphatic language of 9:1–5.[4] Paul feels the need to introduce his statement about his sorrow over the fate of the Jewish people in v. 2 with the assertion: 'I am speaking the truth in Christ, I am not lying; my conscience bears me witness in the Holy Spirit' (v. 1). This emphatic assertion shows his fear lest his readers react to his profession of sorrow with incredulity, because they believe him to be indifferent to his own people. His listing of the privileges of the Jewish people in vv. 4f must again be intended to answer the charge of indifference. This personal involvement in the argument once again becomes clear in 10:1, where Paul writes: 'Brethren, my heart's desire and prayer to God for them is that they may be saved.' Above all, this is true of 11:11ff, where Paul argues that, far from being intended to exalt Gentiles over Jews, his Gentile mission has as its ultimate goal the salvation of the Jews: 'Inasmuch then as I am apostle to the Gentiles, I magnify my ministry *in order to make my fellow-Jews jealous, and thus save some of them*' (11:13b–14).

However, the charge that Paul is an apostate is subordinate to the charge that his view of God's activity in effect makes God an apostate; according to his critics, Paul has made God in his own image. Thus the main subject of Rom. 9–11 is *the consistency of the Pauline view of God's activity with the OT Scriptures*, and not 'Israel's unbelief' *per se*.[5] Everywhere, the presupposition is the Pauline view that God has rejected the majority in Israel and called to himself a new people consisting mainly of Gentiles (although also of a Jewish remnant). The question for Paul and his readers is: Is such a view of God's activity consistent with his revelation of himself in Scripture?[6] This is no mere theoretical discussion. Only if he can convince his readers that on his view God is indeed consistent will they be willing to accept his exhortation in 14:1–15:13 to unite with the Roman Gentile Christians.

2 Election and the consistency of God (Rom. 9:6–29)

The purpose of Rom. 9:6–29 is to prove *the consistency of Paul's view of God's activity with his purpose of election as declared in Scripture*. The aim of this apparently abstract argument about predestination becomes clear in vv. 22–9. Paul claims there that God has rejected the majority of the Jews and called to himself a new people consisting of Gentiles as well as Jews (vv. 22–4). He finds support for this claim in Hosea's prophecy that God would cause those who were not his people to become his people (understood as a reference to the Gentiles), and in Isaiah's prophecies that only a few Jews will be saved (vv. 25–9). Vv. 22–9 thus declare what, according to Paul, God has done, and the purpose of vv. 6–21 is to prove from Scripture his right to do it.[7] In vv. 6–13, Paul attacks the Jewish view that it is the physical descendants of Abraham and of Jacob who are the heirs to the promises of salvation.[8] The very fact that he has to do this proves the falsehood of the view that according to Paul Judaism is a religion of pure 'works righteousness'. Judaism according to Paul has an emphatic theology of grace, and it is precisely this which he is attacking in 9:6ff. He argues first that the true children of Abraham who are heirs to the promise are not his physical descendants – otherwise all of the children of Abraham would have been chosen (Ishmael, and so on), whereas in fact only Isaac was chosen (vv. 6–9). The point of this is that election is not a matter of natural descent but of the activity of God; thus it is quite consistent of God to elect Gentiles as children of Abraham and to reject Jews.[9] This point is repeated with reference to Isaac and his children in vv. 10–13. If election were a matter of natural descent from Isaac, then Esau would have been chosen as well as Jacob. The choice of Jacob alone shows that election is always God's prerogative alone.[10] Once again, the rejection of Jews and the salvation of Gentiles is in the background. Paul is neither constructing a theory of salvation-history[11] nor speaking solely of a Jewish Christian remnant.[12] His aim is to find precedents in Scripture for the kind of activity which he ascribes to God in 9:22ff. Only if he can establish such precedents will his claim that on his view God remains consistent be successful.[13]

9:14–21 continues the argument that it is not inconsistent for the God revealed in Scripture to reject Jews and to call Gentiles, by appealing to the character and nature of the God portrayed in Scripture. As Moses shows, it is a matter of God's free choice alone whom he has mercy on and whom he hardens. If it is his will to have mercy on Gentiles, that is his prerogative. If it is his will to harden Israel as he hardened Pharaoh, that too is his prerogative (vv. 14–18). Mere man is not in a position to criticize the activity of his Creator (vv. 19–21). If it is God's will to reject Jews and call Gentiles, who is in a position to accuse him of injustice? In acting in this way, God is behaving in accordance with his character as revealed in Scripture, i.e. as the Sovereign Lord before whom human beings have no rights.[14]

There is a message in all this for the Roman Jewish Christians. They are wrong to think that the God revealed in the Scripture has committed himself irrevocably to the salvation of the Jewish people, and they are therefore also wrong to regard Paul's view that God has rejected Jews and chosen Gentiles as inconsistent with Scripture.[15] On the contrary, Paul's view of God is precisely the same as that of Scripture. The patriarchal narratives indicate that election is not a matter of natural descent but of God's free choice. Scripture, like

Paul, asserts that God has mercy on whom he wills and hardens whom he wills. Most clearly of all, the prophets proclaim that Gentiles will be saved and most Jews rejected. Despite Paul's acknowledgment of the privileges of Israel in vv. 4f, these privileges prove to be worthless in practice: 'For not all who are descended from Israel belong to Israel, and not all are children of Abraham because they are his descendants' (vv. 6f). The Jewish Christians should realize that their future lies not with their fellow-Jews but with the Gentiles whom God has called (v. 24). Paul's argument therefore has a clear social function.

Scholars for whom Paul's theology is still authoritative have the greatest difficulties with Rom. 9:6ff, and do their utmost to explain away its stark and uncompromising teaching. Thus, it may be claimed that in vv. 6ff, Paul is not really annulling the privileges of the Jewish people; they remain God's elect even in their temporary rejected state.[16] Paul, it may be said, is merely trying to preserve the principle of *sola gratia* in his understanding of salvation-history.[17] God's activity of hardening is not the work of an arbitrary and capricious demon but a paradoxical expression of his mercy.[18] The argument of vv. 21f is hypothetical; it is not said that God really did predestine certain people to destruction.[19] According to M. Barth, the theme of 9:1–29 is that 'God's free election and sovereign faithfulness pertain to a people in revolt and keep it together' (*People*, 34); it argues that the history of the people of God 'included both election and rejection until finally the rejection of the "not-beloved" was overcome by the overwhelming love of God' (40). But such expedients should be rejected. They derive not from the text but from the theological concerns of the commentators – such as the desire to protect Paul from the taint of Calvinism or of anti-Semitism. Rom. 9:6–29 is in fact by Pauline standards a comparatively clear and coherent argument, and an emphasis on its intended social function at least makes it comprehensible even if it cannot make it theologically attractive.

3 Justification and the consistency of God (Rom. 9:30–10:21)

Paul does not elsewhere make much use of a theory of predestination to explain the rejection of Jews and the salvation of Gentiles; he prefers to see this in terms of the faith–works antithesis, and it is this to which he returns in the second part of his argument about the consistency of God, Rom. 9:30–10:21. Here the point is that *Paul's* understanding of the rejection of Jews and the salvation of Gentiles in terms of the faith–works contrast is consistent with the purposes of God declared in the Scriptures. It is not concerned with 'Israel's responsibility', balancing (or contradicting?) the predestinarian language of 9:6ff.[20] As in 9:6ff, the argument is dominated by OT quotations with which Paul seeks to legitimate his understanding of God's activity and of its social consequences. Paul's claim is that Israel failed to accept righteousness by faith because they pursued works of the law (9:31f). The meaning of this is not that the Jews were trying to earn salvation instead of receiving it as a free gift.[21] 'Works' refers to the way of life confined to the Jewish community, and 'faith' refers to a response to God which is open to Gentiles. 'Works' and 'faith' are therefore mutually exclusive because the Jewish way of life is incompatible with the way of life practised by Pauline Gentile Christians. In 9:33, Paul bases his view that Israel has failed to believe because of works on a combination of Is. 28:16 with Is. 8:14: God's salvation will produce both offence and faith, and Paul sees this as realized in the Jewish pursuit of works and Gentile faith, respectively.

In 10:1–13, as in 9:30–3, the contrast between faith and works is primarily a contrast between a way which is open to Gentiles as well as Jews and a way which is confined to Jews, rather than a contrast between receiving salvation as a free gift and earning it by one's own efforts. The former is probably the meaning of the much-disputed v. 4: τέλος γὰρ νόμου Χριστὸς εἰς δικαιοσύνην παντὶ τῷ πιστεύοντι. The phrase παντὶ τῷ πιστεύοντι is also used in 1:16 with the addition of the words, Ἰουδαίῳ τε πρῶτον καὶ Ἕλληνι, and throughout Romans has the pregnant sense of 'Jew and Gentile alike'.[22] V. 4 therefore means that Christ brings to an end[23] the way of life based on the law and practised by the Jewish community (cf. v. 3) in order to make righteousness possible for Gentiles as well as Jews.[24] This bold claim is supported by reference to Scripture in vv. 5–13. It is important to notice that the main characteristic of faith as described here is its *universality*;[25] Is. 28:16 (with the addition of πᾶς) and Jl 3:5 are used (vv. 11, 13) to prove that 'there is no distinction between Jew and Greek; the same Lord is Lord of all and bestows his riches upon all who call upon him' (v. 12).[26] This suggests that in v. 5 the emphasis is not on 'doing' *per se*, but on 'doing *them*', i.e. living the way of life which is confined to the Jewish community, in contrast to the universality of faith.[27]

Scripture has been used to justify Paul's view of both the failure of Israel (9:33) and the salvation of the Gentiles (10:6–13). Paul is trying to show that his view of the rejection of Jews and the salvation of Gentiles is not an arbitrary view of his own which cannot be true because it would involve God in self-contradiction. On the contrary, his view should be accepted because it is in accordance with the purpose of God as declared in Scripture. Rom. 9:30–10:21 should therefore not be regarded as an assertion of 'Israel's responsibility'. That interpretation springs from the mistaken assumption that the main theme of Rom. 9–11 is Jewish rejection of the gospel, which is attributed first to divine predestination (9:6–29) and then to human guilt (9:30–10:21). Rom. 9–11 is in fact an assertion of the congruity between Paul's view of the activity of God in the present and his purposes declared in Scripture.

This point is important in the interpretation of 10:14–21. On the view that the subject of 9:30–10:21 is 'Israel's responsibility', this passage is generally interpreted as a reference to the mission to the Jews: Israel has no excuse because the gospel was duly preached to her.[28] But if Paul is trying to justify his view of the rejection of Jews and the salvation of Gentiles by reference to Scripture, 10:14ff is more likely to be a defence from Scriptural texts of his own Gentile mission. Exegesis confirms this. V. 14 (Πῶς οὖν ἐπικαλέσωνται) follows on directly from v. 13 (πᾶς γὰρ ὃς ἂν ἐπικαλέσηται), and as the emphasis in vv. 11–13 is on the universality of salvation, it is hard to see how v. 14 can be confined to the mission to the Jews (so N. T. Wright, *Messiah*, 178f, to whose arguments the following section is indebted).[29] Its form is dictated by the polemical situation. Paul is addressing the Jewish Christian who rejects the idea of salvation for Gentiles and Paul's mission to them; this accounts for the argumentative style of vv. 14ff, and the frequent use of OT proof-texts. Paul's argument runs: Scripture says that 'everyone who calls on the name of the Lord will be saved'. But how is this possible unless they hear and believe the gospel preached to them by Christ's messengers (vv. 13–15a)? These messengers are spoken of in Scripture (v. 15b). It is true that not all Gentiles have believed; but this was predicted by Isaiah, using words which also confirm that preaching is necessary (vv. 16f).[30] But the Gentiles have heard (v. 18). Israel should have known from her own Scriptures that the Gentiles would enter her heritage while she was rejected, for both Moses and Isaiah spoke of this (vv. 19–21).

This interpretation, according to which 10:14ff is addressed to the Jewish Christian who rejects Paul's Gentile mission, seems to fit his language much better than the view that the section is concerned with the mission to the Jews. As we have seen, the link between vv. 13 and 14 favours this interpretation. The other view also finds vv. 18–21 very hard to explain. According to v. 18, 'they' have heard the gospel,[31] for, as Scripture says, it has been preached throughout the world. This fits the Gentile mission much better than the Jewish mission; the gloss, '... and therefore cannot be supposed not to have been heard by the generality of Jews' (Cranfield, II, 537f),[32] is cumbersome and unnatural. Similarly, in v. 19 Paul claims that Israel should have known, because Scripture (Moses and Isaiah) speaks of the salvation of the Gentiles and the rejection of the Jews (vv. 20f). The natural interpretation is: Israel should have known about God's intention to save the Gentiles at the expense of the Jews. The alternative view requires another unnatural gloss: 'If Gentiles, who, in relation to the knowledge of God, are, compared with Israel, but no-peoples, foolish nations, have come to know, then it certainly cannot be supposed that Israel has not known' (Cranfield, II, 539).[33] But if Paul's point is simply to prove that Israel has heard the gospel, he has made it in a very roundabout way: the Gentiles have heard it, so Israel must also have heard it. It is better to regard the subject throughout 10:14ff as the Gentile mission. Paul's purpose is to argue that the Jews should have known from their own Scriptures that salvation would be preached to the Gentiles, and that this would involve the rejection of the majority of the Jews.

Like the rest of Romans, Rom. 9:30–10:21 is not to be regarded as pure theory, divorced from the situation of the Roman Christians. In discussing 9:6–29, it was suggested that Paul's Roman Jewish Christian readers hold the view that in his covenant with the patriarchs God has committed himself irrevocably to the Jewish people, and so reject Paul's claim that God has chosen Gentiles instead of Jews as involving God in inconsistency. Paul constructs a new view of election from Scripture, based on a stern predestinarianism, to support his own view. 9:30–10:21 counters a different though related Jewish Christian objection to Paul: that his claim about the salvation of the Gentiles cannot be true because it involves setting faith in opposition to the law, the way of life of the Jewish community, again involving God in self-contradiction. Paul argues that salvation for the Gentiles apart from the law, and the Jewish failure to attain salvation because of their loyalty to the law, are not his own arbitrary ideas; for Scripture confirms them. His readers should therefore distance themselves from the Jewish community, which by its very zeal for the law has failed to attain salvation, and accept the legitimacy of the Gentile Christians, and of Paul's work in preaching to them, as true expressions of the will of God as set forth in Scripture. Jews and Greeks should therefore 'call upon the name of the Lord' (10:13) together (cf. 15:7ff).

4 The salvation of Israel and the consistency of God (Rom. 11)

Paul has so far argued that his view of God's activity (i.e. that he has rejected Jews and chosen Gentiles) is consistent with the Scriptural teaching about election and about law and faith. In Rom. 11, Paul argues that *his view of God's activity is consistent with the Scriptural teaching about the final salvation of Israel on the basis of the covenant with the patriarchs*.[34] It is ironic that Paul's arguments for the consistency of God in Rom. 9–11 are apparently themselves inconsistent; for Rom. 11 is based on precisely the definition of Israel, the chosen people who are heirs to salvation, that Rom. 9 (as well as Rom. 4) has rejected so emphatically.[35] The nature of the apparent inconsistency of Rom. 11 with Paul's teaching elsewhere must first be described in more detail, after which it will be argued that the hypothesis about the social function of Romans may be used to resolve the problem.

(i) In 11:1–10, the Jewish Christian remnant is seen as a sign that God has not rejected his people. In 11:1f, 'his people' (τὸν λαὸν αὐτοῦ) refers to the present generation of Jews, and Paul as a representative of them describes himself as 'of the seed of Abraham'. This is diametrically opposed to 9:6ff. In 9:25, λαόν μου refers to Gentile Christians: 'Those who are not my people I will call "my people".' 9:6–9 distinguishes between the natural descendants of Abraham and 'the children of the promise'; it is the latter alone who are the heirs, and it emerges in 9:24 that they are to be identified with Jewish and Gentile Christians. 9:6–29 presents a clear and coherent argument for the view that the salvation of Gentiles and the rejection of Jews was entirely consistent with God's purpose of election as revealed in Scripture. Yet in 11:1f, and indeed throughout this chapter, Paul reverts to the old view of the people of God which he had previously rejected.[36]

(ii) In 11:11–19, 28, 30, a positive salvific role is ascribed to Israel's failure to believe the gospel. In Rom. 9–10, the rejection of Jews and the salvation of Gentiles are simply set alongside one another as independent facts. But in Rom. 11, Israel's failure directly leads to the salvation of the Gentiles: 'Through their trespass salvation has come to the Gentiles' (v. 11; cf. vv. 12, 15, 17, 28, 30). Nowhere else in Paul or in the New Testament is there anything approaching this positive estimate of the value of Israel's failure to believe the gospel.[37] It was suggested in Chapter 2 that these passages give us valuable historical information: Paul and others first preached to the Gentiles as the result of encountering rejection among the Jews. This historical circumstance is given a simple and perhaps primitive theological explanation in vv. 17, 19: branches were broken off the olive tree in order that Gentiles might be grafted in instead; in other words, Israel's failure was needed in order to make room for Gentiles. But despite this historical background, the way in which Israel is in this passage virtually set alongside Christ as the bringer of salvation to the Gentiles is remarkable, and requires explanation.

(iii) The final goal of the Gentile mission is the salvation of the Jews, according to 11:11–16, 25ff. As 11:11 puts it, the purpose of the Gentile mission is that Israel should become jealous and so be saved. Paul expects this to happen to some extent within his own ministry: he preaches to the Gentiles 'in order to make my fellow-Jews jealous, and thus save some of them' (11:13f). It will happen ultimately to τὸ πλήρωμα αὐτῶν (v. 12), which will mean ζωὴ ἐκ νεκρῶν for the world (v. 15).[38] The salvation of 'all Israel' (v. 26) will take place 'by the mercy shown to you' (v. 31). The ultimate purpose of Paul's Gentile mission is thus not the salvation of Gentiles but the salvation of Jews.[39] The Gentiles become the means to an end. Nowhere else does Paul claim that he preaches to the Gentiles in order to secure the salvation of the Jews. Elsewhere, the salvation of the Gentiles, together with the Jewish remnant, is itself seen as the ultimate goal of God's purposes (cf. 4:16f, 9:24ff).

(iv) Gentiles are seen in 11:17ff as a wild olive-shoot which has been grafted into Israel. They are thus seen as proselytes: those who, unlike the Jews, have no claim on the mercy of God by virtue of their birth, but who may nevertheless be incorporated into God's people.[40] Such a view presupposes the old distinction between Jews and Gentiles which Paul has been at such pains to annul throughout the rest of Romans — for example, in 10:12, where he writes, 'There is no distinction between Jew and Greek.'

(v) The promises to the patriarchs guarantee the salvation of the Jewish people as a whole (11:28ff).[41] It is because 'as regards election they are beloved for the sake of their forefathers', and because 'the gifts and call of God are irrevocable' that Paul can be so confident that 'all Israel will be saved' (v. 26),[42] that they too will ultimately receive mercy (v. 31). In v. 16, Paul has grounded his belief in the salvation of Israel (v. 15) in the principle, 'If the root is holy, so are the branches', a probable reference to the patriarchs.[43] Although he acknowledges in vv. 17ff that some of the branches have been broken off in order to make room for the Gentiles, he expresses his hope in vv. 23f that God will graft them back in again. Admittedly, there is a note of caution in v. 23 ('if they do not persist in their unbelief'); but this is no longer evident in vv. 25ff. In Rom. 4 and 9, Paul has argued quite clearly that the promise of salvation to Abraham and to his seed applies not to the Jewish people as a whole but to the Jewish and Gentile Christians whom God has called. But in Rom. 11 the promise to the patriarchs has no direct application to the Gentiles and instead forms the basis for Paul's confidence in the salvation of the Jews.

One may perhaps summarize the problem of Rom. 11 by saying that whereas elsewhere Paul sets his view of the salvation of the Gentiles *in polemical opposition to* the Jewish theology of the covenant, in Rom. 11 he argues that his view of the salvation of the Gentiles is *compatible with* the Jewish theology of the covenant, and may be incorporated into it. The problem is often minimized by those who wish to stress Paul's continuity with Judaism at the expense of discontinuity, but it must be recognized that the clear and coherent argument of Rom. 11 is completely at variance with the equally clear and coherent argument of Rom. 9, not to mention the rest of Romans. Elsewhere in Romans, it is characteristic of Paul's arguments that while they are reasonably consistent internally, it is virtually impossible to relate them satisfactorily to one another. It is, for example, difficult to incorporate Abraham as described in Rom. 4 into the sketch of salvation-history given in 5:12ff.[44] But nowhere is this problem more acute than in Rom. 11. If one is not satisfied with the view that Paul was capable of thinking coherently only for very short periods of time, and if one rejects an artificial harmonizing exegesis, the only possible solution[45] seems to be to examine the social context and function of Romans, to see whether an explanation can be found there.

The most obvious point is that in 11:13ff Paul directly and explicitly addresses the Gentile Christians in Rome. As 14:1–15:13 indicates, the union between Jewish and Gentile Christians there will require a change of heart on both sides: 'Let not him who eats despise him who abstains, and let not him who abstains pass judgment on him who eats' (14:3). In Rom. 11:17ff, Paul emphatically opposes the tendency among Gentile Christians to despise the Jewish community, on the grounds that they (the Gentiles) are supported by the Jewish 'root' (v. 18), that the removal of certain branches because of unbelief ought to serve as a solemn warning and not as a reason for boasting (vv. 19–22), and that God has the power to graft the branches back into the tree (vv. 23f). The 'mystery' of the salvation of Israel is recounted in vv. 25ff 'lest you be wise in your own conceits' (v. 25) – here again, it is the Gentiles who are being addressed (cf. vv. 28–31). The whole chapter may be seen as an attempt to diminish the hostility of the Gentile Christians towards the Jewish Christians,[46] in order to bring the prospect of unity nearer.

This is no doubt correct, but it is insufficient as an explanation of Rom. 11. Throughout Romans, Paul shows himself to be far more concerned to persuade Jewish Christians to accept the legitimacy of his own standpoint (and thus the legitimacy of the Pauline Gentile congregation in Rome) than he is with persuading his own followers to accept the legitimacy of the Jewish congregation. Rom. 11 must therefore have some message for the Jewish Christians. This is confirmed by the fact that the question in v. 1, 'Has God rejected his people?' (or, 'Have they stumbled so as to fall?', v. 11) represents a *Jewish* Christian objection to Paul's teaching. From the Jewish Christian standpoint, Paul's proclamation of the rejection of Jews and the salvation of Gentiles means that God has acted inconsistently in rejecting his people. It also means that Paul himself has rejected his own people, and Paul shows his concern to answer this charge by claiming in vv. 11ff that the goal of his Gentile mission is the salvation of Jews. Paul is overtly addressing Gentile Christians in vv. 13ff, but his argument is surely intended to be read and noted by Jewish Christians.

What would Rom. 11 mean for the Roman Jewish Christians? Elsewhere in Romans, Paul has constantly advocated their separation from the synagogue and their union with the Gentile congregation in which the law is not observed. Does Rom. 11 advocate the same thing, or does the new theological position in Rom. 11 correspond to a different social function? Does Paul perhaps advocate here something other than sectarian separation from the Jewish community? The answer is that from the point of view of its social function, Rom. 11 is no different from the rest of Romans. The reason for this is that there is no change of mind here on the question of the law, the way of life of the Jewish community, observance or non-observance of which determined whether or not one was a member of that community. In 11:5f, Paul explicitly says that the remnant (among whom the Roman Jewish Christians would number themselves) is chosen by grace, and that works are irrelevant to this.[47] In other words, continued observance of the law, and membership of the Jewish community, is inessential to the identity of Jewish Christians, who should rather regard themselves as chosen by grace just as the Gentiles are.[48] Although in vv. 17ff, Paul seems to speak of the Gentile Christians as proselytes who have been incorporated into Israel, there is never the slightest suggestion that they should submit themselves to the law and so join the Jewish community. The point is that, as Gentile Christians who do not observe the law, they are members of 'Israel' despite their empirical separation from the Jewish community; it is the Jewish community, and not the Gentile Christians, who have separated themselves from 'Israel' through their unbelief.

For all its concessions to Jewish Christian theology, Rom. 11 makes no concessions at all on the level of social consequences. Why then does Paul make the remarkable concessions to Jewish Christian theology which have been noted above? The answer seems to lie in Paul's strategy in writing Romans. Elsewhere, his plea for Jewish Christian separation from the synagogue and union with Gentile Christians has involved a great deal of opposition to Jewish and Jewish Christian claims. This has been the case notably with the law, whose function in the Jewish outlook is opposed again and again in the course of the epistle. But it has also been the case in Paul's treatment of election; Rom. 4 and 9 in particular require of Jewish Christians a complete abandonment of the old notion of election as applying to the Jewish community as a whole. In other words, Paul is asking them to make a considerable sacrifice. Belief in divine election, observance of the law, and a basic loyalty to the Jewish community are fundamental elements in their self-understanding which their Christian commitment has not significantly altered. Paul has called for a more-or-less complete abandonment of this old self-understanding, a step which will have painful and disorientating social consequences.

In Rom. 11, Paul adopts a different strategy in calling for the same social reorientation. Instead of opposing the Jewish view of election with his own view, he argues here that *the Jewish view of election is to a large extent compatible with his own view of the failure of Israel and the salvation of the Gentiles*. He seeks to make his own view more attractive and more persuasive by presenting it as far as possible in the context of Jewish Christian beliefs and hopes. The Jewish Christians probably already see themselves as a faithful remnant in the midst of an unbelieving Israel, and they long for the conversion of the rest of Israel. From this standpoint, Paul's Gentile mission would appear irrelevant and dangerous. But Paul argues that the Gentile mission is precisely the means by which God will eventually save all Israel. Its purpose in the present is 'to make my fellow-Jews jealous, and thus save some of them' (v. 14), and ultimately 'that by the mercy shown to you they also may receive mercy' (v. 31). Paul thus justifies his view of the Gentiles by placing it in the context of the hopes and beliefs already held by his Jewish Christian readers. He accepts that the Jewish community is the elect people of God, in distinction from the Gentiles, but adds that God has temporarily set aside many of them in order to make room for Gentiles; this, however, will lead ultimately to the salvation of all Israel.[49] This ingenious interweaving of Jewish Christian and Pauline themes is intended to make separation from the synagogue and union with the Gentile congregation easier to accept.[50] The Jewish Christians are not to regard this social reorientation as apostasy, for these Gentiles are an essential part of the purpose of God which will eventually culminate in the salvation of all Israel.[51] Thus, Paul's view of God's activity of rejecting Jews and calling Gentiles is consistent with the Scriptural promise of the final salvation of Israel.

This completes our discussion of the social context and function of Romans. It has not been possible to show that Romans consists of a single consistent and rationally coherent argument; there are tensions and contradictions between different parts of it, of which the incompatibility of Rom. 9 and 11 is the most obvious. Nevertheless, it has been argued that Romans is a highly coherent piece of writing when considered from the standpoint of its social function. Virtually every part of it (with the exception of the general paraenesis of Rom. 12–13) contributes in some way or other to Paul's attempt to persuade the Jewish Christian congregation in Rome to separate themselves from the Jewish community, to accept the legitimacy of the Pauline Gentile congregation in which the law is not observed, and to unite with it for worship. Paul argues for this from a number of points of view; he anticipates and answers a wide range of objections, and corrects misunderstandings. The three main parts of the argument of Rom. 1–11 (Rom. 1–4; 5–8; 9–11) all fulfil in varying ways this same social function. There is no longer any real problem about the relationship between Rom. 5–8 and 1–4, or about the place of Rom. 9–11 within the whole, for every part of the argument has as its goal the same social reorientation. The fact that Romans apparently contains so much more theoretical discussion than the rest of Paul's letters should not blind us to its thoroughly practical intention. The 'theory' is necessary not because Paul wishes here to expound his gospel in a universally applicable way without regard for concrete circumstances, but because a great deal of theoretical argument will be necessary if the Roman Jewish Christians are to be persuaded to separate themselves from the Jewish community and unite with the Gentiles in a single 'Pauline' congregation in Rome.

Excursus: the collection

The present discussion has repeatedly stressed Paul's emphasis on the need for a radical separation from the Jewish community and from its way of life – an emphasis which led Paul into opposition to the Jerusalem church, which believed that the church's place was still as a reform-movement within the Jewish community. In Rom. 15:25ff, however, Paul speaks of the collection which he is organizing among his Gentile congregations for the benefit of 'the poor among the saints at Jerusalem' (v. 26), for which a rationale is given in v. 27: 'They were pleased to do it, and indeed they are in debt to them, for if the Gentiles have come to share in their spiritual blessings, they ought also to be of service to them in material blessings.' Here, apparently, Paul expresses a deep concern for the unity of the church and a strong sense of solidarity with the Jerusalem Christians. How is this to be reconciled with the view presented here, that there was a fundamental difference of opinion between them about the nature of the church? Does the collection show Paul in a new light, as an ecumenist who, while recognizing the depth of past disagreements, is concerned above all for the unity of the church? To answer these questions, a brief discussion of Paul's most important statements on the collection is necessary.[52]

In Gal. 2:10, Paul recounts the request of the 'pillars' in Jerusalem: 'Only they would have us remember the poor, which very thing I was eager to do.'[53] Despite Paul's initial enthusiasm, this project seems to have fallen into abeyance as a result of the break with the churches of Jerusalem and Antioch described in Gal. 2:11ff, for there is in Galatians no reference to a collection in progress among the Galatian churches.[54] However, in 1 Cor. 16:1 Paul mentions that he has just instituted a collection in Galatia, probably on his second visit to Galatia mentioned in Acts 18:23. (The problems of chronology here were briefly discussed in Chapter 3, where it was argued that the crisis in Galatia preceded the institution of the collection there.) This visit took place fairly shortly after the crisis in Galatia to which Galatians was a response, and this raises the question: Why should Paul have abandoned the hostility towards the Jerusalem church expressed in the letter, in order to resurrect the plan of a collection for that church? There seem to be two possible answers.[55] The first takes a somewhat idealistic view of the apostle: Paul believed that Christians should love one another and that in Christ there is neither Jew nor Greek, and he therefore regarded the collection as a means of healing the church's divisions.[56] This would represent a change of heart since writing Galatians, a conversion from sectarianism to ecumenism. The second possibility is that after his Galatian experience Paul was seriously concerned about the vulnerability of his Gentile congregations to infiltration by the emissaries of Jerusalem, and saw the collection as a means of convincing the Jerusalem church of the legitimacy of the law-free congregations he had founded, so that they would stop trying to undermine them. The advantage of this view is that it is of a piece with Paul's concern in Galatians to preserve his congregations from Judaizing influence. It can also accommodate the fact that (according to the chronology worked out in Chapter 4) Paul expressed his deep anxiety about the possibility of Jewish Christian missionaries infiltrating the Philippian church (Phil. 3) within a few months of his efforts to bring the collection to a successful conclusion (2 Cor. 8–9). Paul was seeking to preserve his congregations in their separation from the synagogue in two different ways: by warnings to his congregations, and by trying by means of the collection to secure Jerusalem's recognition of their legitimacy.

Two passages seem to confirm this interpretation: the first (Rom. 15:31) shows what Paul *fears* may be the outcome of the collection, and the second (2 Cor. 9:12–14) shows what he *hopes* will be its outcome. In Rom. 15:31, Paul requests the prayers of the Romans 'that I may be delivered from the unbelievers in Judaea, and that my service for Jerusalem may be acceptable to the saints'. This verse indicates that relations between Paul and his Gentile congregations on the one hand and the Jerusalem church on the other were still very bad:[57] unless God intervenes in answer to prayer, there is every possibility that the Jerusalem church will refuse to accept the collection,[58] thus signalling their continued refusal to acknowledge the legitimacy of the Pauline Gentile churches, and (presumably) their intention of continuing Judaizing activity within them, as in Antioch and Galatia. Conversely, acceptance of the collection will signify Jerusalem's acknowledgment of the Gentile churches' legitimacy.

The latter point is made explicitly in 2 Cor. 9:12–14, which in Barrett's translation reads as follows:

> For the execution of this act of public service not only supplies the wants of the saints, but also overflows in many thanksgivings to God; they glorify God for the obedience shown in your confession of faith in the Gospel of Christ, proved as it is by this service, and for the integrity of your fellowship with them and with all; and in their prayer for you they long for you on account of the surpassing grace of God bestowed upon you.

Whereas Rom. 15:31 implies the present hostility of the Jerusalem church to the Pauline Gentile congregations, 2 Cor. 9:12–14 shows the change in their attitude which Paul hopes the collection will accomplish: hostility is to give way to recognition of 'the surpassing grace of God bestowed upon you'.[59] Paul's work in the East will thus be safe from the activity of Judaizers, and he will be able to travel to Spain (Rom. 15:28) without anxieties on that score. The stress in Rom. 15:27 on the indebtedness of Gentiles to Jerusalem is therefore not to be understood as an entirely guileless expression of Paul's real feelings,[60] but as a continuation of the strategy of Rom. 11 (cf. also 15:8f): Paul attempts to secure recognition for his congregations by setting his own position in the context of Jewish Christian beliefs (in this case, belief in the supremacy of the Jerusalem church). Paul's collection should therefore not be interpreted idealistically as the first great ecumenical gesture; it was in fact motivated by an intense anxiety about the security of his Gentile congregations.

This means that the collection was intended to accomplish in Jerusalem exactly what the letter to the Romans was intended to accomplish in Rome: recognition by Jewish Christians who observed the law of the legitimacy of Pauline Gentile Christians who did not.

10

CONCLUSION

The present work has attempted to explain Paul's view of Judaism, the law and the Gentiles in a number of comparatively unfamiliar ways. The argument has inevitably been somewhat complicated, and it may therefore be worthwhile in conclusion to summarize its main emphases.

(i) The first aim has been *to uncover the social reality underlying Paul's statements about Judaism, the law and the Gentiles.* On the basis of various Pauline texts, it was possible to reconstruct the process by which Paul arrived at his conviction that Gentiles could be saved apart from the law. He began his Christian career as a missionary to the Jews, but met with so little success that he became convinced that they were subject to divine hardening, and that he was called to preach to Gentiles instead. Full submission to the Jewish law was not required of Gentiles, in order to make conversion more attractive for them. The establishing of mainly Gentile congregations which did not observe the law meant separation from the Jewish community.

Thus what had started as a reform-movement within Judaism became a sect outside it because of the opposition it encountered from the rest of the Jewish community. This sociological process is also exemplified by the Qumran and Johannine communities. However, the problem for Paul was that the church in Jerusalem did not accept his solution to the problem of Jewish unbelief, maintaining that the church should continue to be a reform-movement within the Jewish community, loyal to its traditions. The question which Paul debated with Jewish Christians in Antioch, Galatia and Rome was therefore: Should the church continue as a reform-movement, or should it become a sect according to the Pauline model? Should it remain loyal to the Jewish community, or should it separate itself from that community?

Thus the starting-point for interpreting Paul's statements about Judaism, the law and the Gentiles must be sociological rather than theological. If one presupposes that the law was a problem for Paul primarily for theological and existential reasons, one will misunderstand what he has to say on the subject.

(ii) Paul's theoretical discussions of such themes as the law and works, grace and faith, election and promise, are thus to be regarded as *an attempt to legitimate the social reality of sectarian Gentile Christian communities in which the law was not observed*. Paul sought to construct a theoretical rationale for separation. Any sectarian group must carefully define its relationship to the religious community from which it has separated itself, and this self-definition tends to take three forms: denunciation, antithesis and reinterpretation. Members of the parent religious community are denounced for moral, ritual or theological faults. Antitheses (e.g. between light and darkness, truth and error) express the absolute nature of the gulf which the sect perceives between itself and the community as a whole. Through reinterpretation, religious traditions are reapplied to the sect itself and denied to the wider community. These features are prominent in the ideologies of the Qumran and Johannine communities; and they are also prominent in Paul, especially in Galatians, Phil. 3 and Romans. It is therefore vitally important for the interpreter to bear in mind the social function of what Paul is saying.

(iii) The application of this principle has important results in actual exegesis. This is the case above all with Romans, which has for so long been regarded as the one letter in which Paul is not addressing himself to concrete circumstances in the church to which he is writing, but expounding his gospel in a universally valid way. Exegesis of Rom. 14–16 suggested that there were in Rome two main Christian groups: the Jewish Christians, who constituted the remnant of the original Roman Christian congregation, and Pauline Gentile Christians. Paul's aim was to persuade the Jewish Christians to recognize the legitimacy of the Gentile congregation and to join with it in worship, even though this would inevitably mean a final separation from the synagogue. This interpretation of Rom. 14–16 was then applied systematically to the argument of Rom. 1–11, and it was found that again and again the hypothesis about the social situation in the Roman church and Paul's purpose in writing shed light on the text.

(iv) Attention to the social context and function of Paul's arguments produces an interpretation of Paul in some respects very different from that which stems from the Lutheran tradition. For example, the fundamental antithesis between faith and works is not to be understood as a primarily theological contrast between receiving salvation as a free gift and earning it by one's own efforts, but as a sociological contrast between two different ways of life: 'faith', the way of life practised in the Pauline congregations, marked by the abandonment of certain of the norms and beliefs of the surrounding society, and the adoption of new norms and beliefs; and 'works', the way of life of the Jewish community, which sought to live in conformity with the law of Moses. The two are incompatible not because one stresses grace and the other achievement, but because the law is not observed in the Pauline congregations. If one compares the relationship between divine grace and human obedience in the two communities, the contrast is by no means as absolute as has generally been supposed. Paul acknowledges repeatedly that the Judaism he opposes has its own view of grace (identified with election and the covenant), to which 'works of the law' is the Jew's response. Paul's own soteriology involves a more dynamic view of grace, since the pattern of religion he advocates is conversionist rather than traditional; but he indicates on numerous occasions in many different ways that for him too human obedience as a response to divine grace is a necessary condition of salvation. It is therefore completely wrong to regard the phrase *sola gratia* as the key to Paul's theology; Paul does not believe that salvation is by grace alone. The view that he does so springs from a failure to recognise that the faith–works contrast is primarily sociological rather than theological in meaning. The faith–works contrast is only absolute as a contrast between the incompatible ways of life practised by two different religious communities.

This whole argument represents a plea for the abandonment of Lutheran presuppositions in interpreting Paul. In other areas of New Testament study, historical criticism has long attained the confidence and maturity to free itself from the constraints of ecclesiastical tradition; but in its consideration of Paul's attitude towards Judaism, it has with a few notable exceptions signally failed to do so. F.C. Baur's challenge to interpreters to rid themselves of presuppositions derived from the Reformation was quickly forgotten. The representatives of the 'dialectical theology' which has influenced Pauline studies so deeply for nearly seventy years mistakenly felt that they could combine some of Baur's historical results with an emphatic restatement in contemporary terms of Luther's view of Paul's theology. In an age in which it was becoming increasingly difficult to talk meaningfully about God, it was believed that Paul's gospel would address us and challenge us as it had addressed and challenged

Luther's contemporaries; this outweighed the need for careful investigation of the historical and sociological context of Paul's teaching about justification, law and faith. But the real Paul is not the stranger of Protestant mythology, who was cast into the wilderness by a legalistic early Catholic church, and who returns to the church to preach his gospel anew in times of crisis. He is a stranger only in so far as his activity and teaching belong to a unique and unrepeatable historical situation, in which the church was confronted for the first and only time in its history with the possibilities either of remaining within the Jewish community, or of separation from that community. The identification of the historical Paul with the Lutheran Paul is the result of simplistic and unhistorical thinking. Whatever its theological merits, the Reformation tradition has no right to regard itself as the guardian of authentic Pauline teaching, since its theological concerns have hindered rather than helped a correct understanding of the apostle.

This negative estimate of the Reformation tradition's view of Paul is not intended to imply that, as a general principle, theological concerns are incompatible with the historical study of the New Testament. In practice, it can often be demonstrated that theological concerns *have* led to misunderstanding of the New Testament; but that is not a sufficient reason for a reductionist denial of the legitimacy of all such concerns in New Testament study, since in other cases it is at least arguable that they have led to levels of insight denied to more historically-minded scholarship. The demand for a complete separation between New Testament studies and theology is both narrow-minded and question-begging, since it assumes *a priori* that the question as to the permanent value of the various strands of the New Testament proclamation is not even worth asking. But that is an intolerable position to adopt, not least because of the simple fact that large numbers of people *are* still asking that question.

But to admit the legitimacy of the theological question is not to commit oneself to giving it a positive answer in every case. When the early church accepted the Pauline letters as canonical, it asserted its belief in their permanent value as a normative guide to faith and conduct. That fundamental decision has been maintained by many modern New Testament scholars, who have held that Paul's theology transcends its original historical setting and is still of crucial significance for the modern understanding of God. But if the interpretation of Paul offered here is accepted, it is important to face the question: Can a Paul who devotes his energies to the creation and maintaining of sectarian groups hostile to all non-members, and especially to the Jewish community from which in fact they derived, still be seen as the bearer of a message with profound universal significance? Facing this question will mean that the permanent, normative value of Paul's theology will not simply be *assumed*, as is often the case at present. It must instead be *discussed* – and with genuine arguments, not with mere rhetorical appeals to the authority of the canon, the Reformers, or an *a priori* Christology. Should Paul's thought still be a major source of inspiration for contemporary theological discussion? Or should it be rejected as a cul-de-sac, and should one seek inspiration elsewhere?

NOTES

1. Paul, the Reformation and modern scholarship

1 According to Hübner, in Pauline studies today just as in the sixteenth century, the great question is: 'Is Luther right?' ('Proprium', 445).

2 Ebeling notes that 'in the theology of the Reformers the problems all concentrate themselves so much on the concept of the law that the whole of theology ... stands or falls with it' ('Reflexions', 254).

3 This central aspect of Luther's thought is admirably summarized by the title of an article on justification by G. O. Forde: 'The Exodus from Virtue to Grace'.

4 On Luther's view of the law, see Althaus, *Martin Luther*, and Ebeling, *Luther*.

5 A more detailed survey of dialectical theology's approach to Paul would have to take account of Barth's *Römerbrief*, whose ethos underlies much of the modern Lutheran work on Paul.

6 Because Bultmann so emphatically dissociates himself from Luther at this point, Stendahl is wrong in assuming that Bultmann shares Luther's obsession with guilt and conscience ('Introspective Conscience', 207), as Hübner has pointed out ('Proprium', 446).

7 Althaus writes on Luther's view of sin: 'Man's sin is twofold. First, he does not fulfil the Commandments but transgresses them. And second, he sins against the First Commandment when he attempts to fulfil the Commandments in order to win salvation, since he thereby sins against God as the only God and Creator who alone gives righteousness to men. Man is guilty in relation to God not only when he does not care but also when he is very serious about morality' (*Martin Luther*, 150).

8 This was the case with the autobiographical interpretation, which at one time was widely held; see for example Zahn, *Römer*, 338ff.

9 As Conzelmann points out, the most striking characteristic of Bultmann's theology is the harmony between the exegetical and theological work ('Rechtfertigungslehre', 393). But he begs the question by attributing this harmony to the agreement between Bultmann's theological concerns and those of his subject-matter.

10 Wiles criticizes this view from the standpoint of the patristic interpretation of Paul (*Divine Apostle*, 138f).

11 A similar view of Paul is asserted by Bornkamm, *Paul*, xxvii, and Conzelmann, *Outline*, 238n.

12 Morgan, 'Paulinism', 332.
13 Cf. Ridderbos, *Paul*, 138f. Sanders not unjustly describes Ridderbos' book as 'remarkable for its lack of attention to occasion and context' (*Jewish People*, 51, n. 18).
14 *Paulus und Luther*, 49.
15 'Was heisst bei Paulus', 94.
16 On Baur as a New Testament scholar, see Schweitzer, *Paul and his Interpreters*, 12ff, Kümmel, *The New Testament*, 127ff, Neill, *Interpretation*, 19ff. Neill's discussion is marred by his portrayal of Baur as an anti-Christian extremist whose work from 1833 onwards 'was gravely vitiated by an irrelevant and unproven presupposition' (21), derived from his Hegelianism. Thus, his historical work may be safely dismissed: 'Incautious assumptions at the start lead him into error on every principal point of New Testament criticism' (23), with the result that 'at very few points has investigation proved the rightness of Baur's solutions' (27). It was the work of J. B. Lightfoot to oppose 'the threat presented to the Christian cause by the school of Tübingen' (31); fortunately he was 'less hampered by presuppositions than the representatives of the German schools' (32). But this interpretation of Baur is misleading. While no-one doubts that he was wrong on a large number of historical points, his historical and critical approach to the study of Paul has been of incalculable significance for the study of the New Testament.
17 Wilson cites the comment of Barrett: 'The word religion to me is like a red rag to a bull. It is religion which Paul, as I understand him, energetically attacks' ('Religion', 339). Morgan writes: 'In "dialectical theology", "religion" becomes a bogey word, together with "idealism", "mysticism", "metaphysics", and even "experience"' ('Paulinism', 326). One might add other words to this list: e.g. 'psychological' (or 'psychologizing'), 'objectifying', 'historicizing', 'morality', 'theory', 'salvation history' (except in Käsemann), and 'possession'.
18 Lutheran scholars occasionally admit that this extension of Paul's meaning is problematic (cf. Ebeling, 'Reflexions', 261, Käsemann, *Romans*, 282).
19 Davies' work is part of a much wider movement to re-examine the relationship between Judaism and Christianity, and to replace the old polemical positions with genuine understanding. See C. Klein, *Anti-Judaism*, for a good statement of the problem.
20 G. Klein claims that a phenomenological view of Jewish observance of the law cannot verify or cast doubt on Paul's critique, since it is only Christ who reveals the true nature of Judaism; otherwise the Lutheran standpoint is defenceless ('Präliminarien', 241). But if Paul's critique of Judaism bears no relation to the historical evidence about the nature of first-century Judaism, then it should be rejected as arbitrary.
21 The alternative would be that Paul misunderstood Judaism (so Montefiore, *Judaism and St. Paul*, 12ff, Schoeps, *Paul*, 196ff).
22 Cf. Dunn, 'New Perspective', 119: 'What Jewish scholars rejected

as *Paul's* misunderstanding of Judaism is *itself* a misunderstanding of Paul, based on the standard Protestant (mis)reading of Paul through Reformation spectacles.'

23 See Bibliography for details.

24 Cf. Jewett, 'Major Impulses', who states that the ecumenical dialogue is the background to the work of Stendahl, Minear, Dahl and Wilckens, whereas the dialogue with Judaism is important for Davies and Sanders.

25 This model is applied to Luke–Acts by Esler, 'Community', 103ff (page references to this work are to the doctoral thesis, as yet unpublished). Esler notes that despite the sociological interest in the development of 'sects' into 'churches' (H. R. Niebuhr), little work has yet been done on the development of reform-movements into sects.

26 According to Esler, 'Community', 20, 'Legitimation is the collection of ways in which a social institution is explained and justified to its members'.

27 Holmberg has some excellent comments on the change of perspective required in Pauline research (*Paul*, 205). Discussing 'the fallacy of idealism', he writes: 'Idealism in historical research can be roughly described as the view that the determining factors of the historical process are ideas and nothing else, and that all developments, conflicts and influences are at bottom developments of, and conflicts and influences between ideas.' Unconscious idealism may be traced in the work of Bultmann, Käsemann and others. Great care is taken over historical research, 'but the methodologically fateful step comes with the next stage of the work, where the historical phenomena are often interpreted as being directly formed by underlying theological structures'. Paul's theology is in fact 'a secondary reaction' to 'primary, concrete phenomena in the social world'.

28 Kee rightly protests against the view that New Testament theological affirmations arose from 'a process of intellectual debate – the first-century equivalent of a present-day theological seminar!' (*Community*, 9).

29 Cf. Theissen, 'Sociological Interpretation', 195.

30 Dahl rightly criticizes 'the common but simplistic notion of a contrast between Christian universalism and Jewish particularism'. He writes: 'Jewish monotheism at the time of Paul was universalistic in its own way, and Christian monotheism remained exclusive' ('One God', 191; cf. Sanders, *Jewish People*, 160).

31 For this distinction, cf. Elliott, *Home*, 267ff.

32 Cf. Meeks, *Urban Christians*, 42.

2. The origins of Paul's view of the law

1 Hengel rightly states: 'The *Sitz im Leben* of Paul's theology is the mission of the Apostle to the Gentiles' ('Ursprünge', 37).

2 Haenchen, 359f. Haenchen's whole approach to Acts is attacked by Gasque, *Acts*, 235ff. His commentary is dismissed as 'a historical

phenomenon belonging to one era of the history of exegesis' (243f); it builds on the 'unquestioned assumptions' of older critical orthodoxy, especially *Tendenzkritik*, and also incorporates modern existentialism (250). By contrast, those who accept the historicity of Acts are primarily historians rather than theologians (251). Haenchen and those who think like him exemplify 'the malaise of contemporary Lucan research' (303). In opposition to this polemic against Haenchen, one may note first that those who express very conservative views on N.T. critical questions are not as free of theological preconceptions as they would have us believe; and secondly, that one of the achievements of the dialectical theology represented by Haenchen is that it has given scholars the freedom to discuss historical problems in a thoroughly critical manner. For a more reasoned account of different attitudes towards the historicity of Acts, cf. Mattill, 'Value of Acts'.

3 Its historicity is defended by Marshall, 181ff.

4 Cf. Haenchen, 360f, Esler, 'Community', 143.

5 Hahn agrees with Dibelius that it is possible to recover an earlier narrative underlying Acts 10 (*Mission*, 52). This is denied by Haenchen, 360ff.

6 According to Wilson, Luke justifies the salvation of the Gentiles for the pragmatic reason that they are just as capable of piety as Jews (*Gentile Mission*, 245).

7 Walaskay plausibly argues that Luke's political aim is not so much to commend the church to the Roman authorities (the traditional view) as to commend the Empire to the church (*Rome, passim*). Thus, the point of the concluding chapters of Acts is that 'divine necessity brings Paul and the gospel to Rome under the aegis of Roman law' (58). Julius's action on behalf of Paul in 27:42ff shows that 'the gospel was rescued by Rome' (62).

8 Haenchen, 362.

9 So Wilson, *Gentile Mission*, 174.

10 On the concern of these passages with apostolic legitimacy, see Käsemann, 'Disciples', 143ff.

11 On the significance of anti-Pauline tendencies for the purpose of Acts, see Jervell, *People of God*, 146f, 153f, Wilson, *Law*, 106ff.

12 Cf. Haenchen, 362f.

13 Bultmann, *Theology*, I, 56, Haenchen, 266ff, Hengel, 'Jesus und Paulus', 176.

14 Cf. Bultmann, *Theology*, I, 56, Bornkamm, *Paul*, 13f.

15 A similar account of the Hellenists is given by Simon, *St Stephen*, 5ff, and Wilson, *Gentile Mission*, 142ff.

16 'Jesus und Paulus', 186. The historicity of Stephen's speech is asserted by Simon, *St Stephen*, 39f, and Scharlemann, *Stephen*, 45ff. O'Neill rightly opposes commentators who 'have hoped to discover an esoteric theology in the seemingly harmless details of O.T. history' (*Acts*, 79). Haenchen offers a plausible analysis differentiating an independent sermon of unknown origin from Lucan additions (288f). For a survey of views on Stephen's speech, see Richard, *Acts 6:1–8:4*, 13ff.

17 The historicity of the charge is asserted by Hengel, 'Ursprünge', 26, and Schmithals, *Paul and James*, 27, but denied by Haenchen, 274.

18 Stanton, 'Stephen', 347, rightly emphasizes that Luke intends 6:11, 13f as the accusations of *false* witnesses.

19 Haenchen, 274.

20 There seems little evidence that 'Stephen and the Hellenists must have challenged orthodox Judaism on a sensitive and fundamental point' (Wilson, *Gentile Mission*, 146).

21 On this, see O'Neill, *Acts*, 68f, Wilson, *Gentile Mission*, 239f.

22 Cf. Schmithals, *Paul and James*, 31ff. However, Schmithals argues that the Hellenists originated in or near Antioch, and that some of them moved to Jerusalem to await the Parousia (30).

23 Knox, *Chapters*, 36, Bornkamm, *Paul*, 15, Haenchen, 297; in opposition to this, Hengel, *Acts*, 74.

24 Haenchen, 297.

25 Brandon, *Fall*, 91ff, Haenchen, 91f; against this, Bruce, 'Galatian Problems. 1', 297.

26 There has been a good deal of speculation about the later influence of the Hellenists. Different scholars have suggested links between the Hellenists and Paul's opponents in 2 Corinthians (Friedrich, 'Gegner'), the Johannine community (Cullmann, *Johannine Circle*, 87), Hebrews (W. Manson, *Hebrews*, 36), the Epistle of Barnabas (Barnard, 'St Stephen', 38ff), and the Pseudo-Clementine literature (Schoeps, *Judenchristentum*, 236ff). Such speculations contradict each other and are of little value. Cf. the brief survey by Stanton, 'Stephen', 345f.

27 Saul, introduced in 7:58, was from Tarsus in Cilicia (21:39, 22:3, cf. 9:11,30, 11:25), and is thus probably regarded by Luke as a member of the synagogue for Diaspora Jews which opposed Stephen (6:9ff). If the latter are identified with the Hellenists of 9:29, then the point is that Paul is disputing with his own former associates.

28 Cadbury, *Beginnings*, Part I, Vol. V, 59–74; rejected by Hengel, 'Jesus und Paulus', 161ff, and by most other scholars.

29 Schmithals, *Paul and James*, 26.

30 Hengel, 'Jesus und Paulus', 166ff.

31 Haenchen, 266f.

32 Cf. Simon, *St Stephen*, 4f.

33 The sudden reference to Hebrews and Hellenists in Acts 6:1 is thus not a sign that a new source is being used (against Simon, *St Stephen*, 4, Wilson, *Gentile Mission*, 129).

34 Thus, even Paul is in Acts sent to preach to the Jews first and to the Gentiles second, according to 9:15; 22:15; 26:19ff (so Schmithals, *Paul and James*, 57).

35 Hengel has to resort to guesswork at this point: 'It is very probable that Philip and other "Hellenists" in this area gradually and step by step went over to a mission to the Gentiles which did not involve the law: in the first instance this "freedom from the law" will have been a matter of ignoring the requirement for circumcision and the demands of the ritual law' (*Acts*, 79f).

36 Räisänen gives seven possible explanations for the origin of Paul's view of the law (*Paul*, 229ff): 1. Paul's experience under the law. 2. Application of a current Jewish idea. 3. Influence of OT prophecy. 4. Influence of Jesus traditions. 5. Meditation on Dt. 21:23. 6. Influence of Hellenists. 7. Missionary experience and conflict with Judaizers.

37 Cf. Sanders, *Jewish People*, 187f.

38 2 Cor. 11:24 thus probably does not mean that Paul 'kept attending the synagogue' (Sanders, *Jewish People*, 192).

39 This view is rightly criticized by Schmithals, *Paul and James*, 57, and Sanders, *Jewish People*, 185f.

40 This is not one of the five possible interpretations of the passage listed by Sanders, *Jewish People*, 188, but if one is prepared to question the dogma that the call to preach to the Gentiles was an integral part of Paul's conversion experience, it is much the most plausible view. 1 Cor. 9:20f is usually understood in terms of Paul's 'flexibility' (so Bornkamm, 'Missionary Stance', 197).

41 1 Cor. 9:20 and 2 Cor. 11:24 should therefore not be used as proof-texts for the view that Paul continued to preach to the Jews (against Wilson, *Gentile Mission*, 250).

42 Haenchen rightly remarks that Paul evidently made no great claims for himself on this first visit ('Source Material', 269).

43 Lüdemann argues that the fourteen years of Gal. 2:1 date from the journey to Syria and Cilicia mentioned in 1:21; ἔπειτα in 2:1 refers back to ἔπειτα in 1:21 (*Paul*, 63).

44 Against Schmithals, *Paul and James*, 39f, who thinks that Gal. 1:23f proves that the Judaean churches approved of Paul's law-free gospel to the Gentiles.

45 Borgen, 'Paul Preaches Circumcision', 44, and Tyson, 'Paul's Opponents', 249, rightly link 5:11 to 1:10.

46 Gal. 5:11 is therefore not a reference to Paul's supposed pre-Christian activity as a missionary for Judaism (against Bultmann, 'Paul', 113, Bornkamm, *Paul*, 12).

47 J. T. Sanders rightly argues against the view that Gal. 1–2 is entirely trustworthy historically ('Autobiographical Statements', 336). He points to the contradiction between Gal. 1:11f and 1 Cor. 15:1ff (337ff).

48 Against Munck, *Paul*, 11ff, Stendahl, *Jews and Gentiles*, 7ff, Hahn, *Mission*, 97, Lüdemann, *Paul*, 32f. Hengel allows for development in Paul's understanding of himself as apostle to the Gentiles ('Ursprünge', 21), but he too thinks that Gal. 1:15f and Phil. 3:4ff prove that a law-free gospel was integral to Paul's conversion experience (22). The alternative view is taken by Oepke, *Galater*, 33, and Davies, 'Apostolic Age', 874.

49 Kim, *Origin, passim*, Bultmann, *Theology*, I, 187f, Stuhlmacher, 'Ende des Gesetzes', 30f, Wilckens, 'Bekehrung', 15.

50 Cranfield, following Barth, thinks that it is the Jews' crucifixion of Jesus which leads to the salvation of the Gentiles (*Romans*, II, 556). But (with the dubious exception of the possibly-inauthentic 1 Thes. 2:15) Paul does not elsewhere ascribe the death of Jesus to the Jews.

51 Theissen writes: 'Sooner or later relativizing the Law, which began within the Jesus movement, was bound to relativize the distinction between Gentile and Jew' ('Legitimation', 35). But the evidence is rather of a sharp break with tradition than of a natural and inevitable development.

52 Against Lüdemann, *Paul*, 74, who thinks that only Barnabas was connected with Antioch.

53 It is an exaggeration to say that 'Paul must have been only one of many preachers to the Gentiles' (Lake, *Beginnings*, Part I, Vol. I, 313), if this means that many others shared his rejection of the law.

54 Against Schlier, *Römer*, 328, and others who explain these passages in Rom. 11 by reference to Acts.

55 The Acts view is rejected as unhistorical by Schmithals, *Paul and James*, 53ff, Sanders, *Jewish People*, 179ff, and Meeks, *Urban Christians*, 26, but accepted by M. Barth, *People of God*, 20, Bornkamm, 'Missionary Stance', 200, Munck, *Paul*, 119f. Sanders rightly points out the inconsistency of those scholars 'who would not consider Acts as a source for Paul's thought or for his activity in other respects', but who 'nevertheless regard Acts as reliable for helping to establish Paul's missionary practice' (*Jewish People*, 181).

56 Jervell comments that with regard to the Jewish law Luke has 'the most conservative outlook within the New Testament' (*People of God*, 141). There are at least four possible explanations for the portrayal of Paul in Acts as a law-abiding Jew. 1. According to Jervell, the law is still authoritative for Luke (*People of God*, 144f). 2. Wilson argues that for Luke the law is merely 'the *ethos* of a particular *ethnos*' (*Law*, 103), and that observance of the law 'was an issue of no immediate concern to him or to the communities for whom he wrote' (105). Thus, Luke is concerned with defending Paul against those who reject him, but not with the law *per se* (108f). 3. If Luke–Acts was written in opposition to the Gnostics (so Talbert, *Gnostics, passim*), then the portrayal of Paul may be intended to correct Gnostic misunderstandings of his statements about the law (cf. 2 Pet. 3:15f). 4. Walaskay understands part of the purpose of Acts as a defence of the Empire to the church (*Rome, passim*). If this is correct, then Luke's aim in portraying Paul as a faithful adherent of the Jewish law may be to present him as a model citizen. Throughout Acts 21–6, it is assumed that infringement of the Jewish law is at the same time a crime against Caesar. These four possibilities are not all mutually exclusive, and other views are equally possible.

57 Dunn argues that it was common for less strict Jews to eat with Gentiles, and concludes that at Antioch the Gentiles already observed the basic food-laws, but that the 'men from James' demanded a higher level of ritual purity ('Incident', 23ff). But Esler denies that Jews normally ate with Gentiles, and cites numerous pagan testimonies to this effect ('Community', 122ff). Houlden finds it hard to imagine Paul's doctrine of justification by faith 'ever accommodating a view which expected a partial obedience to the Law from Gentiles who entered the circle of God's people' ('Response', 59).

58 Dunn argues that ἐθνικῶς does not exclude limited observance ('Incident', 25). But Catchpole, 'Apostolic Decree', 440, thinks that Peter had abandoned the law.

59 Barrett comments on 1 Cor. 10:25, 'Paul is nowhere more un-Jewish than in this μηδὲν ἀνακρίνοντες' ('Things Sacrified', 49).

60 That Paul himself abandoned the practice of the Jewish law is put beyond doubt by the passages mentioned above and by 1 Cor. 9:21 (so Räisänen, *Paul*, 73ff). The frequently expressed opinion to the contrary (Davies, *Paul*, 69, 74, Dibelius, *Paul*, 38, Ben-Chorin, *Paulus*, 10f) is based on the evidence of Acts, which in the light of Paul's letters cannot be reliable here (so Vielhauer, 'Paulinism', 38ff).

61 Goppelt writes: 'Christians [at Antioch] had detached themselves from the Law for a reason just as obscure as that which had caused the Jewish believers in Jerusalem to continue to observe it'. Why it should be thought strange that Jewish Christians continued to observe the Law is incomprehensible.

62 This possibility is rejected by Sanders, *Jewish People*, 102f. But Sanders also points out that Paul 'offered no theoretical basis for the *de facto* reduction of the law' (103).

63 Cf. Rutilius Namatianus (early fifth century), *de Reditu Suo* 1.391 (Stern, II, 663): 'the filthy race that infamously practises circumcision'.

64 Cf. 3 Macc. 3:4: the Jews 'held themselves apart in the matter of food; and for this reason they were disliked by some'.

65 Stern, I, 431, II, 102f; cf. also Rutilius Namatianus, *de Reditu Suo*, 1.391 (Stern, II, 663).

66 Examples of spiritualized interpretations of such commandments in Ep. Aris. 139ff (food-laws), Philo, *Spec.* 1.1ff (circumcision), 4.100ff (food-laws), Ep. Bar. 9–10 (polemic against Jewish literal understanding of these laws). Spiritualizing interpretation is often a sign that a tradition has ceased to be credible in its literal form.

67 The situation is succinctly summed up in Sib. Or. 3:272: 'Everyone will be offended at your customs.'

68 Cf. McEleney, 'Conversion', 328ff, Eckert, *Verkündigung*, 53ff on the question of proselytes and circumcision.

69 Dunn argues on the basis of Josephus (*Ap.* 2.38, *BJ* 7.3.3) that Gentile acceptance of Jewish customs was widespread ('Incident', 21ff). He fails here to distinguish between the acceptance of individual customs, such as the observance of the Sabbath, in a syncretistic fashion, and conversion to Judaism through submission to the law and membership of the Jewish community. It may well be that when Greek and Roman writers complain about the influence of Judaism on non-Jews, it is often the former that they have in mind. The attractiveness of certain isolated customs in a syncretistic setting does not mean that conversion to Judaism was attractive.

70 As Chadwick points out, 1 Cor. 9:22 might have been used as evidence against Paul ('All Things to all Men', 263).

71 Cf. Holmberg, *Paul*, 20. The significance of this will be further discussed in Chapter 3.

72 For Judaism the law is an indivisible whole: 'Whoever says, I will take upon me the whole Torah except for this one word, of him it is true: "For he has despised the word of the Lord"' (Sifre Num. 112 to 15:31, cited by Räisänen, *Paul*, 72).

73 Theissen, 'Sociological Interpretation', 181, rightly notes that this implies that Christians 'were not ordinarily distinguished from Jews by a special designation (or set apart within Judaism)'.

74 Betz, *Galatians*, 190.

75 Betz argues that Gal. 3:26—8, 1 Cor. 12:13 and Col. 3:11 reflect a non-Pauline baptismal formula (182ff); cf. Scroggs, 'Eschatological Woman', 292.

76 At Antioch, 'Jews on their own initiative gave up their prerogatives' (Betz, *Galatians*, 191).

77 Against Dunn, who claims that separation from Judaism had not yet taken place ('Incident', 5).

78 Meeks rightly claims that studies of Paul's theology have neglected its social context (*Urban Christians*, 164), and notes that independence from the synagogue is part of that context (168).

79 Sanders rightly states that one should distinguish the reason for which Paul held a view from the arguments he produces in favour of it (*Jewish People*, 4).

80 This sociological model seems preferable to Theissen's suggestion that a tendency in the Jesus-movement away from ethnocentricity and towards the universalization of Judaism reached its logical conclusion with Paul (*First Followers*, 93). The latter model ignores the vitally important factor of tension with the non-Christian Jewish community.

81 Cf. Theissen, *First Followers, passim*, for a sociological description of early Jewish Christianity. His book begins with the sentence: 'Earliest Christianity began as a renewal movement within Judaism brought into being through Jesus' (1).

82 Holmberg makes this point well: 'The first Christians did not regard themselves as a sect or party within Judaism, but rather as the beginning of its total renewal' (*Paul*, 183).

83 In the light of this distinction between reform-movement and sect, it does not appear to be the case that 'the community called into existence by Jesus fulfills the essential characteristics of the religious sect, as defined by recent sociological analysis' (Scroggs, 'Earliest Christian Communities', 1). Jesus no more founded a sect than he founded a church.

84 Gager explains the origins of conflict as follows: 'New religious communities also exemplify the precarious status of all social worlds. By revealing that the legitimacy of the old order is not, after all, inherent in the nature of the universe, they pose a tremendous threat to that order' (*Kingdom*, 11f).

85 Cf. Esler, 'Community', 28.

86 Scroggs lists seven typical characteristics of the sect: 1. It emerges out of protest. 2. It rejects the established view of reality. 3. It is egalitarian. 4. It offers love and acceptance to its members. 5. It is

a voluntary group. 6. It requires total commitment. 7. It may be adventist in orientation ('Earliest Christian Communities', 1ff). The present discussion is concerned chiefly with the alienation from society implied by the first, second and sixth of these points.

87 The term 'ideology' is intended to bring out the close relationship between theoretical statements and the social realities which it is their real (even if hidden) function to justify; cf. the discussion in Elliott, *Home*, 11f.

88 Meeks notes that social cohesion requires boundaries, citing L. Festinger's definition of social cohesion as 'the resultant of all the forces acting on the members to remain in the group' (*Urban Christians*, 85).

89 'The complexities of moral judgments that typify a complex society are resolved into a series of binary oppositions: poor–rich, good–evil, pious–hypocrite, elect–damned' (Gager, *Kingdom*, 25).

90 'Election by God implies or confers status' (Elliott, *Home*, 122f).

91 For a discussion of this twofold function of predestinarian language, cf. F. Watson, 'Social Function', 60ff.

92 Gager writes: 'To the extent that historians in general have stressed the particularity of historical events, they have been disinclined to make use of social scientific disciplines that by their very nature search for common patterns and principles'. He calls for 'a shift of emphasis away from the particularism of most historians of early Christianity' (*Kingdom*, 3).

93 Stanton argues that Matthew's community too 'has recently parted company with Judaism after a period of prolonged hostility' ('Matthew', 273). It is now 'a rather beleaguered "sect"' (277), under threat from Judaism and hostile to the Gentiles, and expressing its alienation from society by means of apocalyptic themes (274ff).

94 So Milik, *Ten Years*, 59, 81.

95 Cf. Milik, *Ten Years*, 76.

96 On this passage, cf. Sanders, *Jesus*, 65f, 338.

97 Elsewhere in the scrolls, light and darkness are both to be found within the heart of the individual (cf. Hengel, *Hellenism*, I, 220).

98 According to Brown, *Community*, 40, conflict with the Jews 'dominates the pre-Gospel phase of the Johannine community'.

99 Suffering is also legitimated by prediction in Mt. 10:17–23 (so Gager, *Kingdom*, 8).

100 Most commentators are agreed that it is the position of the Johannine community which is reflected here (Schnackenburg, II, 250, Bultmann, 335, Brown, I, 379f, Barrett, 299f). J. N. Sanders, 242, is an exception.

101 On these 'crypto-Christians', cf. Brown, *Community*, 71ff.

102 Christology seems to have been the cause of the split with the synagogue (so Brown, *Community*, 43ff), and not the law and the Gentiles, as in the case of Paul.

103 Meeks argues convincingly that their sectarian understanding of themselves determines the nature of their Christology ('Man from Heaven', 49f).

104 Thus, John frequently speaks collectively of 'the Jews', from whom his own community is sharply differentiated (cf. Brown, *Community*, 40ff).

105 Cf. Bultmann, *John*, vii, x.

106 Bultmann's profound existential interpretation of Johannine dualism (e.g. *John*, 140ff, on 3:6) involves an almost complete neglect of this sociological dimension.

107 It is true that the Jews are not the only group from which the Johannine community differentiates itself (Brown, *Community*, 59ff), but they are the most important.

108 Paul's vigorous missionary activity differentiates his form of sectarianism from that of Qumran. One might perhaps make use of the theory of 'cognitive dissonance' to shed light on this. This theory was developed in the field of social psychology, and attempts to explain how religious groups come to terms with the failure of their expectations (cf. the general summary in Carroll, *When Prophecy Failed*, 86ff). One possible response to 'dissonance' is missionary activity (95). In the case of Paul, 'dissonance' occurred when belief that Jesus was the Messiah of Israel was contradicted by Israel's failure to believe this; the Gentile mission would then be a means of relieving this 'dissonance'. Other attempts to apply dissonance theory to the N.T. include Gager, *Kingdom*, 37ff, and Jackson, 'Resurrection Belief'.

109 In interpreting a Pauline text, one should not simply ask about what it *says*. Elliott states that 'sociological exegesis' must ask 'how and why that text was designed to function, and what its impact upon the life and activity of its recipients and formulators was intended to be' (*Home*, 8).

110 Sanders rightly comments that Paul's polemic does not convey objective information (*Jesus*, 338).

3. The Galatian crisis

1 Holmberg too attempts to understand the relationship between Paul and Jerusalem sociologically; he discusses this in terms of the charismatic authority and institutionalization characteristic of both (*Paul*, 150ff). He argues that the primary institutionalization within the Jerusalem church took place before Paul's arrival on the scene (185), so that Paul's innovations occurred 'within an existing tradition without breaking with its fundamental institutions or values' (186). Holmberg thus sets forth a Paul who was bound more closely to Jerusalem than is often recognized. In contrast to this, the present study emphasizes Paul's innovatory role and the tension between himself and Jerusalem.

2 This view has again been set forth in Ebeling's recent book, *Die Wahrheit des Evangeliums* (1981). He argues that, despite the historical differences, 'the fundamental decision for which Paul fought is repeated *mutatis mutandis* in the Reformation's struggle for the truth of the gospel' (viii).

3 Even Betz, whose commentary on Galatians is currently probably the best available, thinks that Luther's 1535 commentary on Galatians 'expresses an extraordinary and profound understanding of what Paul intended to say'; thus, 'Luther speaks as Paul would have spoken had he lived at the time when Luther gave his lectures' (xv).

4 Hengel, *Acts*, 113; cf. Georgi, *Kollekte*, 15, Guthrie, 78.

5 Cf. Lightfoot, 102, Duncan, 46.

6 Lüdemann thinks that the Apostolic Decree is alluded to in Gal. 2:6: the pillars 'added nothing' to *Paul*, but they did 'add something' to Barnabas and Antioch, i.e. they imposed the Decree (*Paul*, 72ff). Catchpole argues that the controversy of Gal. 2:11ff was caused by the Apostolic Decree, which the men from James sought to impose on the church of Antioch ('Apostolic Decree', 441f). However, Houlden attributes the Decree to Lucan theology ('Response', 64f). Since the letter in which the Decree is contained (Acts 15:23–9) is clearly spurious (for example, Paul is one of those responsible for enforcing it, vv. 25f), it is hard to feel much confidence in the historicity of the Decree itself.

7 Betz plausibly suggests that the omission of the negative in v. 5 in part of the textual tradition was influenced by Gal. 5:11 and Acts 16:3 (91).

8 Schmithals thinks that the 'false brethren' were 'Jews officially commissioned to investigate the attitude of the Christian church' (*Paul and James*, 107). But if they were not Christians, why does Paul refer to them as 'brethren'?

9 Lüdemann, *Paul*, 71. Bruce, 'Galatian Problems. 1', 306, van Dülmen, *Gesetz*, 13, and Betz, 90, think that Gal. 2:4 refers to a later period.

10 The problem of why Paul went up to Jerusalem is discussed at length by Schmithals, *Paul and James*, 39ff.

11 Georgi rightly points out that a crisis caused by the 'false brethren' and a revelation given through a prophet are not incompatible as the reason why Paul and Barnabas went up to Jerusalem (*Kollekte*, 16).

12 Cf. Burton, 78.

13 Hahn, *Mission*, 78, and Georgi, *Kollekte*, 15n, regard Acts as accurate at this point. This is denied by Schmithals, *Paul and James*, 108.

14 Betz rightly sees Acts 15:24 as 'apologetic' (108).

15 Cf. Catchpole, 'Apostolic Decree', 442f.

16 Here, 'Luke has turned a disagreement on a matter of principle into a personal quarrel' (Schmithals, *Paul and James*, 71). Cf. Brandon, *Fall*, 132.

17 Against Holmberg, *Paul*, 49.

18 Bruce states: 'It may be that the ψευδάδελφοι claimed the right to exercise "supervision" (ἐπισκοπή), but Paul defines their activity not as authorized ἐπισκοπή but as unauthorized κατασκοπή, "spying"' (113).

19 Burton writes of the 'false brethren' that they were 'distinguished not only from the apostles but from the primitive church in general' (83).

That is certainly Paul's view, but can we assume that his highly polemical language is objective? Acts 21:20ff is tendentious in exactly the same way when it differentiates James, who is on Paul's side, from the 'many thousands' of Jewish Christians who are 'zealous for the law' and opposed to Paul.

20 It seems impossible to distinguish James' position from that of the Judaizers. Hahn claims that 'the Judaizing movement ... did not proceed from the Jerusalem church leaders', but admits that James may have secured for the Judaizers 'a certain influence in the negotiations' (*Mission*, 58).

21 Betz, 107f, and Georgi, *Kollekte*, 16n, deny that the 'false brethren' of 2:4 are the same as the 'men from James' of 2:12.

22 Against Munck, *Paul*, 119, who argues that the Jerusalem church was unconcerned about the Gentile mission, and Schmithals, *Paul and James*, 88, who denies that the Jewish Christians were 'zealots for the law'.

23 There is no good reason for denying that Paul, like Barnabas, was an emissary of the Antiochene church (against Lüdemann, *Paul*, 6).

24 Schmithals argues that Paul sought and obtained an assurance that, since he was no longer to preach to Jews, a parallel mission would be undertaken to the Jews in the cities which he visited − that is the point of Gal. 2:9 (*Paul and James*, 53f). But there is no evidence that such a plan was ever carried out.

25 According to Schmithals, the separation of the two missions mentioned in Gal. 2:7−9 was intended to prevent hostility towards Jewish Christians from non-Christian Jews (*Paul and James*, 47f). But Schmithals is surely wrong to claim that the existence of Gentile Christians who did not observe the law was a matter of indifference to Jews as a whole (25). As he admits when commenting on Rom. 15:30f, solidarity with Paul would be dangerous (82).

26 The latter is the view of most exegetes (e.g. Lightfoot, 116, Burton, 107, Betz, 109, Dunn, 'Incident', 53, Räisänen, 'Legalism', 76n). However, Bruce, 131, Reicke, 'Hintergrund', 177, Munck, *Paul*, 106f, and Schmithals, *Paul and James*, 66ff are exceptions.

27 In Rom. 4:12, τοῖς οὐκ ἐκ περιτομῆς μόνον refers to Jewish Christians, and this suggests that non-Christian Jews would be described as οἱ ἐκ περιτομῆς μόνον. This is therefore likely to be the meaning of τοὺς ἐκ περιτομῆς in Gal. 2:12. It is true that in Acts 11:2, Peter's Jewish Christian critics are described as οἱ ἐκ περιτομῆς, but as so often it is a mistake to rely on Acts at the expense of Paul's own statements.

28 This is denied by Georgi, *Kollekte*, 14f, but on inadequate grounds.

29 So Schmithals, *Paul and James*, 68, Betz, 108f.

30 It is usually claimed that this was the effect of Peter's action but not his intention (so Burton, 112, Oepke, 58, Müssner, 145).

31 There is no evidence for the view of J. B. Lightfoot that 'the men from James' misrepresented him (115).

32 This assumes that the incident at Antioch took place *after* the Jerusalem conference. This is denied by Lüdemann, *Paul*, 75ff,

who argues that ὅτε δέ in Gal. 2:11 does not imply chronological continuity with the preceding narrative (77). But ὅτε δέ in Gal. 1:15; 2:12; 4:4 (cf. 2:14) includes the idea of chronological continuity. Lüdemann's view is also held by Munck, *Paul*, 100ff, Hester, 'Rhetorical Structure', 231n, but opposed by Jewett, *Redating*, 84, and Dunn, 'Incident', 41f.

33 If so, then Gal. 2:7–9 cannot contain a quotation from an official statement (against Klein, 'Galater 2, 6–9', 107, Schmithals, *Paul and James*, 52; cf. Lüdemann, *Paul*, 64ff).

34 Cf. Haenchen, *Acts*, 482.

35 Bruce, 134, Catchpole, 'Apostolic Decree', 439, against Bring, 82.

36 Schütz denies that Paul is disparaging about the 'pillars' in Gal. 2 (*Apostolic Authority*, 141ff).

37 ὁποιοί ποτε ἦσαν probably refers to their relationship to the historical Jesus, although Klein argues that it refers to the fact that since the Jerusalem conference power has shifted from Cephas to James ('Galater 2, 6–9', 111ff).

38 Cf. Barrett, '"Pillar" Apostles', 2f.

39 Cf. Esler, 'Community', 133.

40 Knox, *Chapters*, 68f, Lüdemann, *Paul*, 80ff, Jewett, *Redating*, 95ff.

41 Luke's references to 'the region of Phrygia and Galatia' (Acts 16:6; cf. 18:23) are admittedly somewhat vague (cf. 'the upper country', Acts 19:1, which, as Bruce notes (*Galatians*, 13), could refer to 'more or less any part of inland Asia Minor'). But despite Bruce's argument from geography (10ff), 'Galatia' in these passages cannot refer to Derbe, Lystra, Iconium and Pisidian Antioch (i.e. 'south Galatia'). In Acts 15:36, Paul announces his intention of revisiting those cities, and 16:1 mentions his arrival at Derbe and Lystra, where Timothy was circumcised (16:3). According to 16:4f, he then went through the cities in which there were already churches, delivering the Apostolic Decree. The reference here must be to Iconium and Pisidian Antioch, for Paul had founded churches only there and in Derbe and Lystra (cf. 16:1). Thus, none of these cities can be included within the phrase, 'the Phrygian and Galatian region' in 16:6, which marks a new phase in Paul's travels.

42 The north Galatian view is now accepted by the majority of scholars (cf. Georgi, *Kollekte*, 31, Lüdemann, *Paul*, 138, and Meeks, *Urban Christians*, 42).

43 So Georgi, *Kollekte*, 31.

44 τὸ πρότερον here is not quite clear. It could mean 'the first of two', in which case the two visits are probably those of Acts 16:6 and 18:23 (= 1 Cor. 16:1) – so Kertelge, 'Gesetz', 385. But according to BDF 62, in Hellenistic Greek, πρότερος simply means 'earlier'.

45 Dunn, 'Incident', 70.

46 Lüdemann's view is that on stylistic grounds, Galatians must date from the period of 2 Corinthians and Romans (*Paul*, 85f); cf. Borse, *Standort*, 84ff. But since many commentators have noticed a marked difference in the way Paul treats similar subjects in Galatians and Romans, such stylistic arguments are inconclusive.

47 Lüdemann, *Paul*, 86, Wilckens, 'Abfassungszweck', 135.
48 Against Barrett, *2 Corinthians*, 228, who regards the 'brother' mentioned in 8:19 as the representative of the Macedonian churches.
49 Nickle's view (*Collection*, 18ff) that these unnamed 'brothers' are emissaries from Jerusalem, i.e. 'Judas called Barsabbas and Silas' (Acts 15:22) is implausible. In addition to the total lack of evidence for such an identification, this view is ruled out by Rom. 15:31, where Paul expresses doubts about whether his collection will be accepted in Jerusalem.
50 So Georgi, *Kollekte*, 30, against Lüdemann, *Paul*, 80. For the view that Gal. 6:6–10 refers to the collection, cf. Bruce, 265f.
51 So Georgi, *Kollekte*, 33.
52 In the light of 1 Cor. 16:1, Galatians was therefore presumably successful; Lüdemann's claim that the failure of Galatians is 'more probable in the light of the content and genre of the letter' (*Paul*, 85) is unconvincing.
53 Cf. Betz, 47f.
54 So Dunn, 'Incident', 39 (although Dunn accepts the south Galatian theory).
55 Against Bruce, 84. Duncan, 19, Burton, 29, and Betz, 53f rightly suggest that the reference is to an earlier visit.
56 Such a view contradicts the claim that the Judaizers did not present themselves as in direct opposition to Paul (against Tyson, 'Opponents', 250, Jewett, 'Agitators', 206, Howard, *Crisis*, 44).
57 *Gnostics*, 13–64; cf. Talbert, 'Paul's Visits', *passim*, Schütz, *Apostolic Authority*, 125f; opposed by Vielhauer, 'Gesetzesdienst', 544, Eckert, *Verkündigung*, 64ff, Howard, *Crisis*, 12ff.
58 In a recent article, Schmithals discusses Gal. 3–4 in more detail. He writes: 'In chapters 3 and 4, which form the basis of the Judaizer hypothesis, Paul's argument is wholly derived from tradition, with only a few direct references to the Galatian situation' ('Judaisten', 50). Although Paul's opponents have isolated circumcision from the law, for Paul they belong together, so that an attack on circumcision must involve an attack on the law (51f). Schmithals thus continues to postulate 'a Jewish or Jewish Christian enthusiasm of gnostic provenance' (58). But Paul's argument would surely have been entirely ineffective if he attacked a completely different view of circumcision to the one promulgated by his opponents. Kertelge too thinks that the equation, circumcision = law, is Paul's own ('Gesetz', 386).
59 Cf. Bruce, 'Galatian Problems. 3', 161.
60 Bligh, 233.
61 Paul's opponents in Galatia should therefore not be identified with local non-Christian Jews (Ropes, *Problem*, 45), Paul's own Gentile converts (Munck, *Paul*, 87ff, M. Barth, 'Gesetz', 511), or local Jewish Christians (Tyson, 'Opponents', 252). According to Howard, the agitators did not know of Paul's special commission to preach a law-free gospel, and thought that he preached circumcision (cf. 5:11) and was like them dependent on Jerusalem (*Crisis*, 9). The

purpose of Gal. 1–2 was to explain that he did not tell the Jerusalem apostles about his unique call until his visit after fourteen years (21). Thus, 'while Paul was hostile to the judaizers, there is no indication that they were hostile to him' (11). But if the Judaizers had not previously had the opportunity to hear about Paul's call to preach a gospel without circumcision, why does he abuse them so violently?

62 Esler comments on the Antioch incident of Gal. 2:11ff: 'In sociological terms, it is a clash between someone determined to establish a form of religious belief whose relationship to its mother church can only be described as sectarian, and others who see this new religious impulse as merely an intra-Judaic messianic movement' ('Community', 135).

63 The first anathema of church history, according to Shaw, *Cost*, 44.

64 According to Betz, Paul here uses the public disgust at the castration practised in the cult of Cybele–Attis to discredit his opponents (270).

65 Räisänen, *Paul*, 76.

66 Conversely, Paul exploits the prestige of persecution in 5:11 and 6:17 (cf. Shaw, *Cost*, 41).

67 οἱ περιτεμνόμενοι here may refer to those Galatians who have already succumbed to the Judaizers' teaching (cf. 5:2). There is thus no need to conclude from it that Paul's opponents in Galatia were Gentile Christians (against Munck, *Paul*, 87f, Richardson, *Israel*, 84ff).

68 Against Schmithals, *Gnostics*, 37ff. Räisänen, *Paul*, 96, is correct here.

69 Hostility may thus reinforce the boundary between the minority group and society (so Meeks, *Urban Christians*, 96, Elliott, *Home*, 117).

70 Cf. Elliott, *Home*, 80.

71 It is not necessary to see this as a pragmatic response to increasingly militant Jewish nationalism (Jewett, 'Agitators', 198ff, Dunn, 'Incident', 7f; cf. Dix, *Jew and Greek*, 36f, Reicke, 'Hintergrund', 172ff).

72 Mundle rightly states that 'the Pauline antithesis against works of the law is not a protest against every kind of "human achievement through which one might attain and merit something"; it is a very much more concrete contrast with the Mosaic law and its demands' (*Glaubensbegriff*, 99f).

73 Nor is there any incompatibility between faith and the law in non-Christian Judaism. Thus, 2 Baruch speaks of 'those who subjected themselves to you and your law in faith' (54:5), and states that the law announces 'to those who believe the promise of the reward' (59:2). 4 Ez. 13:23 speaks of those 'who have works and have faith in the Almighty'. 1QpHab 8.1f applies Hab. 2:4 (one of Paul's main proof-texts for righteousness by faith apart from the law, Rom. 1:17, Gal. 3:11) to 'all those who observe the law' and who have 'faith in the Teacher of righteousness'.

74 'For Paul, there is no πίστῳ 'Ιησοῦ Χριστοῦ which does not include the ideas of baptism and joining the Christian community' (Mundle, *Glaubensbegriff*, 84).

75 According to Jewett, 'Agitators', 211, Gal. 6:3ff indicates that the Galatians were 'enthusiasts' who did not believe in the judgment. But this is probably to read too much into the text.

76 This is generally accepted; cf. Burton, 156ff, Duncan, 83f, Oepke, 69, Bring, 111, Guthrie, 95, Becker, 30, Barrett, 'Allegory', 158ff, Zeller, *Juden*, 94. However, it is rejected by Byrne, *'Sons of God'*, 148f.

77 This view thus contrasts with Hübner's existentialist interpretation of the faith–works contrast in Galatians (*Gesetz*, 19). He understands this as a contrast between the 'Gegründetsein in Gott' of those who understand their existence 'nicht im Bedingungsgefüge immanenter Faktoren', and the reliance on the constantly increasing quantity of individual fulfilments of the law of those for whom existence is 'verfügbar'.

78 Cf. Bultmann, *Theology*, I, 283f (in opposition to Mundle), Schlier, *Galater*, 92, *Römer*, 117, Bornkamm, 'Testament', 28f. Bornkamm is typical: 'For Paul, the Jew represents man in general ... This man is indeed not somewhere outside, among unbelievers; he is hidden within each Christian.'

79 On this view, 'works' means adherence to the Jewish way of life and membership of the Jewish community. Observances such as circumcision, the food-laws, the Sabbath and the feast-days, which were 'widely regarded as characteristically and distinctively Jewish' (Dunn, 'New Perspective', 107), thus do not exhaust the meaning of the term.

80 Cf. Sanders' discussion of Paul's transfer terminology (*Jewish People*, 8ff), which indicates how central conversion is to his thought.

81 Meeks describes this as the 'soteriogical contrast pattern' (*Urban Christians*, 95).

82 *Palestinian Judaism*, 552. The value of Sanders' formulation is that it excludes the view that Paul opposed Judaism because of its supposed inherent weaknesses; in fact, 'exclusivist soteriology' (*Jewish People*, 17) is the key to this opposition. Dunn criticizes this replacement of the Lutheran Paul by 'an idiosyncratic Paul who in arbitrary and irrational manner turns his face against the glory and greatness of Judaism's covenant theology and abandons Judaism simply because it is not Christianity' ('New Perspective', 101). Chapter 2 above has attempted to show how Paul reached this position.

83 On this view, παραβάτης refers to Peter's previous conduct seen from the Jewish standpoint (so Oepke, 61, Müssner, 179, Lührmann, 45). In view of the use of ἁμαρτωλός in v. 15 in its Jewish sense, it seems better to take παραβάτης in the same way than as a reference to the real sin of disloyalty to Christ and reversion to the law (the view of Ziesler, *Righteousness*, 173). Schlier thinks that according to v. 18, Peter is restoring the power that condemns transgression (60). But Becker, 30, Bligh, 210, and Müssner, 179, rightly argue that what is 'torn down' and 'built up' is the law regarded as a barrier between Jew and Gentile.

84 V. 15 is concessive (so Burton, 119, Schlier, 53, Müssner, 167, Ebeling, *Wahrheit*, 168): 'We, *although* we are Jews by birth ...'. This strengthens the links with v. 14, where Ἰουδαῖος ὑπάρχων is obviously also concessive.

85 The close link between v. 14 and vv. 15ff makes it hard to justify the view that v. 15 marks the start of a new section (against Müssner, 135, Betz, 113). It cannot be said that from v. 15 onwards, Paul is thinking no longer of Peter but rather of the Galatians (Schlier, 52), for Peter is directly addressed in vv. 15–18. The choice between Antioch and Galatia in these verses is irrelevant because the whole narrative of Gal. 1–2 is aimed at the Galatians (so Ebeling, *Wahrheit*, 164).

86 Ebeling comments on v. 15: 'The divine election has an absolute precedence over everything to which the Jew can point as an achievement. His birth is as little a work as his circumcision eight days afterwards' (*Wahrheit*, 167).

87 As Sanders says, everyone in Galatia was in favour of 'doing' (*Jewish People*, 159).

88 According to Schoeps, *Paul*, 177f, and Sanders, 'Fulfilling the Law', 106, Paul is in Gal. 3:12 actually denying the truth of a passage of Scripture. However, in Romans, Paul asserts that the law's promise of life was genuine (7:10) but that it was unattainable because of the flesh (8:3), and this may be his meaning in Gal. 3:12 as well.

89 'Faith' in Gal. 3 can hardly refer to God's faithfulness (against Howard, *Crisis*, 64).

90 Dunn's distinction ('New Perspective', 117f) between 'works' (which Paul opposes) and 'law' (which he approves of) is unnecessary; the meaning of the faith–works antithesis is exactly the same as the faith–law antithesis.

91 According to Shaw, *Cost*, 44, 'In Paul's hands scripture becomes a ventriloquist's dummy, by which he himself speaks, while attributing responsibility to God.'

92 Bultmann reads ἆρα instead of ἄρα in Gal. 2:17, turning it into a hypothetical assertion ('Galater 2, 15–18', 395f). But Paul's μὴ γένοιτο always follows a question rather than an assertion (Rom. 3:31; 4:6; 6:2, 15; 7:7, 13; 9:14; 11:1, 11; 1 Cor. 6:15; Gal. 3.21; 6:14 is a different usage).

93 Those who seek to be justified in Christ are only sinners from the standpoint of Jews who observe the Torah (Burton, 125ff), and are not really sinners (Müssner, 176, Betz, 119, against Duncan, 67f, Schlier, 58f, Oepke, 60, Becker, 30, van Dülmen, *Gesetz*, 20f), as vv. 18–20 indicate.

94 There is no need to reject Gal. 2:18 as a gloss (against Schmithals, 'Judaisten', 41).

95 'Through the law' probably refers to the death of Christ under the law's curse, referred to in 3:13 (so Schlier, 63, Bring, 96, Bruce, 143, Ebeling, *Wahrheit*, 205, Wilckens, 'Entwicklung', 170, van Dülmen, *Gesetz*, 26): 'I through the law died to the law, because

Christ did' (cf. Byrne, *'Sons of God'*, 155, Dunn, 'Paul's Under-standing', 130).

96   Cf. the discussion in Barrett, 144f, and Conzelmann, 108ff.

97   Cf. Bornkamm, *Paul*, 34, McEleney, 'Conversion', 333.

98   Cf. Bruce, *Paul*, 181.

99   There does not seem to be sufficient evidence for Borgen's claim that, according to his opponents, Paul 'preached circumcision as the removal of the passions and desires' ('Circumcision', 38).

100   Another theological interpretation which should be rejected is the idea that Torah and Christ are mutually exclusive because the former is 'external', a matter of 'rules and regulations', whereas the latter requires a spontaneous, internal response (Drane, *Paul*, 45, 63; cf. Bruce, *Paul*, 200, Duncan, 85f). Drane considers it a problem that 1 Corinthians teaches exactly the 'law-ethics' and legalism which are deprecated in Galatians (64f). But 'law-ethics' is taught even in Galatians (e.g. 5:19–21; 6:1–10). The conflict between 'external' and 'internal' is not prominent in Paul.

101   Barrett writes ('Allegory', 167): 'At the heart of their theology was the concept of the people of God with its origin in Abraham, and the divine promise that constituted it'. Thus, Abraham here is far more than 'an example of righteousness by faith' (against Blank, 'Aus Werken', 93).

102   Wilckens rightly emphasizes the centrality of Christ for Paul's opponents ('Abfassungszweck', 132).

103   Strictly speaking, Paul is combining Gen. 12:3 with 18:18, preferring the term ἔθνη to φυλαί (Bruce, 156).

104   Berger rightly points out that 'in', v. 8, is interpreted as 'with', v. 9 ('Abraham', 51).

105   Barrett, 'Allegory', 160. Barrett also argues that the story of Abraham, Sarah and Hagar, used in Gal. 4:21ff, was first used by Paul's opponents. Its surface meaning supports their case, and Paul would not have referred to it unless forced to do so (161ff). This is possible but uncertain, for Paul uses the story again in Rom. 9.6ff, where he is presumably not compelled to do so.

106   So Barrett, 'Allegory', 159, Wilckens, 'Entwicklung', 165.

107   Cf. Bar. 4:1: Wisdom 'is the book of the commandments of God, and the law that endures for ever. All who hold her fast will live, and those who forsake her will die.'

108   Sanders argues against this interpretation (*Jewish People*, 20ff), claiming that the word 'all' in 3:10 is not significant; Paul wanted a proof-text which would combine 'law' with 'curse', and therefore chose the only LXX passage available. Paul uses Dt. 27:26 simply to 'prove' that those who accept the law are cursed, and if we ask why this is so, the answer is that 'the law is not of faith' (v. 12a), and not that it is impossible to fulfil. Sanders writes: 'What Paul says in his own words is the clue to what he took the proof-texts to mean' (22). That is obviously true; but the text only proves what Paul says in his own words if one emphasizes 'all'. On Sanders' view, Paul's proof-text contradicts what he says in his own words.

In addition, Paul quotes the LXX, which adds 'all' to the Hebrew text, and this too suggests that v. 10 refers to the obligation of perfect fulfilment (Byrne, *'Sons of God'*, 151, Tyson, 'Works', 428). However, that does not mean that Paul is ascribing to Judaism the view that perfect fulfilment of the law is necessary for salvation, but only that this is his own understanding of the law.

109 Schmithals, *Gnostics*, 33, Vielhauer, 'Gesetzesdienst', 545, Jewett, 'Agitators', 201. πάλιν in 5:3 refers back to 3:10 (so Becker, 61, Lührmann, 81, Howard, *Crisis*, 16, Eckert, *Verkündigung*, 41), and not to 5:2 (Lightfoot, 194, Oepke, 118, Bruce, 229), since v. 3 is not a repetition of v. 2, even though they are closely related.

110 Although Sanders rejects this interpretation of Gal. 3:10 (*Jewish People*, 20ff), his own distinction between Paul's arguments and the underlying reason for them (4) is helpful here: Paul *argues* that the law is an absolute demand which no-one can fulfil, but that is not his *reason* for rejecting it. His rejection of it is bound up with his establishment of Gentile congregations separated from the Jewish community; he then requires arguments to justify this.

111 Becker thinks that in Gal. 3, 'the Jew–Gentile problem is lacking' (34). On the contrary, Gal. 3 is discussing nothing else.

112 There is no need to doubt the Judaizers' sincerity, as Georgi does when he refers to their teaching as 'a heresy' whose concern for tradition and the law was only a 'mask' (*Kollekte*, 37).

4. Philippi, Corinth and the Judaizers

1 The argument here presupposes the literary unity of Philippians, which has been challenged by some scholars who believe that Philippians is a collection of two or three letters or fragments of letters. Marxsen regards 4:10–20 as the earliest letter, since Paul would not have allowed the period of time implied in 2:25ff to elapse before thanking the Philippians for their gift (*Introduction*, 61). But Paul could easily have delayed writing to them until Epaphroditus had recovered from a near-fatal illness (2:26f). The Philippians might have known about this illness (2:26) through the return of a companion of Epaphroditus without him, and there is no need to postulate a further message from Philippi expressing their concern (against Roetzel, *Letters*, 77f). The serenity of 4:10–20 contrasts with Paul's anxiety during Epaphroditus' illness (cf. 2:27b). 4:10–20 should therefore not be separated. As regards the separation of 3:1–4:1, 8–9 (Gnilka, 7ff) or 3:1–4:3, 8–9 (Marxsen, *Introduction*, 62), the following points may be made. 1. The occurrence of τὸ λοιπόν in 3:1 does not mean that 3:1 was originally the beginning of the concluding section of a letter (despite 2 Cor. 13:11, Gal. 6:17): NB 1 Thes. 4:1. 2. Rom. 16:17ff is a parallel for an abrupt attack on opponents (so Kümmel, *Introduction*, 333); the question of the original function of Rom. 16 makes no difference to this point (against Gnilka, 7f). 3. The heretics of Phil. 3:2ff are not yet present in Philippi, as 3:18 indicates, and so one would

therefore not necessarily expect references to them in Phil. 1–2 (against Gnilka, 8). 4. In 4:1, Paul calls the Philippians ἐπιπόθητοι, and 1:8 (cf. 1:24–6, 2:24) indicates that this must refer to Paul's longing to visit the Philippians once he is released. The *Sitz im Leben* of 3:1–4:1 is therefore the same as the rest of Philippians. Kümmel rightly states that the arguments for dividing Philippians into two or three letters are 'totally unconvincing' (*Introduction*, 333).

2 Arguments in favour of an Ephesian imprisonment are given by Duncan, *Ephesian Ministry*, 66ff, Gnilka, 20, Marxsen, *Introduction*, 65. Duncan's arguments (which are at times over-elaborate) are criticized by Dodd, 'Mind of Paul, II', 83ff.

3 Against Barrett, who thinks that the reference is to an unknown danger and hardship (*1 Corinthians*, 366).

4 The latter phrase attempts to paraphrase the difficult κατὰ ἄνθρωπον.

5 Duncan also less plausibly refers to Rom. 16:3, 7 and 1 Cor. 4:9 as evidence of an Ephesian imprisonment (*Ephesian Ministry*, 67f).

6 It is probably because he is facing the possibility of death that Paul does not mention the collection in Philippians (so Gnilka, 24, against Robinson, *Redating*, 59, who regards this as an argument against the Ephesian origin of the letter). 2 Cor. 8:1–5, 9:2 indicate that the Philippians did not begin the collection until Paul's arrival after he had left Ephesus.

7 Thus Philippians dates from the end of Paul's Ephesian ministry (cf. Gnilka, 24; against Duncan, *Ephesian Ministry*, 124ff).

8 Cf. Gnilka, 22f.

9 Arguments in favour of the Caesarean and Roman hypotheses are given by Robinson, *Redating*, 57ff, and Beare, 15ff, respectively.

10 Dodd attempts to counter this argument by suggesting that, since Paul's plan to travel to Spain depended on the support of the Roman church, and since (on the Roman hypothesis) Phil. 1:15 and 2:21 show that many in Rome were opposed to him, it is not surprising that Paul should have changed his plans ('Mind of Paul, II', 96). But it would be unlike Paul to accept defeat quite so abjectly.

11 This need not be linked with Timothy's journey of 1 Cor. 4:17, 16:10 (against Duncan, *Ephesian Ministry*, 137). The fact that Acts 19:22, unlike Phil. 2:19, does not imply Timothy's return is hardly a strong reason for not identifying the two journeys (against Kümmel, *Introduction*, 330f).

12 Non-Christian Jews according to Caird, *Letters*, 133; Christian Jews according to Friedrich, 159, Michael, 133.

13 Cf. Mt. 9:37, 38 = Lk. 10:2, 7; 2 Cor. 11:13; 1 Tim. 5:18; 2 Tim. 2:15; Did. 13:2 (so Georgi, *Gegner*, 49ff).

14 Circumcision here is therefore not 'a merely outward act' or 'formalism' (against Martin, 138).

15 There is no good evidence for Marxsen's claim that Paul misunderstood his opponents' view of circumcision (*Introduction*, 63).

16 Jewish examples in SB, I, 724f, III, 621f.

17 So Lohmeyer, 124, Michael, 134f, Friedrich, 159.

18 Staab's comment is thus wide of the mark: 'Er nennt sie "Hünde", wohl deshalb, weil sie immer bellend und beissend hinter ihm herliefen' (*Gefangenschaftsbriefe*, 44).

19 Schmithals, *Gnostics*, 65ff, Koester, 'Pauline Fragment', 324ff; opposed by Klijn, 'Opponents', 278ff.

20 So Jewett, 'Conflicting Movements', 373.

21 Whereas in 3:5ff, the Pharisaic way of life is rejected, in 3:12ff the (Pharisaic) doctrine of resurrection is used to counter 'enthusiasm'. Cf. Acts 23:8, Josephus, *BJ* 7.163, *Ant.* 18.14 for the Pharisaic belief in the resurrection.

22 Collange, *Philippians*, 13, correctly notes that vv. 18f is linked to the preceding; he concludes that the idea of perfection opposed in vv. 12ff was introduced by the opponents described in vv. 18f. But this seems to be excluded by the switch from the second to the third person. It seems more likely that in the course of an attack on Judaizing opponents, Paul takes the opportunity of correcting a rather different error within the congregation.

23 'Heretical libertinists with gnostic tendencies', according to Jewett, 'Conflicting Movements', 382.

24 See n. 19, above.

25 Thus they should not be seen as 'proponents of an obviously lax lifestyle in matters of food and sex' (Kümmel, *Introduction*, 328).

26 δόξα is frequently linked in the LXX to divine manifestation (e.g. Ex. 16:7, 10; 24:16, 17; Ez. 2:1; 3:12; 8:4); ὁ θεός and ἡ δόξα in Phil. 3:19 are thus similar in meaning.

27 Martin, 158. Other suggestions include self-interest (Klijn, 'Opponents', 283) and gluttony (Koester, 'Pauline Fragment', 326).

28 I am indebted to the Rev. C. Mearns for this interpretation of κοιλία. It has this sense in the LXX of 2 Kgd. 7:12 = 1 Chron. 17:11; 2 Kgd. 16:11; 2 Chron. 32:31; Dt. 7:13; 28:4, 11, 18, 53; 30:9; Ps. 131:11.

29 Details and bibliography in *Oxford Classical Dictionary*, 876.

30 3 Kgd. 18:28; Hos. 7:14; Is. 15:2; Jer. 31(48):37; cf. Lev. 19:28.

31 Jewett's objection to the view that 3:18f refers to the Judaizers of v. 2 on the grounds that 'the polemic would be too gross to be effective' ('Conflicting Movements', 379), is therefore not valid.

32 G. Shaw's book, *The Cost of Authority*, is a useful antidote to the tendency to idealize Paul.

33 Against Gnilka, 8.

34 Caird translates βλέπετε in v. 2 not as 'Beware of ...' but as 'Consider ...', on the grounds that βλέπειν with a direct object always means the latter, as in 1 Cor. 1:26; 10:18; 2 Cor. 10:7; Col. 4:17 (*Letters*, 133). But Mk. 4:24, βλέπετε τί ἀκούετε (cited by Lightfoot, 141) seems to justify the traditional interpretation. That Paul here is faced with a real threat is suggested by his 'vicious invective' (Beare, 103).

35 Cf. Beare, 108f.

36 It is this tactical intention that accounts for the 'black and white' nature of Paul's statements here, to which Sanders draws attention (*Jewish People*, 139f).

37 It is clear from this passage that righteous behaviour *'preserves* one's place in the covenant ... but it does not *earn* it' (Sanders, *Palestinian Judaism*, 205).

38 Thus Martin's definition of 'confidence in the flesh' (vv. 3f) is mistaken; he defines it as 'the innate tendency on the part of the religious man to obtain a standing before God and to secure, by his own effort, approval and acceptance with Him' (139f).

39 Martin's claim that σωτηρία here refers not to eschatological salvation but to 'the corporate life of the Philippian church' (111) is artificial. Corporate life is the subject throughout 2:1ff, and the meaning of 2:12 is therefore: 'Behave appropriately in your corporate life, and so ensure your final salvation.'

40 As Sanders writes (*Palestinian Judaism*, 203): 'The general view was that the righteous man was not characterized by perfection ... but by the earnest endeavour to obey the law and by repentance and other acts of atonement in the case of transgression.'

41 The importance of conversion in Paul's thought is stressed by Sanders, *Jewish People*, 6ff, and Meeks, *Urban Christians*, 95.

42 Cf. Elliott, *Home*, 75ff, for a discussion of the 'conversionist response to the world'.

43 For a defence of the view that 2 Cor. 1–9 was written later than 2 Cor. 10–13, which in turn is to be identified with Paul's severe letter to the Corinthians, see F. Watson, '2 Cor. x–xiii'. This article opposes the view that 2 Cor. 10–13 was written *after* 2 Cor. 1–9 (331ff), and the more complex source-analysis of Bornkamm and others (335ff), and argues that 2 Cor. 10–13 exactly fits the description of the severe letter given and implied in 2 Cor. 1–9 (339ff).

44 Barrett argues that Peter had probably visited Corinth in person. He thinks that Peter may be the unnamed individual mentioned in 1 Cor. 3:10–17 ('Cephas', 32f), and 2 Cor. 5:12; 10:7, 10, 11; 11:4, 19f (35f). He writes on 2 Cor. 11:19f: 'The obscurity of the language, and its rapid changes, reflect the confused and embarrassing situation Paul had to deal with' (36) – i.e. the situation of having to oppose Peter. But the fact that Paul does not name his opponent hardly seems sufficient ground for identifying him with Peter. For an alternative view of 2 Cor. 10:7, 10, 11, see Watson, '2 Cor. x–xiii', 343f.

45 So Houlden, 'Response', 66, Meeks, *Urban Christians*, 98; against Barrett, 'Cephas', 33. There seems very little evidence for Barrett's view that Peter or his adherents tried to introduce the Apostolic Decree in Corinth ('Things Sacrificed', 53).

46 The word ἱερόθυτον, which is the correct term for sacrificial meat from a pagan standpoint, suggests that the informant here is a pagan (cf. Conzelmann, 177, Barrett, 241f; against Robertson and Plummer, 221f).

47 Käsemann argues that the superlative apostles (11:5; 12:11) are to be differentiated from the false apostles (11:13): the former are the Jerusalem apostles, whereas the latter were actually present in

Corinth ('Legitimität', 42). This view is accepted by Barrett, 'Paul's Opponents', 64, but rejected by Bultmann, *Probleme*, 20ff. The basis for Käsemann's differentiation is the fact that whereas in 11:4 the opponents are denounced, in 11:5 Paul simply says that he is not inferior to the superlative apostles; thus 11:4, 5 refer to different people. But this is unlikely, for in 11:13–15 Paul denounces the false apostles who, according to 11:12, boast of their authority, and in 11:16–12:13 attacks those who boast (11:18) by boasting himself – i.e. by means of a comparison. These two ways of attacking the same people – one direct, the other indirect – are also apparent in 11:4–6.

48 Käsemann, 'Legitimität', 43ff, Barrett, 'Paul's Opponents', 80, Brandon, *Fall*, 143.

49 Friedrich writes ('Gegner', 192): 'Paul's opponents in II Corinthians cannot be Judaizers like those who had emerged in Galatia. There is no sign of the characteristics of these Jewish Christian nomists, who demand circumcision, observance of the Sabbath and ritual purity. They [i.e. the opponents in 2 Cor.] do not reproach Paul with having rejected the law, nor does Paul polemicize against works-righteousness as the main characteristic of their false theology.'

50 Georgi, *Gegner*, 220ff, describes them as *theioi andres*. Friedrich, 'Gegner', 199ff, links them with Stephen and his circle of Hellenists, as described in Acts 6–7. These two views are opposed by Theissen, 'Legitimation', 65f, and by Barrett, 'Paul's Opponents', 63, respectively.

51 Barrett notes Calvin's question, Why is Apollos not mentioned? (*2 Corinthians*, 76).

52 μυρίους means literally 'tens of thousands', but as Barrett remarks, 'This is rhetoric, not arithmetic' (*1 Corinthians*, 115).

53 Schmithals denies that Apollos was in any sense an opponent of Paul (*Paul and James*, 105); so also Holmberg, *Paul*, 45.

54 Robertson and Plummer think that the criticism is chiefly directed against the Apollos party, although not confined to it (*I Corinthians*, 16).

55 'Wisdom' here is often now understood in terms of 'tendencies of a pneumatic, enthusiastic, individualistic kind' (Conzelmann, *1 Corinthians*, 34, and see the discussion in Barrett, 'Christianity', 6ff, and the literature cited there). However, the 'wisdom' Paul attacks is that of the debaters of this age (1:10), the Greeks (1:22), and the rich, powerful and well-born (1:26), and it is difficult to interpret this in terms of enthusiasm without arbitrary exegesis.

56 According to Barrett, 'The party slogans all bear witness to an over-valuing of human wisdom' (*1 Corinthians*, 51). But it is not at all clear how an attack on the wisdom of the Greeks (1:22) can at the same time be an attack on over-enthusiasm for the version of the gospel taught by one particular teacher. How is Paul's stress on his own preaching (1:17, 21, 23; 2:1–5) compatible with the view that even those who say, 'I belong to Paul' (1:12) are attacked here?

Does 1:18−2:5 really involve a 'critical abrogation of Paulinism' (Conzelmann, 38)? It is simpler to conclude that 1:18−2:5 is directed specifically against the followers of Apollos, who believe that wisdom and the gospel are compatible.

57 Conzelmann, 34, denies the legitimacy of appealing to Acts at this point, though without giving any reasons.

58 Despite his call for unity, he 'cannot ... resist distinguishing himself from all the rest of God's workers in the Corinthian vineyard' (Shaw, *Cost*, 62).

59 Shaw writes on this passage: 'For all his talk of weakness, he is still prepared to invoke avenging power as the ultimate deterrent' (*Cost*, 69). Conzelmann asks, 'Is Paul setting himself up after all as a spiritual strong man?', but answers his question unconvincingly with a negative (93).

60 θέλημα could here refer to God's will; but the context suggests a reference to Apollos, whose reluctance to go to Corinth is implied by πολλὰ παρεκάλεσα αὐτόν.

61 He should not be regarded as a 'travelling evangelist of the Pauline group' (Barrett, 391), but as independent.

62 This contradicts Barrett's claim that Apollos was always Paul's 'friend and colleague' (10).

63 So Friedrich, 'Gegner', 192.

64 So Barrett, 'ΨΕΥΔΑΠΟΣΤΟΛΟΙ', 93.

65 This interpretation is rejected by Hughes on the grounds that 'it attributes to Moses the practising of a subterfuge, and this to Paul would have been unthinkable' (109; cf. Rissi, *Studien*, 30f).

66 According to Cranfield, 'that which passes away' (v. 11) refers 'not to the law or "the whole religious system based on the law"', but to the ministry of Moses at the giving of the law' ('Law', 58). He argues that for polemical reasons, Paul often discusses the law apart from Christ (61), and 'it is this law-apart-from-Christ, this law that is less than its true self, which is temporary' (63). But as the law is here seen purely as the bringer of condemnation, then it must clearly be the law itself which is temporary. τοῦ καταργουμένου here therefore implies that τέλος means 'end', not 'goal' (against Rissi, *Studien*, 38).

67 This has no reference to the eschatological salvation of Israel − against Munck, *Paul*, 58ff.

68 So Wilckens, 'Entwicklung', 163.

69 Beker, *Paul*, 253, Hooker, 'Beyond', 304, Käsemann, 'Spirit', 138ff, Rissi, *Studien*, 35, 37, 41, Collange, *Énigmes*, 85, Windisch, 122. This view is rightly opposed by Bultmann, 90, who points out that 'the παλαιὰ διαθήκη only enters the context as the διακονία of death, of κατάκρισις, as καταργούμενον'.

70 Freedom from the law is thus not freedom from 'legalistically conceived religion' (Barrett, 124) nor from 'all the powers' (Rissi, *Studien*, 38).

71 This is the one Pauline passage which explicitly makes this point (Bornkamm, 'Wandlungen', 108).

72 E.g. 'End of the Law', 41.
73 *Theology*, I, 240, 247, 267; cf. Beker, *Paul*, 81, Cranfield, 'Law', 57f, Lang, 'Gesetz und Bund', 316, Barrett, 113, Héring, 23. But Bultmann is ambivalent at this point. 'The letter kills' (2 Cor. 3:6) by enticing man with the promise of life, so that he 'seeks his own righteousness' and 'boasts' (267); or 'the letter kills' because man 'cannot exhibit "the works of the Law" in their entirety' (263).
74 Windisch, 110, Wilckens, 'Entwicklung', 162. This has nothing to do with remorse and discouragement over one's moral failings (against Plummer, 88).
75 Rissi, *Studien*, 25, points out that νόμος does not occur here or elsewhere in 2 Corinthians, and claims that the gospel is here contrasted with the whole OT. The fact that τὸ γράμμα is linked here with Moses and the Ten Commandments makes this view unlikely.

5. The situation in Rome

1 As Schmithals, *Römerbrief*, 7, notes, whether or not one agrees with Baur, there can be no going back on his view that Romans is to be understood historically.
2 It is typical of this situation that Kettunen devotes only the last few pages of his otherwise useful monograph on the purpose of Romans to Rom. 1:18–11:36 (*Abfassungszweck*, 176ff).
3 Minear is opposed by Drane, 'Romans', 220ff.
4 Cf. W.S. Campbell, 'Romans III', 34ff.
5 Cf. Suggs, '"The Word"', 295ff.
6 Hübner's view of Romans is another attempt to understand it from Paul's own position. Taking as his starting-point the more reflective tone of Romans by comparison with Galatians, he suggests that Paul is responding to James' objections to Galatians, thus moderating his views in the light of them (*Law*, 63). Hübner is thus favourably disposed towards Jervell's position (64f).
7 Donfried comments that despite Baur and historical criticism, Romans has continued to be regarded as a 'christianae religionis compendium', but notes the increasing contemporary interest in its *Sitz im Leben* ('Romans Debate', x–xi).
8 Cf. Dahl, 'Missionary Theology', 78: Romans is not concerned with 'the problems of a local church but the universal gospel and Paul's own mission'.
9 Despite his greater emphasis on the importance of the historical context, Beker is in effect not far from this position. Romans is 'in some sense a "dogmatics in outline"', though it is not 'a timeless theological product' (*Paul*, 77). Beker presumably takes this view because he still reads Romans from the standpoint of dialectical theology; thus he writes in Bultmannian language about the Jew's striving for righteousness, 'All his deeds only promote the attempt to secure his existence before God' (247).
10 Lüdemann rightly argues against the view that he was a Jewish agitator (*Paul*, 169).

11 So Smallwood, *Jews*, 211, Jewett, *Dating*, 37.

12 So Jewett, *Dating*, 38ff.

13 So Smallwood, *Jews*, 215, Jewett, *Dating*, 37f.

14 This identification is also made by Suhl, *Paulus*, 326. However, Suhl accepts Orosius' dating. Stern (II, 116) holds that Claudius did not issue two separate edicts, but that the initial edict of expulsion was reversed.

15 The view that only the main trouble-makers were expelled (Jewett, *Dating*, 37) is possible but uncertain (Haenchen, *Acts*, 65).

16 Hunt and Edgar, *Select Papyri*, II, 212.

17 Cf. Lüdemann, *Paul*, 166ff, on Claudius' attitude towards the Jews.

18 Although Josephus states that Jewish protests were peaceful (*BJ* 2.184–203, *Ant.* 18.261–309), Tacitus speaks of an armed uprising (*Hist.* 5.9.2; Stern, II, 29).

19 Wiefel assumes that because of Claudius' initial tolerance towards the Jews, Dio Cassius' dating of the decree revoking the Roman Jews' right of assembly must be wrong; it must date from *after* the expulsion ('Jewish Community', 110f). Christians therefore could not assemble unless they were without ties to the synagogue, and in this way the independent house-churches mentioned in Rom. 16 arose among Gentile Christians, and Paul is able to assume that they practise freedom from the law (113; cf. Wilckens, 'Abfassungszweck', 120). But the rejection of Dio Cassius seems unnecessary, and an alternative view of the origin of Roman Gentile Christianity will be presented later in the present chapter.

20 Against Hengel, *Earliest Christianity*, 107f, who suggests that the disorders were the result of Hellenists preaching a law-free gospel to Gentiles. The assumption that persecution from Jews only arose when the law was openly abandoned (cf. Bornkamm, *Paul*, 13ff) is erroneous, as the frequent Q passages about persecution indicate.

21 Quoted by Donfried, 'Romans 16', 54. For the Latin original, see *Corpus Scriptorum Ecclesiasticorum Latinorum LXXXI: Ambrosiastri qui dicitur Commentarius in Epistulas Paulinas. Pars.I. In Epistulam ad Romanos*. Vienna 1966, 5f.

22 Cf. Bauer, *Orthodoxy*, xxiii–xxiv, Talbert, *Luke*, 83ff.

23 So also Bornkamm, 'Testament', 28, Furnish, *Love Command*, 115f, Bassler, 'Impartiality', 57n. Drane, 'Romans', 212, describes the whole of Rom. 12–15 as 'vague and general'. This is probably true of Rom. 12–13, but 14:1–15:13 seems considerably more specific.

24 So Käsemann, 366, Wilckens, III, 79.

25 Against Klein, 'Purpose', 40f, Räisänen, *Paul*, 48.

26 Proselytes were actually called 'Jews': according to Dio Cassius, the name 'Jew' 'applies also to all the rest of mankind, although of alien race, who affect their customs' (*Hist. Rom.* 37.16.5–17.1, Stern, II, 351); cf. Epictetus, *Dis.* 2.9.20 (Stern, I, 543).

27 Minear claims that the weak were only vegetarians when eating with Gentile Christians (*Obedience*, 10). This is possible, but Rom. 14

does not indicate that the problem was concerned only with table-fellowship.

28 Thus, Käsemann claims that 'Jewish orthodoxy can be ruled out as a source', since 'general abstinence from meat and wine is not found there' (367).

29 So Barrett, 257f, Schlier, 405f, Käsemann, 368.

30 Schlier's survey of the historical background to Rom. 14 (403ff) surprisingly does not mention most of these texts.

31 Philo, *Leg.* 155, indicates the existence of a definite 'Jewish quarter' in Rome.

32 Cf. Cranfield, II, 695.

33 Cf. Barrett, who thinks that Rom. 14:2 is speaking of the Jew who has been expelled from the synagogue ('Things Sacrificed', 42).

34 There is no need to suppose that abstinence from wine is mentioned only hypothetically (against Cranfield, II, 696).

35 Cf. Cranfield, II, 695f.

36 Käsemann's claim that 14:14 abolishes the age-old boundary between the sacred and the profane (375) is – to say the least – exaggerated, as the most cursory look at the contents of, for example, 1 Cor. 5–11 indicates. The boundary is shifted (in some cases), but by no means abolished. Käsemann's view is accepted by Hübner, *Law*, 84.

37 So Schlier, 407, Barrett, 259, Cranfield, II, 695, Wilckens, III, 83. Käsemann's claim that 'Christians are in view who are convinced that days stand under lucky or unlucky stars' (370) seems unwarranted.

38 The apparent implication in 14:13ff that Gentile Christians should submit to food-laws for the sake of 'peace and mutual upbuilding' (v. 19) does not seem consistent with the exhortation to the weak in v. 3 not to 'pass judgment on him who eats', which implies that Gentile Christians will continue to ignore the food-laws. In vv. 13ff, Paul is perhaps more concerned with explaining the standpoint of the weak to the strong, so as to avoid 'disputes over opinions' (v. 1) than with persuading the strong to adopt the food-laws of the weak.

39 According to 15:7, 'Both groups are to recognize and accept one another' (Cranfield, II, 739). But this suggests that at the time of writing, the two groups do *not* recognize and accept each other, i.e. that they are separated. Käsemann's understanding of the imperative in 14:1 as a call for 'everyday recognition of brotherhood, in the broad sense solidarity' (366), or as 'leaving space for growth and communication' (367), is thus too vague.

40 Rom. 15:6 indicates not that 'conflicts are disturbing worship' (Käsemann, 366), but that common worship does not yet take place at all.

41 Cranfield rightly notes that for Paul the quotation concerned 'the combination of Jews and Gentiles in the believing community' (II, 745).

42 It is therefore not the case that in 15:7ff the tensions of 14:1–15:6 'vanish completely from view' (Käsemann, 384).

43 There is no evidence that these Jewish Christians were in the minority (against Käsemann, 366).

44 Schmithals, *Römerbrief*, 106f, notes that despite the prominence of the strong in 14:1–15:6, nothing is said about these people in Rom. 1–11. He deduces from this that Romans combines two letters sent by Paul to the Roman congregation. On the present hypothesis, however, 14:1–15:6 fits in well with ch. 1–11, as the following chapters will attempt to demonstrate. For a discussion of Schmithals' thesis, cf. Hübner, *Law*, 65ff.

45 Käsemann, 419, Bornkamm, *Paul*, 246, Georgi, *Kollekte*, 79f.

46 Manson, 'Romans', 12ff, opposed by Cranfield, I, 11.

47 So Wilckens, I, 25.

48 The Roman destination of Rom. 16 is asserted by Wilckens, I, 24ff, Cranfield, I, 5ff, Donfried, 'Romans 16', *passim*, Lüdemann, *Paul*, 174f, Meeks, *Urban Christians*, 16, and Kettunen, *Abfassungszweck*, 64ff.

49 So Meeks, *Urban Christians*, 56.

50 So Sanday and Headlam, 423, Cranfield, II, 788f. Others assume that imprisonment with Paul is meant (Barrett, 283, Käsemann, 414, Wilckens, III, 135). Schlier, 444, leaves both possibilities open.

51 Literal imprisonment is presumably meant (against Kittel, TDNT, I, 196f).

52 Cf. Meeks, *Urban Christians*, 56.

53 Acceptance of Paul's doctrine of freedom from the law by Jewish Christians cannot have been common; Col. 4:11 seems to reflect this fact.

54 According to Hübner, 'The polemical thrust of his argument is directed against those Jewish Christians who were making life difficult for the Pauline Gentile Christians' (*Law*, 68). However, he also considers possible the view that the conflict in the Roman congregation was between Gentile Christians and proselytes.

55 Brandon notes that Paul is trying to do in Romans what the Judaizers had tried to do in Galatia: convert the respective congregations to a new understanding of the gospel (*Fall*, 148f). In Rom. 15:15, Paul claims that he has sought merely to 'remind' them of what they already know, but this claim does not carry conviction (so Käsemann, 392).

56 Cranfield thinks it more likely that a woman, presumably Andronicus' wife, is here referred to, on the grounds that there is no evidence elsewhere for 'Junias' as a man's name (II, 788). This receives some support from Paul's statement in 1 Cor. 9:5 that other apostles were accompanied by their wives. Cf. also Wilckens, III, 135f.

57 Against Wilckens, III, 136, who thinks that Andronicus and Junia were 'Paul's fellow-workers in the Gentile mission'.

58 Kettunen thinks that they may have been sent there from Jerusalem (*Abfassungszweck*, 77). However, he regards them as members of the 'Hellenist' group there (76), for whom circumcision was 'in principle meaningless'; despite this, they were welcomed by many in the synagogue (80). The very existence of a Hellenistic group with

views such as these is more than doubtful, and it is hard to see why Roman Jews should have welcomed people for whom the sign of the covenant had become meaningless.

59 So Sanday and Headlam, 425, Cranfield, II, 791f. Aristobulus is mentioned by Josephus (*BJ* 2.221–2; *Ant.* 18.273–6; 20.13).

60 It is therefore not the case that 'the characteristic and peculiar thing about Romans' is 'the fact that it was not, or was only in slight degree, aimed at circumstances within a certain congregation' (Nygren, 4).

61 According to Schlier, the imperatives make the Roman congregation the 'Übermittlerin' of Paul's greetings (442f).

62 Käsemann gives the contrast between the violence of 16.17–20 and the rest of the letter as an additional reason for separating ch. 16 (419). But Kettunen points out that it fits just as badly into ch. 16 itself (*Abfassungszweck*, 67).

63 Kettunen, *Abfassungszweck*, 67, identifies 'the doctrine you have been taught' with 'the pattern of faith delivered to you' (6:17). If so, then Paul is maintaining the fiction of 15:15 that he is merely 'reminding' them of things with which they are already familiar. Those who dissent from his teaching are thus seen as dissenting from 'the pattern of faith delivered to you'.

64 Schmithals, *Gnostics*, 222ff, Dodd, 244f, Käsemann, 418.

65 According to Kettunen, 1:5f,13–15; 11:13; 15:16,18 clearly indicate that the readers were Gentiles (*Abfassungszweck*, 27). But in no case is this certain. Even 11:13 could easily imply that elsewhere Paul has been speaking primarily to Jews – otherwise he would not have to single out the Gentiles for special mention.

66 So Sanday and Headlam, 12, Barrett, 22, Käsemann, 15, Schlier, 30.

67 So Cranfield, I, 20, Wilckens, I, 67.

68 Cf. Cranfield, I, 67f.

69 If the primary addressees were Jewish, this resolves the problem posed by Zeller, *Juden*, 38f, Schmithals, *Römerbrief*, 24, and Kettunen, *Abfassungszweck*, 22, that a letter supposedly written to Gentile readers is concerned with Jewish problems. Schmithals' solution is that the readers were former God-fearers (83,90,93).

70 Against Klein, 'Purpose', 45.

71 Cf. Klein, 'Purpose', 36, Wilckens, 'Abfassungszweck', 114ff. Schmithals, *Römerbrief*, 167ff, tries to solve this problem by means of source criticism.

72 Cf. Hübner, *Law*, 69: despite Rom. 15:20, Paul still sees Rome as his mission field 'as his Paulinist followers live there'.

73 Most commentators hold that Romans is addressed to a predominantly Gentile readership: so Sanday and Headlam, xxxiii, Barrett, 22, Schlier, 5, Käsemann, 15. Cranfield argues that both Jewish and Gentile Christians were numerous in the Roman church (21ff). Baur, *Paul*, I, 321ff, and W. Manson, *Hebrews*, 172ff, argue for a Jewish Christian readership.

74 Cf. Klein, 'Purpose', 47.

75 So Wilckens, 'Abfassungszweck', 115.

76 This seems more likely than Käsemann's theological interpretation: 'Paul gives Judaism precedence for the sake of the continuity of the plan of salvation' (23). The context suggests that the historical reality of the Roman church is in view.

77 Cf. Georgi, *Kollekte*, 90.

78 For this identification, cf. Watson, '2 Cor. x–xiii'.

6. The social function of Romans: Rom. 2

1 According to Lüdemann, *Antipaulinismus*, 158f, Baur's view of Romans as addressed to Jewish Christians in Rome is hardly represented any more in modern scholarship. It will be the argument here that Baur's approach (unlike any other) does at least show how the contents of Romans might be relevant to its recipients. I regret not having had access to Lüdemann's book during the preparation of earlier chapters.

2 For example, Conzelmann denies that Paul's views on justification and the law can be derived from his historical situation, and adds: 'The doctrine of the law must be understood in specifically theological terms' (*Outline*, 221).

3 Thus, according to Nygren, the fact that Romans was not aimed at circumstances within the Roman congregation gives it 'a uniquely objective character' (5).

4 Minear, *Obedience*, is exceptional in this respect. However, his claim that in, for example, 2:1–6,17–24, the 'weak in faith' are *directly* addressed (46) seems an over-simplification.

5 Against Wilckens, 'Abfassungszweck', 126, who denies any close connection between Rom. 14–15 and Rom. 1–11.

6 The words, ἵνα μὴ ἃ ἐὰν θέλητε ταῦτα ποιῆτε are sometimes understood as a reference to moral failure along the lines of Rom. 7 (Dunn, 'Rom. 7,14–15', 267, opposed by Wenham, 'Christian Life', 83). But the point here is that the Spirit *does* restrain the flesh, as v. 16 indicates. V. 16 is a promise, not a command as in RSV; cf. Betz, 278, Bruce, 243, BDF, 365. In none of the other 18 occurrences of οὐ μή in the NT (Mt. 16:22; 21:19; 24:2,21; 25:9; Mk 13:19; Jn 6:35,37; 10:5,28; 13:8; 16:7; Rom. 10:18,19; 1 Cor. 11:22; Rev. 9:6; 18:7; 21:25) is there a clear imperative sense.

7 Barrett finds evidence of four main charges against Paul in his letters: (i) He is not truly an apostle, (ii) he is a man-pleaser, (iii) he is an antinomian who hates his own people, (iv) he is dishonest (ΨΕΥΔΑΠΟΣΤΟΛΟΙ, 99). Cf. Stuhlmacher, *Paulus*, 23ff. As Bauer comments, 'The apostle Paul was the only heresiarch known to the apostolic age' (*Orthodoxy*, 236).

8 According to Lüdemann, *Antipaulinismus*, 159f, Rom. 3:8 is the only place where we can definitely see evidence of anti-Paulinism in Romans. But the parallels to the Jewish Christian objections in Galatians suggest that there is much more evidence than that. Again and again, Paul answers objections which have been made by Jewish Christians, and which he assumes will also be made by the Jewish Christians of Rome.

9 Bornkamm, 'Revelation', 50ff, Sanday and Headlam, 51f.

10 For Jewish condemnation of homosexuality, see Apoc. Abr. 24:8, Ep. Aris. 152, Sib. Or. 3:595ff.

11 Lüdemann, *Antipaulinismus*, 159, cites Bornkamm's claim that the use of the diatribe genre makes it impossible to reconstruct concrete circumstances which Paul is addressing. But apparently-general arguments may well have a very specific purpose.

12 Barrett, 43, Leenhardt, 72f, Franzmann, 44,48, Pregeant, 'Grace', 75, Wright, *Messiah*, 67, Dahl, 'Missionary Theology', 79, Hahn, 'Gesetzesverständnis', 31.

13 This seems more likely than Kuss's suggestion that Paul here addresses the Jew as 'man' in order to emphasize the removal of the absolute privileges he claims (I, 60).

14 Cf. Bornkamm, 'Anakoluthe', 76, Dahl, 'Missionary Theology', 80.

15 Bassler understands 2:12–29 as a single section, manifesting a chiastic structure ('Impartiality', 49f). But the supposed correspondences (e.g. vv. 17–24 = v. 25) are not convincing.

16 Cf. Käsemann, 68.

17 So Cranfield, I, 138f.

18 The importance of comparison with the Gentiles in Rom. 2 is stressed by Mauser, 'Universalität', 264.

19 I.e. in a quite literal sense (cf. 2:21ff), and not in the sophisticated sense suggested by Barrett: the act of judging is the same as idolatry because both cases reveal 'man's ambition to put himself in the place of God' (44). Paul is not against judging *per se* – indeed, in Rom. 1:18–3:20, he seems to cast himself in the role of 'God's prosecutor' (Shaw, *Cost*, 149).

20 V. 4 refers to salvation-historical privileges denied to the Gentiles (so Wilckens, I, 124).

21 Hübner, *Law*, 114, rightly points out that the Jew in 2:1–3:8 boasts of his possessing of the law, not of doing it.

22 So Bläser, *Gesetz*, 20, Schlier, 77.

23 καυχᾶσαι here does not have a derogatory sense (so Käsemann, 69, against Barrett, 55f).

24 Cf. Käsemann's perceptive comments about Paul's rhetoric in 2:17ff (69).

25 This is of course polemic rather than objective description, and is not evidence of a 'terrible degradation of Jewish morals in the period preceding the Destruction of the Temple' (Dodd, 64).

26 These charges are to be understood literally (against Barrett, 56ff); the problem of their function in Paul's argument is discussed later in the chapter.

27 Hübner, *Law*, 113f, cites ExR 19 (81c) as a possible background for Rom. 2:25ff: 'The circumcised do not go down into Gehenna.'

28 Wilckens writes (I, 177): 'One should note that it is precisely Paul who insists on works as the single criterion for the justification of the righteous, whereas his opponent insists throughout on his salvation-historical privileges (2:12–29; 3:1ff), which Paul contests.'

29 Barrett finds an attack on earning salvation in the word ἐριθεία (2:8), which refers to 'those who are out for quick and selfish profit on

their own account', i.e. 'those who look on their works as achievements of their own' (47f). But this reads too much theology into a single word.

30 When Conzelmann states (*Outline*, 249) that the theme of Rom. 1–3 is 'the crisis of Israel (in so far as Israel wants to exist by its own achievements)', he misses the point of Rom. 2. This is well stated by Wright, *Messiah*, 97: 'The Jews were not trying to "earn" salvation *de novo* by good works: they were presuming upon it as an ancestral right.'

31 According to Räisänen, *Paul*, 101, 'Paul's argument is here simply a piece of propagandist denigration.'

32 However, there is a surprising parallel in Philo, *Vir.* 226–7, where Philo's opposition to the view that punishment and salvation are apportioned according to the virtues of one's ancestors is probably to be understood as an attack on the Jewish theology of the covenant (against Sanders, 'Covenant', 28).

33 It is therefore not simply 'a concrete attack on the Jews' (Käsemann, 68).

34 Horace, *Serm.* 1.4.142f, 1.9.68ff (Stern, I, 323,325), Juvenal, *Sat.* 14.96ff (Stern, II, 102f). As early as 139 BC, Cornelius Hispalus 'banished the Jews from Rome, because they attempted to transmit their sacred rites to the Romans' (Valerius Maximus, *Mem.* 1.3.3; Stern, I, 358). According to Dio Cassius, *Hist. Rom.* 57.18.5a (Stern, II, 365), Tiberius expelled the Jews in AD 19 because they 'flocked to Rome in great numbers and were converting many of the natives to their ways' (cf. Josephus, *Ant.* 18.81ff). Proselytes were expelled too, according to Suetonius, *Vit. Tib.* 36 (Stern, II, 112f). Those in Rome who had adopted the Jewish way of life were severely punished by Domitian (Dio Cassius, *Hist. Rom.* 67.14.1–3, Stern, II, 379ff – there is no evidence that Christianity is here referred to).

35 Cicero, *Flac.* 28.66, and Tacitus, *Hist.* 5.1 indicate the irritation felt by the Romans at the Jewish success in persuading large numbers of converts to send money for the support of the temple in Jerusalem (Stern, I, 197, II, 26).

36 ἱεροσυλεῖς; could have the wider meaning, 'Do you commit sacrilege?' (Barrett, 57, Cranfield, I, 169f). According to Sanday and Headlam, 66, Schlier, 86, Käsemann, 71, and Wilckens, I, 150, the reference here is to Jewish complicity in theft from pagan temples, which Acts 19:37 and Josephus, *Ant.* 4.207 show to have been a possibility. The latter view agrees well with, 'You who abhor idols'. But this phrase is also consistent with robbery of the Jerusalem temple, which proves that apparent concern for the worship of the true God was fraudulent. Cf. Bruce, 93.

37 Martial speaks of 'the lecheries of circumcised Jews' (*Epig.* 7.30.5, Stern, I, 524f), but it is not clear whether this was a widespread pagan idea about Jews.

38 Räisänen, 'Theological Difficulties', 309, exaggerates at this point.

39 According to Minear, in Rom. 2 Paul attacks Jewish *Christian* condemnation of Gentile life (*Obedience*, 51). But Rom. 2 does not have to be directly addressed to the Roman Jewish Christians to be relevant to them.

40 Cf. for example 1 En. 95:5; 100:7; Ps. Sol. 17:10; 4 Ez. 7:35.

41 'The analysis of works presupposed by vv. 7f has the important consequence of dissolving the barrier between Jew and Gentile' (Barrett, 48); cf. van Dülmen, *Gesetz*, 74.

42 Cf. 2 Bar. 15:5ff.

43 Bassler, 'Impartiality', 54, rightly notes that Rom. 1–2 is more concerned with divine impartiality than with the universality of sin.

44 The acknowledgment in 4 Ez. 3:36 of the existence of righteous Gentiles probably refers to proselytes (cf. 2 Bar. 41:4).

45 This seems preferable to the view that v. 14 is linked to v. 12 (Barrett, 51, Käsemann, 62, Bornkamm, 'Gesetz', 99, Walker, 'Heiden', 304).

46 So Kuss, 69, Schlatter, 95. But Käsemann, 66, Cranfield, I, 162, Schlier, 79f, Wilckens, I, 136, think that the reference here is to a purely internal process.

47 The view that v. 16 is to be linked with v. 12 or v. 13, and that the intervening material is a parenthesis (Riedl, 'Auslegung', 278) is too cumbersome to be plausible.

48 ἐνδείκνυνται is regarded as future in sense by Leenhardt, 84, Cranfield, I, 162, Wilckens, I, 135, Franzmann, 51; as present by Kuss, 71, Michel, 69f.

49 Cranfield refers the Gentiles' deeds to the present (I, 158), but the witness of conscience and the λογισμοί to the Day of Judgment (161f). V. 15b seems to be linked so closely to v. 15a that such an abrupt change of subject seems unlikely.

50 Bultmann, 'Glossen', 282ff.

51 Cf. Cranfield, II, 808f, Käsemann, 423, Barrett, 286. Nygren, 457, and Bruce, 282, are exceptions.

52 Käsemann claims that v. 16 is an integral part of the argument on the grounds that Paul here 'protects himself against a psychological misunderstanding of the anthropology of v. 15' (67). Such a view is motivated by dialectical theology's hostility towards natural theology, and leaves the precise meaning of vv. 14f unclear.

53 Bornkamm states that 'if it cannot be said of the Gentile that he knows God's law, God's punishment, to which he is liable and which regards him as guilty, would not be justified' ('Gesetz', 98). But the point of 2:14f is more positive: Gentiles may do good and be saved.

54 Cf. Sanders' discussion of the various interpretations of this passage in *Jewish People*, 123ff. His own solution to its problems is that it uses material from Diaspora Judaism (127f).

55 Cf. Schlier, 72.

56 Schlier's comment on vv. 28f illustrates the confusion which results from this type of interpretation: 'Here Paul has already left behind the pre-Christian moral argument. But it is still not clear from which standpoint he is judging' (90).

57 Cf. Mundle, 'Auslegung', Flückiger, 'Werke', Barth, *Shorter*, Minear, *Obedience*, 47.
58 Cf. Mundle, 'Auslegung', 251, Bläser, *Gesetz*, 20, Flückiger, 'Werke', 26, Wright, *Messiah*, 117.
59 Cf. Mundle, 'Auslegung', 251, Flückiger, 'Werke', 34, K. Barth, *Shorter*, 36.
60 Cf. Mundle, 'Auslegung', 254, Barth, *Shorter*, 38f.
61 Wilckens mentions the characteristic Protestant embarrassment about Rom. 2 (I, 144).
62 The typically Protestant anxiety lest faith should become a work (Doughty, 'Priority', 165ff), thus becomes superfluous.
63 Meeks rightly sees baptism as marking 'an extraordinarily thorough resocialization' (*Urban Christians*, 78).
64 'The faith which Paul preaches ... in no sense contains a fundamental, far-reaching denial of all human activity' (Wilckens, I, 145).
65 So, for example, Pfleiderer, *Paulinismus*, 280ff (cited by Wilckens, I, 144n). Cf. Synofzik, *Gerichtsaussagen, passim*.
66 Donfried argues that according to Paul 'God can and will reject disobedient Christians' ('Justification', 107). N. Watson attributes the alleged tension between the ideas of justification and judgment to 'the occasional nature of Paul's letters' and the difference in the addressees ('Antinomy', 213f).
67 This means that justification should not be seen as an eschatological concept (except in the very general sense that virtually no Pauline idea is entirely free from eschatological overtones): so Lyonnet, 'Gratuité', 101f; against Bultmann, *Theology*, I, 274ff, Kertelge, *Rechtfertigung*, 112ff, Mattern, *Gericht*, 121, N. Watson, 'Antinomy', 209f.
68 Cf. Donfried, 'Justification', *passim*, for criticism of Protestant scholarship at this point. Donfried describes much discussion of this problem as 'rambling, repetitive and contradictory' (91).
69 Thus, Rom. 2–3 does not arise from a constructive tension between 'the logic of grace' and 'the logic of recompense', which cannot be combined into a systematic unity, but which must both be maintained (against Pregeant, 'Grace', 85ff). On this view, 'It is more important that the reader experience both the event of grace and accountability for his or her deeds than to be able to order all elements of these realities into a conceptually unified whole' (87).
70 These passages do not mean that it is central to Paul's thought that 'the law should be fulfilled' (against Sanders, *Jewish People*, 93ff), that 'in discussing the behaviour appropriate to being Christian, Paul saw no incongruity between "living by faith" and "fulfilling the law"' (114). Paul might have made the law the basis for his ethical instruction, but on the whole he does not do so – probably because the law was for him indivisible and inseparable from the Jewish community.
71 Bassler points out that Rom. 1–2 provides no real basis for the summarizing statement of 3:9 ('Impartiality', 53). As Räisänen puts it, 'some' to 'every' is 'a blatant non sequitur' (*Paul*, 99).

72 Paul does not 'concede' the possibility of good works in 2:7–10 (Jüngel, 'Adam', 73); he *affirms* it.

73 Thus, although the motif of the circumcision of the heart is derived from Jewish tradition (cf. Lev. 26:41; Dt. 10:16; 30:6; Jer. 4:4; 6:10; 9:25; Ez. 44:7,9; 1QS 5:5; 1QH 18:20; Od. Sol. 11:1–3; Philo, *Mig.* 92; *Spec.* 1.6.305), the radical conclusions here drawn from it – that circumcision is unnecessary for the obedient Gentile, and that it is not one of τὰ δικαιώματα τοῦ νόμου – are distinctive.

74 Against Räisänen, *Paul*, 106, who claims that Paul has no real interest in the Gentiles of Rom. 2.

7. The social function of Romans: Rom. 3–4

1 Cf. Williams, ' "Righteousness" ', 268f, Campbell, 'Romans III', 33, Hall, 'Romans 3.1–8', 184f.

2 3:1ff can hardly be entitled 'der Rechtsstreit Gottes mit der Welt' (C. Müller, *Gerechtigkeit*, 57), for it is concerned with τὸ περισσὸν τοῦ 'Ιουδαίου.

3 Thus, 3:1–8 should not be regarded as a 'digression' (Kuss, 59, 99, Cranfield, I, 183, Schlier, 97), unless exegesis makes this absolutely necessary.

4 So Barrett, 64, Leenhardt, 92f, Cranfield, I, 184, Lagrange, 65, Stuhlmacher, *Gerechtigkeit*, 85, Kertelge, *Rechtfertigung*, 64, Bornkamm, 'Teufelskunst', 144.

5 'At this point Paul's thought takes an unexpected turn' (I, 183); cf. Kuss, 102.

6 Against Michel, 80, who thinks that Paul may be showing that his opponent is not capable of serious discussion.

7 Dodd, 69f, Lagrange, 66. Bornkamm, 'Teufelskunst', 145, finds here the idea that God must be acknowledged, not theologized about.

8 So Käsemann, 81f, Stuhlmacher, *Gerechtigkeit*, 85, Kertelge, *Rechtfertigung*, 65, Bornkamm, 'Teufelskunst', 144, Hahn, 'Gesetzesverständnis', 34, Müller, *Gerechtigkeit*, 67. It is true that πᾶς ἄνθρωπος cannot refer simply to the Jews (against Hall, 'Romans 3.1–8', 186).

9 So Käsemann, 81, Wilckens, I, 165.

10 Cf. Käsemann, 79, Kertelge, *Rechtfertigung*, 67, Stuhlmacher, *Gerechtigkeit*, 85f, Williams, 'Righteousness', 184; against Bornkamm, 'Teufelskunst', 145. But despite seeing the importance of God's covenant with Israel in this passage, Käsemann, Stuhlmacher and Kertelge insist that vv. 4–8 are concerned with humanity as a whole.

11 Moxnes comments on 3:5,7: 'In the first part of each verse, the arguments from Paul's opponents draw on the "dogma" stated in 3:1–4, that God is faithful to his promises. However, they then make the inference that therefore God should not inflict his wrath upon the Jews' (*Theology*, 58; cf. Hall, 'Romans 3.1–8', 184f, on v. 5).

12 The form of the question in v. 5b indicates that Paul himself is speaking, and not the objector (Schlier, 91, Hall, 'Romans 3.1–8', 190). But this does not mean that Paul has no objector in mind (against Hall). We may paraphrase: 'Surely you do not mean to tell me that God would be unjust to inflict wrath on us?' This explains the addition of κατὰ ἄνθρωπον λέγω.

13 'In Rom. 3.1–8 Paul is trying to reconcile two seemingly inconsistent ideas: on the one hand, God's faithfulness to his covenant promises to the Jewish nation; on the other hand, God's impartiality towards Jew and Gentile, both in mercy and in judgment, which he has just described in ch. 2' (Hall, 'Romans 3.1–8', 183).

14 Hall, 'Romans 3.1–8', 192; mentioned as a possibility by Barrett, 64.

15 So Hall, 'Romans 3.1–8', 191.

16 Against Barrett, 64, and Käsemann, 83, who regard it as irrelevant.

17 Hall understands v. 7 not as an objection but as Paul's own comment: 'If God's faithfulness increases to his glory, the more unfaithful I am to the covenant, how do you account for the fact that I, Paul, a Jew, come under the judgment of God just as much as a Gentile sinner?' ('Romans 3.1–8', 195). But on this view, v. 7b disputes the claim of v. 7a that our unfaithfulness shows forth God's faithfulness, which is one of the main themes of 3:1–8.

18 So Cranfield, I, 187, Hall, 'Romans 3.1–8', 194; against this, Kuss, 104, Barrett, 65, Käsemann, 84, Wilckens, I, 167.

19 Lüdemann, *Antipaulinismus*, 160, rightly emphasizes that this is probably a Jewish *Christian* objection.

20 Dahl argues that προεχόμεθα refers not to Jews but to all men ('Romans 3.9', 185), and is to be connected to τί οὖν and translated: 'What, then, do we plead as a defence?' (194). This is a rhetorical question needing no answer, and οὐ πάντως is an early gloss (195). But Cranfield's argument in favour of the active meaning (I, 188ff) is convincing. This interpretation is accepted by almost all commentators (e.g. Käsemann, 86, Wilckens, I, 172, Barrett, 68, Leenhardt, 95), though not by Franzmann, 61, who takes the verb to be passive.

21 It is possible that the application of such texts (mainly from the psalms) to the Jews is the result of the early Christian identification of the innocent sufferer of the psalms with the crucified and risen Jesus. Once that identification had been made, it would be natural to identify those who persecute the righteous man with the Jews, who were regarded as responsible for the crucifixion of Jesus. Whether or not Rom. 3:10ff is a pre-Pauline early Christian psalm (so Michel, 85), it may at least testify to a pre-Pauline way of understanding the psalms. Cf. Hanson, 'Reproach', 20ff.

22 In ὅσα ὁ νόμος λέγει, νόμος is equivalent to γραφή (cf. 1 Cor. 14:21 – Michel, 86); in ἐν τῷ νόμῳ, it has the more usual restricted meaning of 'Torah', as also in v. 20.

23 The view of Sanders, *Jewish People*, 82; opposed by Bläser, *Gesetz*, 9.

24 So Bornkamm, *Paul*, 120f, Hahn, 'Gesetzesverständnis', 59, Bandstra, *Elements*, 63, Jüngel, 'Gesetz', 52.

25 Cf. Sanday and Headlam, 81, Dodd, 72, Barrett, 71, Robinson, *Wrestling*, 37.

26 The view of Bultmann, *Theology*, I, 264, Schlier, 101, and Käsemann, 89f, is that 3:20b, like 7:7f, refers to the law's function of provoking sin. But there is nothing in the context to indicate that this is the meaning (so Cranfield, I, 199n).

27 This view of 3:20a is rightly criticized by Wilckens, I, 176ff, on the grounds that the context shows that Paul is speaking of actual transgressions of the law, and not of a striving to fulfil the law which is itself sinful.

28 This is a more accurate statement of the purpose of Rom. 1:18–3:20 than the usual view that this section is 'a demonstration of the universality of sin' (Bultmann, *Theology*, I, 250). Cf. Bassler, 'Impartiality', 54.

29 δικαιοσύνη θεοῦ appears to have the same reference to God's faithfulness to his covenant in 3:21ff as it does in 3:5 (so Käsemann, 'Righteousness', 169, Williams, 'Righteousness', 271; opposed by Bultmann, 'ΔΙΚΑΙΟΣΥΝΗ', 12, Conzelmann, 'Rechtfertigungslehre', 399; cf. also the discussion in Hübner, *Law*, 124ff, and Wilckens, I, 202ff).

30 So Käsemann, 'Römer 3,24–26', 96ff, Kertelge, *Rechtfertigung*, 48ff, Michel, 92f, Wilckens, I, 83f, Pluta, *Bundestreue, passim*, Stuhlmacher, 'Römer 3,24–26', *passim*.

31 Ziesler rightly states that 'righteousness' in 3:25b,26 means God's covenant loyalty (*Righteousness*, 194).

32 Cf. Rom. 15:8, where Paul himself says that 'Christ became a servant to the circumcised to show God's truthfulness, in order to confirm his promises given to the patriarchs.'

33 Mundle, *Glaubensbegriff*, 87f, rightly asks why Paul should have been interested in the latter.

34 Cf. Wright, *Messiah*, 99.

35 Cf. Howard, 'Romans 3:21–31', *passim*.

36 One cannot speak unreservedly about 'Pauline universalism' in this context. Shaw comments: 'The "all" is deceptive. It is inclusive in relation to sin, but has a much more selective sense in relation to the justified' (*Cost*, 151).

37 Bassler sees the main theme of the whole of Rom. 1–3 as God's impartiality ('Impartiality', 55).

38 Thus, the reinterpretation in vv. 21–4,26 of the Jewish Christian tradition of v. 25 is to be understood as a call for social reorientation rather than as an existentialist interpretation of 'objectivising terms from the inherited tradition' (Hübner, *Law*, 115).

39 So Michel, 95, Kuss, 176, van Dülmen, *Gesetz*, 87; against this, Friedrich, 'Röm. 3,27', 401ff, Cranfield, I, 220, Wilckens, I, 245.

40 Barrett, 82, regards 3:28 as a 'footnote' to 3:27.

41 Against Friedrich, 'Röm. 3.27', and Rhyne, *Faith*, 67ff, who argue that the two senses of νόμος derive from 3:21, where the righteousness of God is both 'apart from law' and 'attested by the law and the prophets'.

42 In the light of 3:29f, ἄνθρωπος in v. 28 probably has the sense of 'Jew and Gentile alike' (so Bultmann, *Theology*, I, 231, Klein, 'Römer 4', 171n).

43 A similar view is taken by Via, 'Structuralist Approach', 213: 'Faith then is the subjective situation of the alazon or boaster of comedy after he has been deflated – that is, saved – by the ironical God whose humble foolishness is wisdom'.

44 Cf. Moxnes, *Theology*, 40, Howard, 'Romans 3:21–31', 232, Wilckens, I, 244, Sanders, *Jewish People*, 33, Räisänen, *Paul*, 170ff.

45 Käsemann is one of the few commentators in the Reformation tradition who recognizes the importance of vv. 29f; he notes that 'the full force of this revolutionary statement is seldom perceived' (104). But he still interprets the passage with Reformation presuppositions when he writes: 'The monotheistic confession shatters a conception of the law which makes salvation a privilege of the religious' (104). The equation, Jew = religious person, is unquestioned.

46 Robinson recalls Dodd's comment on this verse during the translation of the NEB: 'What rubbish!' (*Wrestling*, 51).

47 There is therefore no need to regard continuity and discontinuity as mutually exclusive interpretative possibilities (against Rhyne, *Faith*, 1, 121); Paul's sectarian stance requires both.

48 The most common interpretation of v. 31 refers back to v. 21, where it is said that the righteousness of God is attested by the law and the prophets (so Michel, 97, Barrett, 84,86, Käsemann, 250, Wilckens, I, 250, Ziesler, *Righteousness*, 195). Van Dülmen, *Gesetz*, 88, thinks that 3:31 points towards 8:4. But 3:21 understands 'law' in the broader sense of 'the Pentateuch', and probably refers to such passages as Gen. 15:6, discussed at length in Rom. 4. The two occurrences of νόμος must both have the same sense and refer to the law of Moses, i.e. to God's commandments to Israel.

49 Cf. Klein, 'Römer 4', 148.

50 The relationship between vv. 27f and vv. 29f is stressed by Howard, 'Romans 3:21–31', 232, Sanders, *Jewish People*, 33f, Moxnes, *Theology*, 30, Wilckens, I, 244, Bläser, *Gesetz*, 24.

51 It is often seen as a scriptural proof of 3:28 (Eichholz, *Paulus*, 222, Schlier, 121, Hübner, *Law*, 118) or of 3:31 (Kümmel, *Römer 7*, 5f, Wilckens, 'Rechtfertigung', 41f).

52 Robinson too regards Rom. 4 as an 'excursus' (*Wrestling*, 52).

53 Bassler denies that Rom. 4 is a mere scriptural proof for justification by faith, and asserts that like Rom. 1–3 its main theme is God's impartiality towards Jews and Gentiles ('Impartiality', 56).

54 If Hengel's attractive view of Sirach as a response to the encroachments of Hellenism is correct (*Hellenism*, I, 138ff), then the portrayal of Abraham here may be determined by the controversy with Hellenism (152). Nickelsburg, *Jewish Literature*, 64, claims to the contrary that Sirach is 'striking for its lack of specific, pointed, and explicit polemics against Hellenism'.

55 Cf. the Hellenized version of this theme in Philo, who argues that 'before any at all of the particular statutes was set in writing',

Abraham and the other patriarchs 'followed the unwritten law with perfect ease' (*Abr.* 5).

56 Here, the use of the figure of Abraham in opposition to Hellenism seems clear, especially since Abraham was a key figure in liberal Palestinian Judaism (cf. Hengel, *Hellenism*, I, 88ff).

57 Abraham also symbolizes separation from the Gentiles in the interpretation of his migration as the abandonment of idolatry (Jub. 12, Apoc. Abr. 1–8) or of polytheism and astrology (Philo, *Abr.* 68ff, *Mig.* 176ff).

58 Cf. the discussion of Abraham in Jubilees in Nickelsburg, *Jewish Literature*, 75f.

59 The view that Gen. 15:6 is not confined to a single episode but summarizes Abraham's whole life is thus not confined to Paul. Cf. Jas. 2:21ff.

60 The theme of Abraham's ten trials (Jub. 19:8) occurs also in mAb. 5:3: 'With ten temptations was Abraham our father tempted, and he stood steadfast in them all.'

61 Here the promise to Abraham of the land (Gen. 15:18ff) becomes a promise to inherit the world, under the influence of Ps. 72:8.

62 There is no need to regard Azariah's prayer as 'a previously existent composition reused for its present purpose' (Nickelsburg, *Jewish Literature*, 28). It seems to be a straightforward addition to Daniel, composed for the purpose, which regards the narrative of Dn. 3 as paradigmatic of the plight of Israel (cf. Tob. 13). Vv. 15–17 are intended to give it verisimilitude, and are not a sign of composition during Antiochus' persecution between 167 and 164 BC (against Nickelsburg, *Jewish Literature*, 29).

63 Thus, in Abraham's vision of the judgment in Apoc. Abr. 22, those who are saved are 'the ones I have prepared to be born of you and to be called my people' (22:5).

64 Bornkamm rightly states that Rom. 4 is polemical throughout (*Paul*, 144).

65 'Critical though he may be towards his Jewish religious inheritance, he still wishes to legitimate his new position in terms which are derived, however tendentiously, from his previous one' (Shaw, *Cost*, 152).

66 This interpretation of ὑπακοὴν πίστεως in 1:5 is accepted by Cranfield, I, 66f, who states that 'the equivalence for Paul of faith in God and obedience to Him may be illustrated again and again from this epistle'. He cites 1:8 with 16:19, 10:16a with 10:16b, 11:23 with 11:30 and 11:31, and 15:18 with 1:5 (66). This is a strong argument in favour of regarding faith for Paul as a comprehensive term, including acceptance of a new way of life as well as new beliefs.

67 The distinction betwen Abraham as a model and as recipient of the promise is somewhat blurred in 4:9–12, where the theme of Abraham's fatherhood implies the promise to him and to his seed (cf. 4:13ff). Nevertheless, the former theme is predominant in this passage.

68 According to Shaw, in Rom. 4 'Abraham gives legitimacy to the mixed communities which have been established as a result of Paul's preaching' (*Cost*, 154).

69 According to Minear, *Obedience*, 53, Paul is in Rom. 4 saying to the 'weak in faith', 'You must accept the strong in faith as children of Abraham and heirs to the promise of Abraham.'

70 There is nothing in the text to support Hübner's claim that Abraham was ungodly because he wanted to be justified by works (*Law*, 121).

71 Cf. Sanders, *Jewish People*, 35.

72 Protestant scholars are often reluctant to admit that faith for Paul is the condition for salvation, insisting that it is only God who justifies (cf. Hübner, *Law*, 140).

73 Cf. Bultmann, *Theology*, I, 112. Zeller's analysis is more satisfactory: vv. 1–8 answer the question of v. 1, and vv. 9–25 are concerned with the question, 'To whom?' (*Juden*, 100); cf. also Müller, *Gerechtigkeit*, 51.

74 As Sanders points out, Paul in 4:9ff attacks not self-righteousness but privileged status (*Jewish People*, 34).

75 According to Hübner, *Law*, 53, the comparatively positive view of circumcision here is 'radically new in contrast to Galatians'. Hübner rejects the view that this might be due to the differences in the situations of the addressees (53f), and attributes it to 'a far from trivial process of reflection and development in Paul the theologian' (54), stimulated in part by critical responses to Galatians from the Jerusalem church (55).

76 In 4:12, πατέρα περιτομῆς τοῖς οὐκ ἐκ περιτομῆς μόνον ἀλλὰ καὶ τοῖς στοιχοῦσιν κτλ. suggests as it stands that two separate groups of Jewish Christians are referred to: (i) those who are not of circumcision alone, and (ii) those who follow in Abraham's footsteps. This is obviously impossible, and the second τοῖς is commonly regarded as a mistake, either by Paul or by his copyist (so Kuss, 186, Schlier, 128, Cranfield, I, 237, Wilckens, I, 266).

77 Thus, as Sanders states, Paul is in Rom. 4 'primarily interested in the status of the Gentiles', and 'in denying that those who are "of the law" (Jews) are privileged' (*Jewish People*, 34).

78 According to Byrne, *'Sons of God'*, 149, and Moxnes, *Theology*, 43f, the description of Abraham as 'ungodly' in 4:5 means that he is regarded as a Gentile.

79 The view that Paul is opposing here is summed up by 2 Bar. 44:15, according to which it is those 'who have preserved the truth of the Law' (i.e. remained faithful members of the Jewish community) to whom 'the coming world will be given'.

80 So Käsemann, 121, Cranfield, I, 242, Wilckens, I, 271f. Michel, 123, and Schlier, 131, take the phrase, οὐ τῷ ἐκ τοῦ νόμου μόνον, as a reference to Jews in general; but this does not accord with the context.

81 The fact that Paul regards the church as the seed of Abraham does not mean that he regards it as existing in a salvation-historical continuum with Israel, as Wilckens has argued ('Rechtfertigung', 41ff). Klein opposes this view ('Römer 4'), although Käsemann, 'Abraham',

argues that Klein goes too far in the opposite direction to Wilckens. Cf. also Wilckens, 'Römer 3,21–4,25', Klein, 'Römer 3,21–4,25'.
82 The quotation from Gen. 17:5 in Rom. 4:17 is parenthetic (so Schlier, 131; opposed by Wilckens, I, 274).
83 Shaw comments on Rom. 4 that, in contrast to Abraham, 'the Christian surrenders himself in theory to Christ, but in practice to his apostle' (*Cost*, 153). While this may be an exaggeration, it at least recognizes that there is a practical strategy underlying the text.

8. The social function of Romans: Rom. 5–8

1 Cf. Kettunen, *Abfassungszweck*, 76.
2 This explanation of the differences between Galatians and Romans is rejected by Hübner, *Law*, 53f, who postulates a 'process of reflection and development in Paul the theologian' (54).
3 Cf. Nygren 193f, on the textual problem here.
4 Cf. Cranfield, I, 256f.
5 So Nygren, 205, Käsemann, 138.
6 A subjective genitive (so Barrett, 105, Schlier, 150, Käsemann, 135, Cranfield, I, 262, Wilckens, I, 293f).
7 Bultmann, *Theology*, I, 252, 'Adam', 143ff, Dahl, 'Missionary Theology', 82, Jüngel, 'Gesetz', 49, Schnackenburg, 'Römer 7', 286f.
8 So Käsemann, 387. However, on Käsemann's view, 15:9–13 is to do with turning away from liturgy to everyday life (387) – an antithesis which is surely alien to Paul.
9 Cf. Meeks, *Urban Christians*, 162.
10 Cf. Elliott's comments on suffering as a threat to sectarian groups, *Home*, 101.
11 Meeks stresses the way in which ritual speech and music, the reading of Scripture and preaching promote social cohesiveness (*Urban Christians*, 145f).
12 Hübner, *Law*, 81, denies that in Rom. 5:12ff Paul is writing 'objectifying' salvation history. The catch-word 'objectifying', much beloved by scholars influenced by dialectical theology, seems to refer to the conversion of the existential decision required by the kerygma into a non-existential theory about history. This dichotomy has a great deal to do with modern controversy about the nature of theological knowledge, but little to do with Paul.
13 It is not stated here that the sphere of the law is universal (against Jüngel, 'Gesetz', 52).
14 Cf. the traditional Jewish Christian language used by Paul himself in 15:8.
15 Beker, *Paul*, 85, rightly stresses that 'the Jewish question' is still present in Rom. 5.
16 Beker sees Rom. 5:12ff as a summary of the argument so far and a transition to the next stage of the argument (*Paul*, 85). But the notion of a single, gradually unfolding argument derives from the view that Romans is a systematic dogmatic treatise, and should be rejected.

17 According to Minear, Rom. 6 is addressed to 'the strong in faith who scorned and despised the weak in faith', and who object to the idea that they should become 'righteous by the Law's standards' (*Obedience*, 63). But 3:8 suggests that ch. 6 is a response to a Jewish Christian objection to Paul.

18 This is a more probable explanation of the origins of the objection in 6:1 than the view that it is a reaction to Paul's supposed doctrine of salvation by grace alone (against Nygren, 231f, Barrett, 120f, Cranfield, I, 297f).

19 'Righteousness' in Rom. 6 means 'behaviour acceptable to God', as in Jewish usage; the view that here 'righteousness is the power of God which has come on the scene in Christ' (Käsemann, 177) is not justified exegetically, since 'slavery' to sin and to righteousness is simply a metaphor (cf. 6:19a).

20 According to Hübner, *Law*, 131, righteousness in Rom. 6 cannot be 'even only in part a deed or achievement of man' – that is, 'unless we wish to reverse the whole drift of Pauline theology'. But Rom. 6 poses the question of whether this Lutheran approach has misunderstood 'the whole drift of Pauline theology'.

21 Thus, it is not merely the case in Rom. 6 that Paul derives an imperative from an indicative (against Bultmann, 'Ethik', 182, Ziesler, *Righteousness*, 203); the imperative is also the condition of the (future) indicative.

22 Rom. 6 is ostensibly addressed to Gentiles, as vv. 17, 19, 20 suggest; but its main function is to correct a Jewish Christian misunderstanding of Paul's teaching, as 3:8 indicates.

23 Kaye states that 'throughout the letter law is the possession of the Jew' (*Thought Structure*, 110).

24 Rom. 7 is therefore not concerned with 'man's situation' but with the Jewish situation (against Kümmel, *Römer 7*, 134, Bornkamm, *Paul*, 126, Hahn, 'Gesetzesverständnis', 57).

25 That Rom. 7 is addressed to Jewish Christians is recognized by Minear, *Obedience*, 62, Bläser, *Gesetz*, 29f, Schneider, 'Finis', 416, Wright, *Messiah*, 147. This is preferable to the view of Scroggs, that Rom. 7 rejects a possible solution to the problem of enthusiasm ('Rhetorician', 288).

26 Cf. the careful discussion by Cranfield, I, 334f.

27 Minear's view, that the sin aroused by the law is the sin of condemning one's Christian brothers (*Obedience*, 67), is unlikely, since in 7:7ff 'sin' is identified with 'desire'.

28 Hübner, *Law*, 71f, rightly stresses the active nature of sin and the passive nature of the law in this passage, and contrasts this with Gal. 3:19 (78). But he denies that in this respect Rom. 7:7ff also contrasts with Rom. 4:15 and 5:20 (79ff), thereby emphasizing differences between Romans and Galatians at the expense of differences within Romans itself.

29 So Fuchs, *Freiheit*, 56f, Käsemann, 193, Furnish, *Ethics*, 141.

30 Cf. Gundry, 'Frustration', 232f.

31 'Passions' (Rom. 7:5) and 'desire' (Rom. 7:7) are also linked to Gal. 5:24.

32 Cranfield, I, 337f, M. Barth, 'Gesetz', 504, Guthrie, *Theology*, 692n, Räisänen, *Paul*, 142.
33 Bultmann, 'Romans 7', 155, Bornkamm, 'Sin', 96, Conzelmann, *Outline*, 227, Käsemann, 194, Hübner, *Law*, 72ff.
34 There is a full discussion in Räisänen, 'EPITHYMIA', 85ff.
35 E.g. Bruce, *Paul*, 194, Davies, *Rabbinic Judaism*, 32, Wedderburn, 'Adam', 420f, Bornkamm, 'Sin', 94, Käsemann, 195f; opposed by Kümmel, *Römer 7*, 86f, Bläser, *Gesetz*, 114f, Gundry, 'Frustration', 231.
36 Adam must be in mind here, since only he lived before the law was given (so Käsemann, 196). Fuchs thinks that Paul is here taking up the gnostic myth of the pre-existent soul (*Freiheit*, 58ff). Gundry objects that 'the command came right after the creation and setting of man in Eden: there is no hint of an interval without law' ('Frustration', 231). But it is enough for Paul that Genesis does not exclude the possibility of such an interval.
37 Cf. Bar. 3:9, 'the commandments of life'; Ps. Sol. 14:1f.
38 'The work of the law as a spur to sin can be demonstrated only by Adam' (Käsemann, 196).
39 The tenth commandment is similarly understood as forbidding 'desire' in 4 Macc. 2:4ff.
40 An autobiographical reference is thus superfluous (against Davies, *Rabbinic Judaism*, 24ff, Gundry, 'Frustration', 232, and older commentators such as Sanday and Headlam, 186f, Zahn, 343f). Kümmel's arguments against this view are still compelling (*Römer 7*, 81ff).
41 Rom. 7:7ff draws an analogy between Gen. 2−3 and life under the law, but is not thinking in salvation-historical terms of Eden and Sinai (against Campbell, 'Identity', 57, 61; opposed by Conzelmann, 'Rechtfertigungslehre', 402).
42 Kümmel, *Römer 7*, 8, Bultmann, 'Romans 7', 153, Beker, *Paul*, 238. Räisänen prefers to call it, 'An apology of his theology of the law' (*Paul*, 67).
43 So Käsemann, 192.
44 Schoeps, *Paul*, 183, Davies, 'Law', 8ff, Drane, *Paul*, 74, Hübner, *Law*, *passim*. According to Davies, in Galatians, 'Paul views the Law with the cold eyes of an antagonist' (8), whereas 'in Romans Paul approaches the Law not as if he were viewing it clinically, from outside, but experientially, from the inside' (9).
45 Hübner, *Law*, 63, denies that Paul's concessions to Jewish Christians were made for tactical reasons. The widespread failure to recognize the importance of tactical considerations for Paul is the outcome of an idealized and uncritical view of the apostle.
46 This view of the purpose of Rom. 7 makes discussion of the extent to which 'man under the law' is aware of his 'desperate plight' (Hübner, *Law*, 76ff) superfluous.
47 Nygren, 288f, Mitton, 'Romans vii', Packer, 'Wretched Man', Dunn, 'Rom. 7,14−25', *passim*.
48 Barrett finds the link between v. 13 and vv. 14ff in the idea of the goodness of the law (146).

49 These two phrases are parallel (so Wilckens, II, 84).

50 So Wright, *Messiah*, 151.

51 The usual view is that these phrases refer not to the law of Moses but to the authority of sin. 'Law' is thus used metaphorically; this is 'a forceful way of making the point that the power which sin has over us is a terrible travesty, a grotesque parody, of that authority over us which belongs by right to God's holy law' (Cranfield, I, 364). However, Wilckens, II, 90, Hahn, 'Gesetzesverständnis', 46, and Wright, *Messiah*, 153, have claimed that 'the law of sin which is in my members' is a reference to the Torah as it is misused by sin. The context suggests that the former view is right: v. 22 derives from 'the good that I want' (v. 19a), and v. 23 derives from 'the evil I do not want' (v. 19b). It is natural to identify 'the law of sin which is in my members' with 'sin which dwells within me' (vv. 17,20).

52 Against Cranfield, I, 344f, Packer, ' "Wretched Man" ', 624; cf. Nygren, 288f.

53 Against Dunn, 'Rom. 7,14–25', 262, Cranfield, *Romans*, I, 345, Packer, ' "Wretched Man" ', 625. Bultmann considers both 7:25b and 8:1 to be glosses ('Glossen', 279). Dodd, 132, and Eichholz, *Paulus*, 257, place v. 25b immediately after v. 23. Such expedients are unnecessary.

54 Cranfield, I, 346, Packer, ' "Wretched Man" ', 625f.

55 There is no need to suppose, as Bandstra does (*Elements*, 141), that the Jew here becomes aware of his position as he comes to Christ – i.e. that 7:14ff portrays the moment of conversion.

56 This interpretation is preferable to the view that whereas Rom. 7:14ff depicts the Christian who lives 'in his own strength', 8:1ff describes the victory over sin gained through the Spirit (Mitton, 'Romans vii', *passim*, Bruce, 150ff).

57 Althaus, *Paulus*, 46ff, Räisänen, *Paul*, 110, and Sanders, *Jewish People*, 78, raise the problem of whether Rom. 7:14ff is an exaggeration

58 One of the many ways in which the influence of the Reformation has adversely affected the interpretation of Paul is that its rejection of asceticism has led scholars to overlook the strongly ascetic and anti-sexual tendency of Paul's teaching.

59 Schneider, 'Finis', 416, claims unconvincingly that Paul is speaking here about two different entities; cf. Hübner, *Law*, 145f.

60 So Lyonnet, 'Gratuité', 108, Bandstra, *Elements*, 107, Keck, 'Justification', 202.

61 Hübner claims that 8:1–4 is speaking of the liberation of the law from 'the perversion and legalisation to which up till now it has been subject' (*Law*, 147). But nothing in this context suggests that Paul is even aware of the Lutheran problem of 'legalism'.

62 Klein is working with entirely inappropriate theological categories when he claims that Rom. 5–8 is developing the anthropological implications of justification ('Römer 4', 148).

63 The view of Scroggs that the problem of Israel is absent in Rom. 5–8 ('Rhetorician', 281) should be rejected.

64 The view that Rom. 1–4 uses 'juridical' language, whereas Rom. 5–8 is mystical (Sanders, *Palestinian Judaism*, 434ff, 503ff, following Schweitzer; Conzelmann, 'Problems', 134; rejected by Käsemann, 'Justification', 76ff, Beker, *Paul*, 259f) ignores the common social function of these two sections. The same is true of Scroggs' view that Rom. 1–11 comprises two originally independent homilies, Rom. 1–4 and 9–11 on the one hand, and Rom. 5–8 on the other ('Rhetorician', 271ff).

65 On the social function of a doctrine of predestination for sectarian groups, see Watson, 'Social Function', 60ff.

9. The social function of Romans: Rom. 9–11

1 Sanders sees Rom. 9–11 as 'Paul's reflection on and anguish over' the failure of the mission of Peter and others to the Jews (*Jewish People*, 185); cf. Nygren, 354, Barrett, 175. But Rom. 9–11 concerns Paul much more directly than this suggests.

2 Cf. Schlier, 284, Wilckens, II, 189f.

3 Baur protests against the view that Rom. 9–11 is a mere appendix to Rom. 1–8, and describes it as 'der Mittelpunkt und Kern des Ganzen' ('Zweck und Veranlassung', 157f). He is followed by Stendahl, *Jews*, 28f, Beker, *Paul*, 87, and Ellison, *Mystery*, 27f. But this view is as exaggerated as the view of Dodd that Rom. 9–11 is a mere excursus (161ff): Rom. 9–11 is an integral part of the argument of Romans, neither more nor less important than Rom. 1–8.

4 So Michel, 223, Wilckens, II, 189f; opposed by Cranfield, II, 453f.

5 Käsemann sees this section as an assertion of the significance of salvation-history as opposed to mere individualism: it proves that 'the apostle's thought and work do not circle around anthropology but around the conquest of the world' (296, cf. 255f, 264, 314, etc.; 'Abraham', 88). His emphasis on the world (also apparent in his reinterpretation of δικαιοσύνη θεοῦ) enables him to stress the significance of Rom. 9–11 within the argument of Romans despite his passionate commitment to the Lutheran standpoint. But this leads him to interpret Rom. 9–11 as pure theology, with little reference to any social context and function. Müller adopts a similar position: 'Romans 9–11 creates the possibility of freeing the Pauline doctrine of justification from the Procrustes-bed of individualism' (*Gerechtigkeit*, 27).

6 Shaw, *Cost*, 167, perceptively entitles Rom. 9–11, 'The quest for legitimacy: the dependence of the new on the old'.

7 Cf. Müller, *Gerechtigkeit*, 32.

8 So Wilckens, II, 209; against Kümmel, who claims that Rom. 9–11 is non-polemical ('Probleme', 26).

9 Paul's problem is not, 'Can God in his freedom reject those who were once elected?' (against Plag, *Wege*, 16f), for the point of 9:6ff is to deny that the Jewish people were *ever* elected for salvation; their privileges (9:4f) are in the sphere of σάρξ (9:8).

10 Rom. 9:6ff indicates that the privileges of 9:4f have been forfeited (Dodd, 168), or at least that they are of no avail for salvation. Paul is not saying that Israel retains her privileges but that they are opened out to others also (against Richardson, *Israel*, 131).

11 Against Käsemann, 255f, 264, Kertelge, 103; opposed by Klein, 'Präliminarien', 235ff, Luz, *Geschichtsverständnis*, 67, 70, 72.

12 Against Käsemann, 263, Müller, *Gerechtigkeit*, 29, Richardson, *Israel*, 132, Hübner, *Law*, 58; opposed by Wright, *Messiah*, 194f.

13 There do not seem to be sufficient grounds for claiming, as Hübner does (*Law*, 59), that Paul is positive about the history of Israel in Rom. 9 in a way which represents 'a deliberate rejection' of what he had said in Galatians.

14 Shaw comments on this: 'The exaltation of Paul's God demands the demeaning of man' (*Cost*, 169).

15 According to Baur, 'Zweck und Gedankengang', 160, Paul is here arguing against the view of the Roman Jewish Christians that Gentiles could not participate in salvation until the Jews accepted it.

16 Cranfield argues that the subject of 9:6ff is different forms of election, rather than election and non-election (II, 471).

17 Conzelmann, *Outline*, 250ff, Dinkler, 'Prädestination', 257, Müller, *Gerechtigkeit*, 78.

18 According to Cranfield, in v. 18 'the double θέλει is controlled by the words quoted in v. 15' (II, 488). This hardening is only temporary, and 9:30–11:36 shows how 'vessels of wrath' become 'vessels of mercy' (497). Cranfield is seeking to provide exegetical support for K. Barth's opposition to Calvin's notion of 'an altogether un-qualified, indeterminate, absolute will, which moves now in one direction, now in another, capriciously' (488). In doing so, he finds the theology of Rom. 11 in Rom. 9. But this exegesis is only con-vincing if one holds that Rom. 9 *must* agree with Rom. 11. If the two passages are expounded on their own terms, they contradict each other; the nature of this contradiction will be discussed later in the present chapter.

19 Robinson, *Wrestling*, 117.

20 Against Barrett, 'Romans 9:30–10:21', 132ff, Dinkler, 'Prädestina-tion', 254, Dodd, 173, Käsemann, 276, Schlatter, 307. However, Wright, *Messiah*, 212, regards this as an 'alien theological theme'.

21 Luz is therefore wrong to state that in Rom. 9:30ff Paul discusses 'die Gesetzesgerechtigkeit, hier exemplarisch durch Israel vertreten' (*Geschichtsverständnis*, 156f).

22 Williams points out the significance of πᾶς in Romans ('Righteous-ness', 247).

23 The view that τέλος in Rom. 10:4 means 'end' is represented by Käsemann, 282f, Schlier, 311, Wilckens, II, 222f, van Dülmen, *Gesetz*, 126f, Räisänen, *Paul*, 53ff. Campbell, 'Christ', argues that we should 'bear in mind the normal Jewish revulsion against any suggestion that the Law should be abolished' (76). But Paul as a Christian was no longer motivated by normal Jewish feelings about the law.

24 Cf. Howard, 'Christ', 336, Sanders, *Jewish People*, 37f.

25 Or, according to Shaw, its *apparent* universality, which 'only intro-duces a more radical cleavage between those who have faith and those who have not' (*Cost*, 169).

26 In 10:11–13, πᾶς is four times used in the sense of 'Jew and Gentile alike' (so Zeller, *Juden*, 124).

27 The view that Rom. 10:5 refers to Christ (Cranfield, II, 521f, M. Barth, *People*, 39, Bandstra, *Elements*, 104) is rightly rejected by Räisänen as 'eccentric' (*Paul*, 55).

28 So Cranfield, II, 533ff, Dodd, 179, Käsemann, 294, Leenhardt, 273ff, Schlier, 316.

29 Cf. also Richardson, *Israel*, 134.

30 V. 17 is unnecessarily rejected as a gloss by Bultmann, 'Glossen', 199.

31 The assumption that 'they' here means 'Israel' (e.g. Barrett, 205) ignores the contrast between 'they' in v. 18 and 'Israel' in v. 19.

32 Cf. Wilckens, II, 230.

33 Cf. Dodd, 181, Kuss, 779.

34 There is no justification for the view of Bornkamm (*Paul*, 151) that in Rom. 11 Israel represents man in general.

35 Against Cranfield, who insists that Rom. 9–11 constitutes a single argument (II, 447f).

36 Cf. Dodd, 192, Wilckens, II, 185, 197, Bultmann, 'History', 12, Müller, *Gerechtigkeit*, 27, 38, 92f, Zeller, *Juden*, 115. Hickling, 'Centre', 201, argues that Rom. 9–11 forms a unity but contradicts Rom. 4–5 and Galatians in its view of salvation-history.

37 The difference between Rom. 11 and Rom. 9 at this point is far greater than the difference that Hübner finds between Rom. 9 and Galatians (*Law*, 57ff). On his view, Paul exemplifies the fact that 'theological reflection to a great extent also means departing from theological ideas which at one time have gained favour' (60). Can such a view account for fundamental differences within the same writing?

38 Wright argues that 'all Israel' in 11:26 means the whole Christian church, not the Jewish people (*Messiah*, 200ff). This argument rests on the assumption that a reference to the eschatological salvation of the Jewish people would contradict 11:11–24, which is speaking of 'a steady flow of Jewish conversions to Christian faith during the course of the Gentile mission' (201). That is certainly the argu-ment of 11:13f, but can it really account for 11:12,15? In v. 12, Paul speaks of the riches which the world has received as the result of Israel's trespass as less than the riches resulting from τὸ πλήρωμα αὐτῶν, and in v. 15 this is made more specific by a comparison between reconciliation and life from the dead. Vv. 12,15 can only be speaking of a future, eschatological reality, for the 'steady flow of Jewish conversions' has no such dramatic effect. In addition, 11:28f favours the view that the subject of 11:26f is the Jewish people; cf. Hahn, 'Römer 11.26a', *passim*, in opposition to J. Jeremias.

39 Plag argues that the problem of Rom. 9–11 is not the tension between ch. 9–10 and ch. 11, but between ch. 9–11 as a whole and

11:25–7, and so regards 11:25–7 as a gloss (*Wege*, 41ff). He claims that two different ways of salvation for Israel are set forth in Rom. 11: salvation through the Gentile mission (vv. 11ff), and a quite independent eschatological salvation (vv. 25–7). But this distinction is untenable, for in vv. 11ff Paul speaks not only of the salvation of some Jews through the Gentile mission (vv. 13f) but also of the final eschatological salvation of the whole people (vv. 12,15).

40 Käsemann finds here the idea that 'for the apostle there is no salvation apart from the history of Israel' (309f), but apparently does not recognize the extent to which Paul here contradicts what he has said elsewhere.

41 Against Müller, *Gerechtigkeit*, 99f, who thinks that the salvation of Israel is here grounded in the promise of a new creation; as he puts it, 'Gottesvolksgedanke' is 'Schöpfungsgedanke' (99).

42 For the apocalyptic background to 11:26, cf. Müller, *Gerechtigkeit*, 38ff.

43 So Schlier, 332, who also identifies the 'root' with the 'first-fruits'.

44 So Goppelt, 'Heilsgeschichte', 325, Berger, 'Abraham', 74.

45 Unless one accepts Dodd's claim that in Rom. 11 Paul's emotion triumphs over his logic (192).

46 Cf. Cranfield, II, 568. Schlier, 333, rejects the idea that Gentile Christian anti-Semitism is present here.

47 Paul's association of himself with the Jewish remnant (11:1) may be compared to his references to certain individuals as 'fellow-countrymen' (16:7,11): in both cases, Paul stresses his solidarity with the Roman Jewish Christians.

48 Thus, 'works' here should not be paraphrased as 'their own meritorious achievement' (against Cranfield, II, 547).

49 This view of the Gentile mission has been formulated for apologetic reasons, and tells us nothing about Paul's real missionary strategy (against Ben-Chorin, *Paulus*, 17, Stuhlmacher, *Paulus*, 30).

50 Paul is therefore not motivated in Rom. 11 by the desire to show how his theological doctrine of the justification of the ungodly applies also to Israel (against Käsemann, 317).

51 Rom. 11:25ff is not 'derived from speculative fantasy' (against Bultmann, *Theology*, II, 132). It is motivated by strategy, not speculative interest.

52 For a history of research into Paul's collection, see Georgi, *Kollekte*, 9ff.

53 Bruce's claim (*Galatians*, 126) that the aorist means that Paul had *already* gathered a collection (Acts 11:30) is unwarranted; the verb is not a pluperfect.

54 So Georgi, *Kollekte*, 30ff.

55 Georgi argues that Paul took up again the idea of the collection so as to oppose tendencies towards mysticism in Galatia and Corinth by stressing salvation-historical links with Israel (*Kollekte*, 37ff). But that can hardly have been his main aim.

56 Nickle, *Collection*, 111, describes the collection as 'both a charitable expression of Christian fellowship and a tangible witness to the

solidarity of all believers within the Body of Christ'. Cf. Bornkamm, *Paul*, 92.

57 Schmithals, *Paul and James*, 81f, tries unconvincingly to evade this conclusion.

58 Lüdemann, *Antipaulinismus*, 94ff, argues that the collection was indeed rejected, on the grounds of the silence of Acts 21. He argues that Luke deliberately omits references in his source to the rejection of the collection, transferring the collection to Acts 11:27ff (96f), and notes that nothing is said in Acts 21–8 about the Jerusalem Christians supporting Paul (97). He concludes that they were predominantly anti-Pauline (98).

59 Barrett suggests (following Windisch) that the possibility of hostility (Rom. 15:31) is not mentioned in 2 Cor. 9 'because it would discourage Corinthian generosity' (*2 Corinthians*, 241).

60 Shaw is therefore wrong to state that this passage refers to 'Gentile tribute' to 'the ecclesiastical reality of Jewish privilege' (*Cost*, 168).

BIBLIOGRAPHY

1 Primary sources

Quotations from extra-biblical works are taken from the following:

Charles, R. H. (ed.) *The Apocrypha and Pseudepigrapha of the Old Testament in English: With Introductions and Critical and Explanatory Notes to the Several Books*, two vols., Oxford, 1913

Charlesworth, J. H. (ed.) *The Old Testament Pseudepigrapha. Vol. I: Apocalyptic Literature and Testaments*, London 1983

Colson, F. H., Whitaker, G. H. and Marcus, R. *Philo*, twelve vols., LCL, London 1929–62

Danby, H. *The Mishnah. Translated from the Hebrew with Introduction and Brief Explanatory Notes*, Oxford 1933

Hunt, A. S. and Edgar, C. C. *Select Papyri II. Non-Literary Papyri: Public Documents*, LCL, London 1977

Lake, K. *The Apostolic Fathers*, two vols., LCL, 1912–13

Lohse, E. *Die Texte aus Qumran. Hebräisch und Deutsch*, Munich 1981[3]

RSV. *The Apocrypha/Deuterocanonical Books*

Stern, M. *Greek and Latin Authors on Jews and Judaism*, two vols., Jerusalem, 1974–80

Strack, H. L. and Billerbeck, P. *Kommentar zum Neuen Testament aus Talmud und Midrasch*, six vols., Munich 1922–61

Thackeray, H. St J. et al. *Josephus*, ten vols., LCL, London 1926–63

Vermes, G. *The Dead Sea Scrolls in English*, London 1975[2]

2 Secondary literature

Althaus, P. *Paulus und Luther über den Menschen*, Gütersloh 1950
   The Theology of Martin Luther, ET Philadelphia 1966

Bammel, E., Barrett, C. K. and Davies, W. D. (eds.) *Donum Gentilicium. New Testament Studies in Honour of David Daube*, Oxford 1978

Bandstra, A. J. *The Law and the Elements of the World. An Exegetical Study in Aspects of Paul's Teaching*, Kampen 1964

Banks, R. (ed.) *Reconciliation and Hope: New Testament Essays on Atonement and Eschatology Presented to L. L. Morris on his 60th Birthday*, Exeter 1974

Barnard, L. 'St. Stephen and Early Alexandrian Christianity', *NTS* 7 (1960–61), 31–45

Barrett, C. K. *A Commentary on the Epistle to the Romans*, BNTC, London 1957

The Gospel according to St John, London 1958

A Commentary on the First Epistle to the Corinthians, BNTC, London 1971[2]

A Commentary on the Second Epistle to the Corinthians, BNTC, London 1973[2]

Essays on Paul, London 1982: 'Cephas and Corinth', 28–39; 'Things Sacrificed to Idols', 40–59; 'Paul's Opponents in 2 Corinthians', 60–86; 'ΨΕΥΔΑΠΟΣΤΟΛΟΙ (2 Cor. 11.13)', 87–107; 'Romans 9.30–10.21: Fall and Responsibility of Israel', 132–53; 'The Allegory of Abraham, Sarah, and Hagar in the Argument of Galatians', 154–70

'Paul and the "Pillar" Apostles', in *Studia Paulina*, ed. J. N. Sevenster and W. C. van Unnik, Haarlem 1953, 1–19

Barth, K. *The Epistle to the Romans*, ET London 1933

A Shorter Commentary on Romans, ET London 1959

Barth, M. *The People of God*, *JSNT* Supplement 5, Sheffield 1983

'The Kerygma and Galatians', *Int.* 21 (1967), 131–46

'Jews and Gentiles: The Social Character of Justification', *JES* 5 (1968), 241–67

'Die Stellung des Paulus zu Gesetz und Ordnung', *EvTh* 33 (1973), 496–526

Bassler, J. M. 'Divine Impartiality in Paul's Letter to the Romans', *NovT* 26 (1984) 43–58

Batey, R. (ed.) *New Testament Issues*, London 1970

Bauer, W. *Orthodoxy and Heresy in Earliest Christianity*, ET Philadelphia 1971, ed. R. A. Kraft and G. Krodel

Baur, F. C. *Paul the Apostle of Jesus Christ*, ET London/Edinburgh, Vol. I, 1873

The Church History of the First Three Centuries, Vol. I, ET London/Edinburgh 1875

'Über Zweck und Veranlassung des Römerbriefs und die damit zusammenhängenden Verhältnisse der römischen Gemeinde', *Tübinger Zeitschrift für Theologie*, 1836, Heft 3, 59–178, reprinted in *Ausgewählte Werke in Einzelausgaben. 1. Historisch-kritische Untersuchungen zum Neuen Testament*, Stuttgart 1963

'Über Zweck und Gedankengang des Römerbriefs, nebst einer Erörterung einiger paulinische Begriffe, mit besonderer Rücksicht auf die Kommentare von Tholuck und Philippi', *Theologisches Jahrbuch* 16, Tübingen 1857, 60–108, 184–208

Beare, F. W. *The Epistle to the Philippians*, BNTC, London 1959

Becker, J., Conzelmann, H. and Friedrich, G. *Die Briefe an die Galater, Epheser, Philipper, Kolosser, Thessalonicher, und Philemon*, Das Neue Testament Deutsch 8, Göttingen 1976

Beker, J. C. *Paul the Apostle. The Triumph of God in Life and Thought*, Edinburgh 1980

Ben-Chorin, S. *Paulus. Der Völkerapostel in jüdischer Sicht*, Munich 1980

Berger, K. 'Abraham in den paulinischen Hauptbriefen', *MTZ* 17 (1966), 47–89

Betz, H.D. *Galatians. A Commentary on Paul's Letter to the Churches in Galatia*, Hermeneia, Philadelphia 1979

Betz, O., Hengel, M. and Schmidt, P. *Abraham unser Vater* (Festschrift for O. Michel), Leiden/Köln 1963

Blank, J. 'Warum sagt Paulus: "Aus Werken des Gesetzes wird niemand gerecht"?', EKKNT, Vorarbeiten Heft I, 79–95

Bläser, P. *Das Gesetz bei Paulus*, Münster 1941

Blass, F., Debrunner, R. and Funk, R.W. *A Greek Grammar of the New Testament and Other Early Christian Literature*, Chicago 1961

Bligh, J. *Galatians: A Discussion of St Paul's Epistle*, London 1969

Borgen, P. 'Paul Preaches Circumcision and Pleases Men', in *Paul and Paulinism*, ed. M. Hooker and S.G. Wilson, London 1982

Bornkamm, G. *Paul*, ET London 1971

    Early Christian Experience, London 1969: 'The Revelation of God's Wrath', 47–70; 'Sin, Law and Death: An Exegetical Study of Romans 7', 87–104

    Das Ende des Gesetzes. Paulusstudien, BevTh 16, Munich 1966: 'Paulinische Anakoluthe im Römerbrief', 76–92

    Studien zu Antike und Urchristentum, BevTh 28, Munich 1970: 'Gesetz und Natur (Röm 2,14–16)', 93–118

    Geschichte und Glaube 2, BevTh 53, Munich 1971: 'Wandlungen im alt- und neutestamentlichen Gesetzesverständnis', 73–119; 'Theologie als Teufelskunst (Römer 3,1–9)', 140–8

    'The Letter to the Romans as Paul's Last Will and Testament', in *The Romans Debate*, ed. K.P. Donfried, Minneapolis 1977, 17–31

    'The Missionary Stance of Paul in I Corinthians 9 and in Acts', in *Studies in Luke–Acts*, ed. L.E. Keck and J.L. Martyn, London 1968, 194–207

Borse, U. *Der Standort des Galaterbriefes*, BBB, Köln/Bonn 1972

Brandon, S.G.F. *The Fall of Jerusalem and the Christian Church*, London 1957²

Bring, R. *Commentary on Galatians*, ET Philadelphia 1961

Brown, R.E. *The Gospel according to John*, AB (two vols.), London 1971

    The Community of the Beloved Disciple, London 1979

Bruce, F.F. *Romans: An Introduction and Commentary*, TNTC, London 1963

    The Epistle of Paul to the Galatians. A Commentary on the Greek Text, NIGTC, Exeter 1982

    Paul: Apostle of the Free Spirit, Exeter 1977

    'Galatian Problems. 1. Autobiographical Data', *BJRL* 51 (1968–69), 292–309

    'Galatian Problems. 3. The "Other" Gospel', *BJRL* 53 (1970–71), 253–71

Bultmann, R. *Theology of the New Testament*, two vols., ET London 1952–55

    The Gospel of John, ET Oxford 1971

    Faith and Understanding I, ET London 1969: 'Liberal Theology and the Latest Theological Movement', 28–52

    Existence and Faith, London 1961: 'Paul', 111–46; 'Romans 7 and the Anthropology of Paul', 147–57

Essays Philosophical and Theological, ET London 1955: 'Christ the End of the Law', 36–66

'History and Eschatology in the New Testament', *NTS* 1 (1954–55), 5–16

'Adam and Christ according to Romans 5', in *Current Issues in New Testament Interpretation*, ed. W. Klassen and G. F. Snyder, London 1961, 143–65

'Das Problem der Ethik bei Paulus', repr. in *Das Paulusbild in der neueren Deutschen Forschung*, ed. K. H. Rengstorf, Darmstadt, 1969, 179–99

'Zur Geschichte der Paulus-Forschung', as above, 304–37

Exegetica, Tübingen 1967: 'Glossen im Römerbrief', 278–84; 'Zur Auslegung von Galater 2,15–18', 394–9

Der Zweite Brief an die Korinther, KEKNT, Göttingen 1976

Exegetische Probleme des zweiten Korintherbriefes, Upsala 1947

'ΔΙΚΑΙΟΣΥΝΗ ΘΕΟΥ', *JBL* 83 (1964), 12–16

Burton, E. de W. *A Critical and Exegetical Commentary on the Epistle to the Galatians*, ICC, Edinburgh 1921

Byrne, B. *'Sons of God'* – *'Seed of Abraham'*, AnBib 83, Rome 1979

Cadbury, H. J. 'The Hellenists', in *The Beginnings of Christianity*, ed. F. J. Foakes-Jackson and K. Lake, Pt. I, Vol. V, London 1933, 59–74

Caird, G. B. *Paul's Letters from Prison*, Oxford 1976

Campbell, D. 'The Identity of ἐγώ in Romans 7:7–25', *StBib* III (1978), 57–64

Campbell, W. S. 'Christ the End of the Law: Romans 10:4', *StBib* III (1978), 73–8

'Romans III as a Key to the Structure and Thought of the Letter', *NovT* 23 (1981), 22–40

Carroll, R. P. *When Prophecy Failed. Reactions and Responses to Failure in the Old Testament Prophetic Traditions*, London 1979

Catchpole, D. R. 'Paul, James and the Apostolic Decree', *NTS* 23 (1976–77), 428–44

Chadwick, H. ' "All Things to All Men" (I Cor. ix.22)', *NTS* I (1954–55), 261–75

Collange, J. F. *Énigmes de la Deuxième Épître de Paul aux Corinthiens*, SNTSMS 18, Cambridge 1972

The Epistle of Saint Paul to the Philippians, ET London 1979

Conzelmann, H. *An Outline of the Theology of the New Testament*, ET London 1969

I Corinthians, Hermeneia, Philadelphia 1975

'Die Rechtfertigungslehre des Paulus: Theologie oder Anthropologie?', *EvTh* 28 (1968), 389–404

'Current Problems in New Testament Research', in *New Testament Issues*, ed. R. Batey, London 1970

Cranfield, C. E. B. *A Critical and Exegetical Commentary on the Epistle to the Romans*, ICC, two vols., Edinburgh 1975–79

'St. Paul and the Law', *SJT* 17 (1964), 43–68

Cullmann, O. *The Johannine Circle*, Philadelphia 1976

Dahl, N. A. *Studies in Paul*, Minneapolis 1977: 'The Missionary Theology in the Epistle to the Romans', 70–94; 'The Doctrine of Justification: Its Social Function and Implications', 95–120; 'The One God of Jews and Gentiles (Rom. 3:29–30)', 178–91

'Romans 3.9: Text and Meaning', in *Paul and Paulinism*, ed. M.D. Hooker and S.G. Wilson, London 1982

Davies, W.D. *Paul and Rabbinic Judaism. Some Rabbinic Elements in Pauline Theology*, London 1970³

'Paul and the People of Israel', *NTS* 24 (1977–78), 4–39

'Paul and the Law. Reflections on Pitfalls in Interpretation', in *Paul and Paulinism*, ed. M.D. Hooker and S.G. Wilson, London 1982

'The Apostolic Age and the Life of Paul', in *Peake's Commentary on the Bible*, London 1977, 870–81

Dibelius, M. *Studies in the Acts of the Apostles*, ed. H. Greeven, London 1956: 'The Conversion of Cornelius', 109–22

Dibelius, M. and Kümmel, W.G. *Paul*, ET London 1953

Dinkler, E. *Signum Crucis. Aufsätze zum Neuen Testament und zur christlichen Archäologie*, Tübingen 1967: 'Prädestination bei Paulus – Exegetische Bemerkungen zum Römerbrief', 241–69

Dix, G. *Jew and Greek. A Study in the Primitive Church*, London 1953

Dodd, C.H. *The Epistle to the Romans*, MNTC, London 1932 (1959 ed.)

New Testament Studies, Manchester 1953: 'The Mind of Paul, II', 83–128

Donfried, K.P. 'Justification and Last Judgment in Paul', *ZNW* 67 (1976), 90–110

The Romans Debate (ed.), Minneapolis 1977: 'The Nature and Scope of the Romans Debate', ix–xvii; 'A Short Note on Romans 16', 50–60; 'False Presuppositions in the Study of Romans', 120–48

Doughty, D.J. 'The Priority of ΧΑΡΙΣ', *NTS* 19 (1972–73), 163–80

Drane, J.W. *Paul: Libertine or Legalist? A Study of the Major Pauline Epistles*, London 1975

'Why did Paul write Romans?' in *Pauline Studies*, ed. D.A. Hagner and M.J. Harris, Exeter 1980, 208–27

Dülmen, A. van *Die Theologie des Gesetzes bei Paulus*, SBM, Stuttgart 1968

Duncan, G.S. *St. Paul's Ephesian Ministry. A Reconstruction with Special Reference to the Ephesian Origin of the Imprisonment Epistles*, London 1929

The Epistle of Paul to the Galatians, MNTC, London 1934

Dunn, J.D.G. 'Rom. 7,14–25 in the Theology of Paul', *TZ* 31 (1975), 257–73

'Paul's Understanding of the Death of Jesus', in *Reconciliation and Hope*, ed. R. Banks, Exeter 1974, 125–41

'The Incident at Antioch (Gal. 2:11–18)', *JSNT* 18 (1983), 3–57

'The New Perspective on Paul', *BJRL* 65 (1982–83), 95–122

Ebeling, G. *Word and Faith*, ET London 1963: 'On the Doctrine of the Triplex Usus Legis in the Theology of the Reformation', 62–78; 'Reflexions on the Doctrine of the Law', 247–81

Luther: An Introduction to his Thought, ET London 1970

Die Wahrheit des Evangeliums. Eine Lesehilfe zum Galaterbrief, Tübingen 1981

Eckert, J. *Die Urchristliche Verkündigung im Streit zwischen Paulus und seinen Gegnern nach dem Galaterbrief*, Munich 1971

Eichholz, G. *Die Theologie des Paulus im Umriss*, Neukirchen-Vluyn 1977²

Elliott, J.H. *A Home for the Homeless. A Sociological Exegesis of I Peter, its Situation and Strategy*, London 1982

Ellis, E. E. and Grässer, E. (eds.) *Jesus und Paulus. Festschrift für Werner Georg Kümmel am 70. Geburtstag*, Göttingen 1975

Ellison, H. L. *The Mystery of Israel*, Exeter 1976[3]

Esler, P. F. 'Community and Gospel in Luke–Acts. The Social and Political Motivations of Lucan Theology', Oxford D. Phil. thesis, 1984

Flückiger, F. 'Die Werke des Gesetzes bei den Heiden (nach Röm. 2,14ff)', *TZ* 8 (1952), 17–42

Foakes-Jackson, F. J. and Lake, K. (eds.) *The Beginnings of Christianity*, Pt. I, Vol. I, London 1920; Pt. I, Vol. V, London 1933

Forde, G. O. 'The Exodus from Virtue to Grace: Justification by Faith Today', *Int.* 34 (1980), 32–44

Franzmann, M. H. *Romans*, Concordia Commentary, St Louis/London 1968

Friedrich, G. *Der Brief an die Philipper*, in J. Becker, H. Conzelmann and G. Friedrich, *Die Briefe an die Galater ... Philemon*. Das Neue Testament Deutsch 8, Göttingen 1976

'Das Gesetz des Glaubens, Röm 3,27', *TZ* 10 (1954), 401–17

'Die Gegner des Paulus im 2. Korintherbrief', in *Abraham unser Vater*, ed. O. Betz, M. Hengel and P. Schmidt, Leiden/Köln 1963, 181–215

Fuchs, E. *Die Freiheit des Glaubens. Römer 5–8 ausgelegt*, Munich 1949

Furnish, V. P. *Theology and Ethics in Paul*, Nashville 1968

The Love Command in the New Testament, Nashville 1972

Gager, J. G. *Kingdom and Community. The Social World of Early Christianity*, New Jersey 1975

Gasque, W. W. *A History of the Criticism of the Acts of the Apostles*, Tübingen 1975

Georgi, D. *Die Gegner des Paulus im 2. Korintherbrief. Studien zur religiösen Propaganda in der Spätantike*, WMANT, Neukirchen 1964

Die Geschichte der Kollekte des Paulus für Jerusalem, Hamburg 1965

Gnilka, J. *Der Philipperbrief*, HTKNT, Freiburg/Basel/Wien 1968

Goppelt, L. *Apostolic and Post-Apostolic Times*, ET London 1970

'Paul and Heilsgeschichte. Conclusions from Romans 4 and I Corinthians 10.1–13', *Int.* 21 (1967), 315–26

Gundry, R. H. 'The Moral Frustration of Paul before his Conversion: Sexual Lust in Romans 7:7–25', in *Pauline Studies*, ed. D. A. Hagner and M. J. Harris, Exeter 1980, 228–45

Guthrie, D. *New Testament Introduction*, London 1970[3]

Galatians, NCBC, London 1973

New Testament Theology, London 1981

Haenchen, E. *The Acts of the Apostles: A Commentary*, ET Oxford 1971

'The Book of Acts as Source Material for the History of Early Christianity', in *Studies in Luke–Acts*, ed. L. E. Keck and J. L. Martyn, London 1968, 258–78

Hagner, D. A. and Harris, M. J. (eds.) *Pauline Studies. Essays Presented to F. F. Bruce on his 70th Birthday*, Exeter 1980

Hahn, F. *Mission in the New Testament*, SBT 47, ET London 1965

'Das Gesetzesverständnis im Römer- und Galaterbrief', *ZNW* 67 (1976), 29–63

'Zum Verständnis von Römer 11,26a: "... und so wird ganz Israel gerettet werden"'', in *Paul and Paulinism*, ed. M.D. Hooker and S.G. Wilson, London 1982

Hall, D.R. 'Romans 3.1–8 reconsidered', *NTS* 29 (1982–83), 183–97

Hamerton-Kelly, R. and Scroggs, R. (eds.) *Jews, Greeks and Christians. Religious Cultures in Late Antiquity. Essays in Honour of W.D. Davies*, Leiden 1976

Hammond, N.G.L. and Scullard, H.H. (eds.) *The Oxford Classical Dictionary*, Oxford 1970²

Hanson, A.T. *Studies in Paul's Technique and Theology*, London 1974: 'The Reproach and Vindication of the Messiah', 13–51

Hengel, M. *Judaism and Hellenism*, two vols., ET London 1974
  Acts and the History of Earliest Christianity, ET London 1979
  'Zwischen Jesus und Paulus. Die "Hellenisten", die "Sieben" und Stephanus', *ZTK* 72 (1975), 151–206
  'Die Ursprünge der christlichen Mission', *NTS* 18 (1971–72), 15–38

Héring, J. *The Second Epistle of Saint Paul to the Corinthians*, ET London 1967

Hester, J.D. 'The Rhetorical Structure of Galatians 1:11–2:14', *JBL* 103 (1984), 223–33

Hickling, C.J.A. 'Centre and Periphery in the Thought of Paul', *StBib* III (1978), 199–214

Holmberg, B. *Paul and Power. The Structure of Authority in the Primitive Church as Reflected in the Pauline Epistles*, Coniectanea Biblica NT Series 11, Lund 1978

Hooker, M.D. 'Beyond the Things that are Written? St. Paul's Use of Scripture', *NTS* 27 (1980–81), 295–309

Hooker, M.D. and Wilson, S.G. (eds.) *Paul and Paulinism. Essays in Honour of C.K. Barrett*, London 1982

Houlden, J.L. 'A Response to James D.G. Dunn', *JSNT* 18 (1983), 58–67

Howard, G. *Paul: Crisis in Galatia*, SNTSMS 35, Cambridge 1979
  'Christ the End of the Law', *JBL* 88 (1969), 331–7
  'Romans 3:21–31 and the Inclusion of the Gentiles', *HTR* 63 (1970), 223–33

Hübner, H. *Das Gesetz bei Paulus. Ein Beitrag zum Werden der paulinischen Theologie*, FRLANT 119, Göttingen 1978
  ET: *Law in Paul's Thought*, SNTW, Edinburgh 1984
  'Pauli Theologiae Proprium', *NTS* 26 (1979–80), 445–73

Hughes, P.E. *Paul's Second Epistle to the Corinthians*, NLC, London 1962

Jackson, H. 'The Resurrection Belief of the Earliest Christians. A Response to the Failure of Prophecy?', *JR* 55 (1975), 415–25

Jervell, J. *Luke and the People of God. A New Look at Luke–Acts*, Minneapolis 1972
  'The Letter to Jerusalem', in *The Romans Debate*, ed. K.P. Donfried, Minneapolis 1977

Jewett, R. *Dating Paul's Life*, London 1979
  'Conflicting Movements in the Early Church as Reflected in Philippians', *NovT* 12 (1970), 362–90
  'The Agitators and the Galatian Congregation', *NTS* 17 (1971), 198–212
  'Major Impulses in the Theological Interpretation of Romans since Barth', *Int.* 34 (1980), 17–31

Jüngel, E. 'Das Gesetz zwischen Adam und Christus: eine theologische Studie zu Röm 5, 12–21', *ZTK* 60 (1963), 42–74

Karris, R. J. 'Romans 14:1–15:13 and the Occasion of Romans', in *The Romans Debate*, ed. K. P. Donfried, Minneapolis 1977, 75–99

Käsemann, E. *Commentary on Romans*, ET London 1980

Essays on New Testament Themes, SBT 41, London 1964: 'The Disciples of John the Baptist in Ephesus', 136–48

New Testament Questions of Today, ET London 1969: '"The Righteousness of God" in Paul', 168–82; 'Paul and Israel', 183–7; 'Paul and Early Catholicism', 236–51

Perspectives on Paul, ET Philadelphia 1971: 'Justification and Salvation-History in the Epistle to the Romans', 60–78; 'The Faith of Abraham in Romans 4', 79–101; 'The Spirit and the Letter', 138–68

'Die Legitimität des Apostels', *ZNW* 41 (1942), 33–71

Exegetische Versuche und Besinnungen, I, Göttingen 1970[6]: 'Zum Verständnis von Römer 3,24–26', 96–100

Kaye, B. N. *The Thought Structure of Romans with Special Reference to Chapter 6*, Austin, Texas 1979

Keck, L. E. 'Justification of the Ungodly and Ethics', in *Rechtfertigung*, ed. J. Friedrich, W. Pöhlmann and P. Stuhlmacher, Tübingen 1976, 199–209

Keck L. E. and Martyn J. L. (eds.) *Studies in Luke–Acts*, London 1968

Kee, H. C. *Community of the New Age. Studies in Mark's Gospel*, London 1977

Kertelge, K. *"Rechtfertigung" bei Paulus. Studien zum Struktur und zum Bedeutungsgehalt des paulinischen Rechtfertigungsbegriffs*, Münster 1967

'Gesetz und Freiheit im Galaterbrief', *NTS* 30 (1983–84), 382–94

Kettunen, M. *Der Abfassungszweck des Römerbriefes*, Helsinki 1979

Kim, S. *The Origin of Paul's Gospel*, WUNT, Tübingen 1981

Kittel, G. and Friedrich, G. (eds.) *Theological Dictionary of the New Testament*, 1933–73, ET Grand Rapids, Michigan 1964–73

Klassen, W. and Snyder, G. F. (eds.) *Current Issues in New Testament Interpretation*, London 1962

Klein, C. *Anti-Judaism in Christian Theology*, ET London 1978

Klein, G. *Rekonstruktion und Interpretation. Gesammelte Aufsätze zum Neuen Testament*, Munich 1969: 'Galater 2,6–9 und die Geschichte der Jerusalem Urgemeinde', 99–128; 'Römer 4 und die Idee der Heilsgeschichte', 145–69; 'Exegetische Probleme in Römer 3,21–4,25. Antwort an Ulrich Wilckens', 170–9

'Präliminarien zum Thema "Paulus und die Juden"', in *Rechtfertigung*, ed. J. Friedrich, W. Pöhlmann and P. Stuhlmacher, Tübingen/Göttingen 1976, 229–43

'Paul's Purpose in Writing the Epistle to the Romans', in *The Romans Debate*, ed. K. P. Donfried, Minneapolis 1977

Klijn, A. F. J. 'Paul's Opponents in Philippians III', *NovT* 7 (1964–65), 278–84

Knox, J. *Chapters in a Life of Paul*, London 1954

Koester, H. 'The Purpose of the Polemic of a Pauline Fragment (Philippians III)', *NTS* 8 (1961–62), 317–32

Kuhr, F. 'Römer 2,14f und die Verheissung bei Jeremia 31,31ff', *ZNW* 55 (1964), 243–61

Kümmel, W. G. *The New Testament. The History of the Investigation of its Problems*, ET London 1973

Introduction to the New Testament, ET London 1975

Römer 7 und die Bekehrung des Paulus, Leipzig 1929, repr. Munich 1974

'Die Probleme von Römer 9–11 in den gegenwärtigen Forschungslage', in *Die Israelfrage nach Röm. 9–11*, ed. L. de Lorenzi, Rome 1977, 13–33

Kuss, O. *Der Römerbrief*, 3 vols., Regensburg 1957–78

Lagrange, M. J. *Saint Paul – Épître aux Romains*, Paris 1950

Lang, F. 'Gesetz und Bund bei Paulus', in *Rechtfertigung*, ed. J. Friedrich, W. Pöhlmann and P. Stuhlmacher, Tübingen/Göttingen 1976, 305–20

Leenhardt, F. J. *The Epistle to the Romans*, ET London 1961

Lightfoot, J. B. *St Paul's Epistle to the Galatians*, Cambridge/London 1865

Lohmeyer, E. *Der Brief an die Philipper*, KEKNT, Göttingen 1928

Lüdemann, G. *Paul, Apostle to the Gentiles. Studies in Chronology*, ET London 1984

Paulus, der Heidenapostel, Band II. Antipaulinismus im frühen Christentum, Göttingen 1983

Lührmann, D. *Der Brief an die Galater*, ZBK, Zurich 1978

Luther, M. *Lectures on Galatians (1535), Chapters 1–4*, LW 26, St Louis 1963

The Freedom of a Christian (1520), LW 31, St Louis 1957

De Servo Arbitrio (1526), LW 33, St Louis 1972

Luz, U. *Das Geschichtsverständnis des Paulus*, BevTh 49, Munich 1968

Lyonnet, S. J. 'Gratuité de la Justification et Gratuité du Salut', in AnBib 17–18, I, 95–110

McEleney, N. J. 'Conversion, Circumcision and the Law', *NTS* 20 (1973–74), 319–41

Manson, T. W. 'St. Paul's Letter to the Romans – and Others', *BJRL* 31 (1948), 3–19

Manson, W. *The Epistle to the Hebrews*, London 1951

Martin, R. P. *Philippians. An Introduction and Commentary*, TNTC, London 1959

Mattern, L. *Das Verständnis des Gerichtes bei Paulus*, AThANT, Zurich/Stuttgart 1966

Mattill, A. J. 'The Value of Acts as a Source for the Study of Paul', in *Perspectives on Luke–Acts*, ed. C. H. Talbert, Danville/Edinburgh 1978, 76–98

Marshall, I. H. *Acts. An Introduction and Commentary*, TNTC, Leicester/Grand Rapids 1980

Marxsen, W. *Introduction to the New Testament*, ET Philadelphia 1974

Mauser, U. 'Galater III.20: Die Universalität des Heils', *NTS* 13 (1966–67), 258–70

Meeks, W. *The First Urban Christians. The Social World of the Apostle Paul*, New York/London 1983

'The Man from Heaven in Johannine Sectarianism', *JBL* 91 (1972), 44–72

Michael, J. H. *The Epistle of Paul to the Philippians*, MNTC, London 1928

Michel, O. *Der Brief an die Römer*, KEKNT, Göttingen 1955

Milik, J. T. *Ten Years of Discovery in the Wilderness of Judaea*, SBT, London 1959

Minear, P. S. *The Obedience of Faith*, SBT 2nd Series, London 1971

Mitton, C. L. 'Romans vii Reconsidered', *ExT* 65 (1953), 78–81,99–103, 132–5

Montefiore, C. G. *Judaism and St. Paul: Two Essays*, London 1914

Morgan, R. 'The Significance of "Paulinism"', in *Paul and Paulinism*, ed. M. D. Hooker and S. G. Wilson, London 1982, 320–38

Moxnes, H. *Theology in Conflict. Studies of Paul's Understanding of God in Romans, NovTSup* LIII, Leiden 1980

Müller, C. *Gottes Gerechtigkeit und Gottes Volk. Eine Untersuchung zu Römer 9–11*, FRLANT 86, Göttingen 1964

Munck, J. *Paul and the Salvation of Mankind*, ET London 1959

Mundle, W. *Der Glaubensbegriff des Paulus*, Leipzig 1932

'Zur Auslegung von Röm 2,13ff', *TB* 13 (1934), 249–56

Müssner, F. *Der Galaterbrief*, HTKNT, Freiburg/Basel/Vienna 1974

Neill, S. C. *The Interpretation of the New Testament 1861–1961*, London 1964

Neusner, J. (ed.) *Christianity, Judaism and Other Greco-Roman Cults* (FS for Morton Smith), Leiden 1975

Nickelsburg, G. W. E. *Jewish Literature between the Bible and the Mishnah*, London 1981

Nickle, K. F. *The Collection. A Study in Paul's Strategy*, SBT 48, London 1966

Nygren, A. *Commentary on Romans*, ET London 1952

Oepke, A. *Der Brief des Paulus an die Galater*, THKNT, Berlin 1955[2]

O'Neill, J. C. *The Theology of Acts in its Historical Setting*, London 1970[2]

Packer, J. I. 'The "Wretched Man" in Romans 7', *StEv* II (1964), 621–7

Pedersen, S. (ed.) *Die Paulinische Literatur und Theologie*, Århus/Göttingen 1980

Plag, C. *Israels Wege zum Heil. Eine Untersuchung zu Römer 9 bis 11*, Stuttgart 1969

Plummer, A. *A Critical and Exegetical Commentary on the Second Epistle of St Paul to the Corinthians*, ICC, Edinburgh 1915

Pluta, A. *Gottes Bundestreue: ein Schlüsselbegriff in Röm.3,25a*, SBS, Stuttgart 1969

Pregeant, R. 'Grace and Recompense: Reflections on a Pauline Paradox', *JAAR* 47 (1979), 73–96

Räisänen, H. *Paul and the Law*, WUNT 29, Tübingen 1983

'Paul's Theological Difficulties with the Law', *StBib* III (1978), 301–15

'Legalism and Salvation by the Law. Paul's Portrayal of the Jewish Religion as a historical and theological Problem', in *Die Paulinische Literatur und Theologie*, ed. S. Pedersen, Århus/Göttingen 1980, 63–83

'Zum Gebrauch von EPITHYMIA und EPITHYMEIN bei Paulus', *StTh* 33 (1979), 85–99

Reicke, B. 'Der geschichtliche Hintergrund des Apostelkonzils und der Antiochia-Episode', in *Studia Paulina*, ed. J. N. Sevenster and W. C. van Unnik, Haarlem 1953, 172–87

Rengstorf, K. H. (ed.) *Das Paulusbild in der neueren Deutschen Forschung*, Darmstadt, 1969
Rhyne, C. T. *Faith Establishes the Law*, SBL Diss. Series 55, Chico 1981
Richard, E. *Acts 6:1–8:4. The Author's Method of Composition*, SBL Diss. Series, Missoula, Montana 1978
Richardson, P. *Israel in the Apostolic Church*, SNTSMS 10, Cambridge 1969
Ridderbos, H. *Paul: An Outline of his Theology*, ET Grand Rapids 1975
Riedl, J. 'Die Auslegung von R2,14–16 in Vergangenheit und Gegenwart', AnBib 17–18, I, 271–81
Rissi, M. *Studien zum zweiten Korintherbrief*, AThANT 56, Zurich 1969
Robertson, A. and Plummer, A. *A Critical and Exegetical Commentary on the First Epistle of St Paul to the Corinthians*, ICC, Edinburgh 1911
Robinson, J. A. T. *Redating the New Testament*, London 1976
Wrestling with Romans, London 1979
Ropes, J. H. *The Singular Problem of the Epistle to the Galatians*, Cambridge, Mass. 1929
Sanday, W. and Headlam, A. C. *A Critical and Exegetical Commentary on the Epistle to the Romans*, ICC, Edinburgh 1902[5]
Sanders, E. P. *Paul and the Palestinian Judaism: A Comparison of Patterns of Religion*, London 1977
Paul, the Law and the Jewish People, Philadelphia 1983
Jesus and Judaism, London 1985
'On the Question of Fulfilling the Law in Paul and Rabbinic Judaism', in *Donum Gentilicium*, ed. E. Bammel, C. K. Barrett and W. D. Davies, Oxford 1978, 103–126
'The Covenant as a Soteriological Category and the Nature of Salvation in Palestinian and Hellenistic Judaism', in *Jews, Greeks and Christians*, ed. R. Hamerton-Kelly and R. Scroggs, Leiden 1976, 11–44
Sanders, J. N. and Mastin, B. A. *The Gospel according to St John*, BNTC, London 1968
Sanders, J. T. 'Paul's "Autobiographical" Statements in Galatians 1–2', *JBL* 85 (1966), 335–43
Scharlemann, M. H. *Stephen: A Singular Saint*, AnBib 34, Rome 1968
Schlatter, A. *Gottes Gerechtigkeit. Ein Kommentar zum Römerbrief*, Stuttgart 1935
Schlier, H. *Der Brief an die Galater*, KEKNT, Göttingen 1949[1]
Der Römerbrief, HTKNT, Freiburg/Basel/Vienna 1979[2]
Schmithals, W. *Paul and James*, SBT 46, London 1965
Paul and the Gnostics, ET Nashville 1972
Der Römerbrief als historisches Problem, StNT 9, Gütersloh, 1975
'Judaisten in Galatien?', *ZNW* 74 (1983), 27–58
Schnackenburg, R. *The Gospel according to St John*, 3 vols., ET Tunbridge Wells 1968–82
'Römer 7 im Zusammenhang des Römerbriefes', in *Jesus und Paulus*, ed. E. E. Ellis and E. Grässer, Göttingen 1975, 283–300
Schneider, E. E. 'Finis Legis Christus – Röm.10,4', *TZ* 20 (1964), 410–22
Schoeps, H. J. *Paul: the Theology of the Apostle in the Light of Jewish Religious History*, ET London 1961
Theologie und Geschichte des Judenchristentums, Tübingen 1949

Schütz, J. H. *Paul and the Anatomy of Apostolic Authority*, SNTSMS 26, Cambridge 1975
Schweitzer, A. *Paul and his Interpreters*, ET London 1912
Scroggs, R. 'The Earliest Christian Communities as Sectarian Movement', in *Christianity, Judaism and Other Greco-Roman Cults*, ed. J. Neusner, Leiden 1975
'Paul and the Eschatological Woman', *JAAR* 40 (1972), 283–303
'Paul as Rhetorician: Two Homilies in Romans 1–11', in *Jews, Greeks and Christians*, ed. R. Hamerton-Kelly and R. Scroggs, Leiden 1976, 271–98
Sevenster, J. N. and van Unnik, W. C. *Studia Paulina in Honorem J. de Zwaan*, Haarlem 1953
Shaw, G. *The Cost of Authority*, London 1983
Simon, M. *St Stephen and the Hellenists in the Primitive Church*, London 1958
Smallwood, E. M. *The Jews under Roman Rule*, Leiden 1976
Staab, K. *Die Thessalonicherbriefe, Die Gefangenschaftsbriefe*, Regensburger NT, Regensburg 1969[5]
Stanton, G. N. 'Stephen in Lucan Perspective', *StBib* III (1978), 345–60
'The Gospel of Matthew and Judaism', *BJRL* 66 (1984), 264–84
Stendahl, K. 'The Apostle Paul and the Introspective Conscience of the West', *HTR* 56 (1963), 199–215
Paul among Jews and Gentiles and Other Essays, London 1977
Stuhlmacher, P. *Gottes Gerechtigkeit bei Paulus*, Göttingen 1965
' "Das Ende des Gesetzes". Über Ursprung und Ansatz der paulinischen Theologie', *ZTK* 67 (1970), 14–39
'Zur neueren Exegese von Röm 3,24–26', in *Jesus und Paulus*, ed. E. E. Ellis and E. Grässer, Göttingen 1975
Stuhlmacher, P. and Lapide, P. *Paulus, Rabbi und Apostel. Ein jüdisch-christlicher Dialog*, Stuttgart/Munich 1981
Suggs, M. J. ' "The Word is Near You": Romans 10:6–10 within the Purpose of the Letter', in *Christian History and Interpretation*, ed. W. R. Farmer, C. F. D. Moule and R. R. Niebuhr, Cambridge 1967, 289–312
Suhl, A. *Paulus und seine Briefe: Ein Beitrag zur paulinischen Chronologie*, StNT 11, Gütersloh 1975
Synofzik, E. *Die Gerichts- und Vergeltungsaussagen bei Paulus. Eine traditionsgeschichtliche Untersuchung*, Göttingen 1977
Talbert, C. H. (ed.) *Perspectives on Luke–Acts*, Danville/Edinburgh 1978
Luke and the Gnostics, Nashville/New York 1966
'Again: Paul's Visits to Jerusalem', *NovT* 9 (1967), 26–40
Theissen, G. *The First Followers of Jesus. A Sociological Analysis of the Earliest Christianity*, ET London 1978
The Social Setting of Pauline Christianity, ET Edinburgh 1982: 'Legitimation and Subsistence: An Essay on the Sociology of Early Christian Missionaries', 27–67; 'The Sociological Interpretation of Religious Traditions', 175–200
Tyson, J. B. 'Paul's Opponents in Galatia', *NovT* 10 (1968), 241–54
Via, D. O. 'A Structuralist Approach to Paul's Old Testament Hermeneutic', *Int.* 28 (1974), 201–20

Vielhauer, P. 'On the "Paulinism" of Acts', in *Studies in Luke–Acts*, ed. L. E. Keck and J. L. Martyn, London 1968, 33–50

'Gesetzesdienst und Stoicheiadienst im Galaterbrief', in *Rechtfertigung*, ed. J. Friedrich, W. Pöhlmann and P. Stuhlmacher, Tübingen/ Göttingen 1976, 543–55

Walaskay, P. W. *'And So We Came to Rome'*, SNTSMS, Cambridge 1983

Walker, R. 'Die Heiden und das Gericht', *EvTh* 20 (1960), 302–14

Watson, F. B. '2 Cor. x–xiii and Paul's Painful Letter to the Corinthians', *JTS* 35 (1984), 324–46

'The Social Function of Mark's Secrecy Theme', *JSNT* 24 (1985), 49–69

Watson, N. M. 'Justified by Faith, Judged by Works – An Antinomy?', *NTS* 29 (1982–83), 209–21

Wedderburn, A. J. M. 'Adam in Paul's Letter to the Romans', *StBib* III (1978), 413–30

Wenham, D. 'The Christian Life: A Life of Tension?', in *Pauline Studies*, ed. D. A. Hagner and M. J. Harris, Exeter 1980, 80–105

Wiefel, W. 'The Jewish Community in Ancient Rome and the Origins of Roman Christianity', in *The Romans Debate*, ed. K. P. Donfried, Minneapolis 1977

Wilckens, U. *Der Brief an die Römer*, 3 vols., EKKNT, Zurich/Neukirchen 1978–82

Rechtfertigung als Freiheit, Neukirchen 1974: 'Die Bekehrung des Paulus als religionsgeschichtliches Problem', 11–32; 'Die Rechtfertigung Abrahams nach Römer 4', 33–49; 'Zu Römer 3,21–4,25. Antwort an G. Klein', 50–76; 'Was heisst bei Paulus: "Aus Werken des Gesetzes wird kein Mensch gerecht"?', 77–109; 'Über Abfassungszweck und Aufbau des Römerbriefs', 110–70

'Zur Entwicklung des paulinischen Gesetzesverständnisses', *NTS* 28 (1981–82), 154–90

Wiles, M. F. *The Divine Apostle*, Cambridge 1967

Williams, S. K. 'The "Righteousness of God" in Romans', *JBL* 99 (1980), 241–90

Wilson, S. G. *The Gentiles and the Gentile Mission in Luke–Acts*, SNTSMS, Cambridge 1973

Luke and the Law, SNTSMS, Cambridge 1983

'Paul and Religion', in *Paul and Paulinism*, ed. M. D. Hooker and S. G. Wilson, London 1982, 339–54

Windisch, H. *Der zweite Korintherbrief*, KEKNT, Göttingen 1924

Wright, N. T. *The Messiah and the People of God*, Oxford D. Phil. thesis, 1980

Zahn, T. *Der Brief des Paulus an die Römer*, Leipzig 1910

Zeller, D. *Juden und Heiden in der Mission des Paulus. Studien zum Römerbrief*, Stuttgart 1973

Ziesler, J. A. *The Meaning of Righteousness in Paul. A Linguistic and Theological Inquiry*, SNTSMS, Cambridge 1972

INDEX